MATHEMATICS RESEARCH DEVELOPMENTS

PARALLEL PROGRAMMING

PRACTICAL ASPECTS, MODELS AND CURRENT LIMITATIONS

Mathematics Research Developments

Additional books in this series can be found on Nova's website
under the Series tab.

Additional e-books in this series can be found on Nova's website
under the e-book tab.

MATHEMATICS RESEARCH DEVELOPMENTS

PARALLEL PROGRAMMING

PRACTICAL ASPECTS, MODELS AND CURRENT LIMITATIONS

MIKHAIL S. TARKOV
EDITOR

nova publishers
New York

NOTICE TO THE READER

LIBRARY OF CONGRESS CATALOGING-IN-PUBLICATION DATA

Parallel programming : practical aspects, models and current limitations / [edited by] Mikhail S. Tarkov (Institute of Semiconductor Physics, Siberian Branch, Russian Academy of Sciences, Russia).

pages cm -- (Mathematics research developments)

Includes bibliographical references and index.

ISBN 978-1-63321-957-1 (hardcover)

1. Parallel programming (Computer science) I. Tarkov, Mikhail S., editor.

QA76.642.P356 2014

005.2'75--dc23

2014034859

Published by Nova Science Publishers, Inc. † New York

CONTENTS

PREFACE

Parallel programming is designed for the use of parallel computer systems for solving time-consuming problems that cannot be solved on a sequential computer in a reasonable time.

These problems can be divided into two classes:

1. Processing large data arrays (including processing images and signals in real time).
2. Simulation of complex physical processes and chemical reactions.

For each of these classes prospective methods are designed for solving problems. For data processing one of the most promising technologies is the use of artificial neural networks. Method of particles-in-cell and cellular automata are very useful for simulation.

Problems of scalability of parallel algorithms and the transfer of existing parallel programs to future parallel computers are very acute now. An important task is to optimize the use of the equipment (including the CPU cache) of parallel computer. Along with parallelizing information processing it is essential to ensure the processing reliability by the relevant organization of systems of concurrent interacting processes. From the perspective of creating qualitative parallel programs it is important to develop advanced methods of teaching parallel programming.

The above reasons are the basis for the creation of this book, chapters of which are devoted to solving these problems.

The first chapter (by Dr. Mikhail S. Tarkov) is devoted to mapping neural networks onto regular structures (hypercube, torus) of distributed computer systems (CS). These structures are now used not only in supercomputers but also serve as a basis for the construction of parallel systems for VLSI chips (System-on-Chip). As a result of mapping neural networks on such a structure we can obtain an effective solution of the problem of organizing interactions between the neurons within chip and within the entire distributed CS.

The second chapter (by Dr. Mikhail S. Tarkov) examines the possibility of using the Hopfield recurrent neural network for mapping structures of parallel programs onto the structures of distributed CS. It is shown that such a network can be successfully used for mapping of parallel programs on a multicore computer and for constructing Hamiltonian cycles in the structure of distributed CS. In the last case the neural network algorithms are not inferior in speed than the permutation ones.

The third chapter (by Dr. Alexey Snytnikov) investigates the relaxation processes in high-temperature plasma caused by the propagation of the electron beam. The mathematical Particle-In-Cell (PIC) model is used in the problem. To achieve high performance both large-scale and fine-grain parallelization techniques are used. Large-scale parallelization is achieved by domain decomposition on computing nodes of the cluster supercomputer. Fine-grain parallelization is done by implementing the computation of motion of each particle as a separate stream. Thus, the highest performance is achieved by hybrid supercomputers with GPU.

The fourth chapter (by Dr. Igor Kulikov et al.) describes the technology of numerical modeling of astrophysical flows on the hybrid supercomputer with NVIDIA accelerators. To solve this problem the software packages GPUPEGAS (modeling of astrophysical objects), AstroPhi (simulation of the dynamics of stars and molecular clouds), PADME (simulation of the formation of planetary systems) are developed.

The fifth chapter (by Dr. Mikhail A. Marchenko) focuses on the problems of using the Monte Carlo method (method of numerical stochastic modeling) on supercomputers. An effective approach is proposed for parallel stochastic modeling and its application in practice, in particular in the problem of modeling the evolution of electron avalanches in gases. On the basis of this approach the software library PARMONC was created. The results of the study on the scalability of parallel algorithms of stochastic modeling are presented.

The sixth chapter (by Dr. Yuri Medvedev) presents the development of cellular automata models of gas flows. Transitions from Boolean models to integral models, from two-dimensional models to three-dimensional models, and from gas flow models to models of multiphase flows are considered. Implementation of models on a cluster using the MPI library is proposed. The problem of dynamic load balancing is solved for multiple cores of the cluster in the implementation of models with integer alphabet.

The seventh chapter (by Dr. Konstantin Kalgin) is devoted to the modeling of parallel asynchronous cellular automata. A comparative analysis of their parallel implementations is done. Parallel algorithms on the model of physical and chemical process of surface CO + O2 reaction are tested on different parallel computers: a computer with shared memory, a cluster (distributed memory computer), and GPU. The specialized language CACHE and programs for conversion of this language to C language are proposed for cellular automata models of physical and chemical processes.

In the eighth chapter (by Dr. Nader Khammassi and Prof. Jean-Christophe Le Lann) the parallel programming model XPU is suggested. It facilitates the programming of parallel computations without loss of performance. The XPU technology is based entirely on traditional parallel programming language C^{++} and can be easily integrated into many systems. The XPU uses methods of C^{++} metaprogramming in order to simplify the creation of various kinds of parallelism (task parallelism, data parallelism, temporal parallelism) at all levels of granularity.

In the ninth chapter (by Dr. Igor N. Skopin) a robust approach to the construction of systems of interacting processes is proposed. It is shown how the successive solution of some problems can be naturally represented as a system of interacting concurrent processes. Such representation improves the robustness of computations.

Tenth (final) chapter (by Dr. Igor N. Skopin) considers the problems associated with learning parallelism. A new efficient approach is proposed to learning parallel programming. This approach is based on constructing program sketches, which does not take into account any restrictions on concurrency, and the subsequent mapping of the sketches on a real computer.

We hope this book will be of interest to researchers, students and all those who work in the field of parallel programming and high performance computing.

Mikhail S. Tarkov, Ph.D.
Institute of Semiconductor Physics SB RAS
Novosibirsk, Russia
Tel: +7 (383) 330-84-94
Fax: +7 (383) 330-52-56
Email: tarkov@isp.nsc.ru

In: Parallel Programming
Editor: Mikhail S. Tarkov
ISBN: 978-1-63321-957-1

Chapter 1

MAPPING DATA PROCESSING NEURAL NETWORKS ONTO DISTRIBUTED COMPUTER SYSTEMS WITH REGULAR STRUCTURES

Mikhail S. Tarkov *
Institute of Semiconductor Physics SB RAS, Novosibirsk, Russia

Abstract

The methods for efficient mapping data processing neural networks onto robust distributed computer systems (CS) are proposed. Cellular neural networks are mapped onto the graphs of parallel programs with structures "mesh" and "line". The efficiency of the proposed methods for neural networks with global connections (Hopfield network, Kohonen network, and multilayer perceptron) is based on a butterfly scheme and mapping this scheme onto hypercube with subsequent embedding of the hypercube onto a torus. This networks are mapped onto regular graphs of parallel programs ("line", "ring", "mesh", "hypercube", "torus") intended for implementation on distributed computer systems.

Keywords: neural networks, distributed computer systems, mapping, hypercube, torus

1. Introduction

Currently, there is a steady growth in the volume of processed measurement information (signals and images) in modern information systems. This also increases the performance requirements for such systems.

Neural networks realize a perspective model of parallel computations [1-9]. The artificial neural networks are based on the following features of live neural networks allowing them to cope with irregular tasks:

* E-mail address: tarkov@isp.nsc.ru

- a simple processing element, the neuron;
- huge number of neurons are participated in information processing;
- each neuron is connected to many other neurons (global connections);
- huge number of inter-neuron connections with changing weights;
- massive parallelism of information processing.

The network possessing of these properties belongs to the class of connectionist models of information processing. Their main feature is the use of weighed connections between processing elements as a means of storing information. The processing is carried out at the same time by a large number of neurons, and each neuron is connected to many other neurons; so, the neural network is resistant to malfunctions and is capable of fast computing. To create a neural network for a specific task is to determine:

- a neuron model;
- connection topology;
- connection weights.

Neurocomputer is a device that contains a neural network as the major component and has applications in many areas:

- artificial intelligence: pattern recognition, image processing, reading handwritten characters, etc;
- control system and technical control;
- creation of special parallel computers;
- study of the human brain.

Neural networks are different not so much in their neuron model as the topology of connections and rules determining the weights (training rules). The neural network structures are divided into single-layer structures and multi-layer ones. Single-layer networks are cellular neural networks, Hopfield and Kohonen networks.

Multi-layer network has an input layer, output layer and hidden layers. The input layer receives input data; the output layer generates the output result of processing and hidden layers are involved in processing information.

Unlike traditional means of information processing, the neural network programming performed implicitly in the training process. Training is constructed as follows. There is a training set, i.e., given a set of examples with answers. These examples are presented to the neural network. The neurons receive conditions of the example and transform them. Then the neurons are communicated repeatedly by transformed signals and, finally, give a response in the form of an output set of signals. A deviation of an output from the correct answer is penalized. Training is meant to minimize the penalty as an implicit function of weights of neuronal interconnections.

Traditional computer systems have the following problems:

1. They need a precise description of the algorithm (the computer is oriented to character processing).
2. The data must be exact. The equipment is easily damaged. A destruction of the main elements of memory makes the system faulty.
3. Each object to be processed must be explicitly specified in the memory.
4. It is difficult to build a good algorithm for pattern recognition and associative sampling.

In neurocomputers (neural networks):

1. The method of data processing is more similar to signal processing. Instead of the program there is a set of neuron weights; instead of programming there is a training of neurons (adjustment of neuron weights).
2. The neural network is tolerant to noise; data distortion does not substantially affect the result (including the failure of individual neurons).
3. Processed objects are represented implicitly by neuron weights. As a result, the network can work with the objects not previously come across and is capable of training results generalization.
4. The neural network is good for solving the problems of perception and associative sampling.

Real time image and signal processing require the creation of a highly parallel data processing means. Autonomous means of a computer image and signal processing require not only high performance of computing facilities, but also their high reliability and the ability to learn and generalize the training outcomes in relation to new situations that arise in the process of information processing. Artificial neural networks to be implemented in hardware have all these qualities.

The enormous number of global interneuron connections (synapses) complicates the neural network implementation as a VLSI layout because their connection length is inevitably increased, which makes it necessary to reduce the clock frequency of operation of the digital devices. On the other hand, increasing the degree of VLSI integration requires a larger amount of clock generators on the chip, i.e., leads to the distributed processing of the information that means the information processing by multiple cooperating processors (elementary computers).

A system of interacting elementary computers (ECs) is a subject scalable to its homogeneity (ECs are all the same). Scaling is possible only if means of communications between processors are distributed, which, for a given technology of VLSI production, leads to the interprocessor network representation in the form of a regular graph with a vertex of a bounded degree.

Due to the rapid development of VLSI manufacturing technologies, a question of combining the components in large systems on a chip is aroused. The most common approach, using the principle of a common bus, shows a lack of scalability and a decrease in throughput with increasing number of connected elements. One of the methods to eliminate such deficiencies may be the use of network technology to exchange the data between subsystems of the VLSI chip. The concept of combining computing cores in the network – NoC (Network-on-Chip) is originated. The essence of this approach is to combine the kernels, typically processor cores with local memory and additional devices by specialized routers. This approach to communication in VLSI has the advantages of scalability (the increasing size of the network increases its bandwidth) and parallelism (data in different network segments are transmitted simultaneously). The structures of such networks are regular and have a limited degree of the node (hypercube, torus). The most common structures in such networks are multi-dimensional tori.

The advantage of this concept over the classic alone is that the point-to-point links between routers provide a high throughput by the presence of intermediate registers in the signal path, and the data on different network segments are transmitted and switched simultaneously. It provides high performance, capacity and resource savings, making the research and development of new network architectures on a chip topical. A modern VLSI chip is no longer seen as a monolithic block of synchronous hardware where all state transitions occur simultaneously. Most of VLSI chips now are regarded as distributed systems of interacting subsystems - System-on-Chip (SoC) and Network-on-Chip (NoC) [10, 11].

In this chapter, algorithms for mapping neural networks of signal and image processing onto distributed computer systems with a regular structure are proposed. The algorithms for mapping neural networks onto hypercube and torus are investigated.

2. Distributed Computer System Topology

A distributed computer system (DCS) [12–17] is a set of elementary computers (ECs) connected by a network program-controlled by these computers. Every elementary computer includes a computing unit (CU) and a system device (SD) (a router). The system device works under CU control and has input and output poles connected accordingly to the output and input poles of the neighboring ECs. The DCS structure is described by a graph $G_s(V_s, E_s)$ where V_s is a set of ECs and $E_s \subseteq V_s \times V_s$ is a set of connections between ECs.

For a distributed computer system, a graph $G_p(V_p, P_p)$ of a parallel program is usually defined as a set V_p of the program branches (virtual elementary computers) communicating to each other by point-to-point principle, i.e., by transferring messages across logical (virtual) channels (one- and two-directed) of a set $E_p \subseteq V_p \times V_p$. In a general case, nodes $x, y \in V_p$ and edges (or arcs) $(x, y) \in E_p$ are weighed by numbers characterizing computing complexities of the branches and intensities of communications between them.

There are many factors that must be taken into consideration for a choice of the DCS architecture to be used for image processing. The most popular types of the DCS topology are hypercubes and tori [12–17].

In d-dimensional hypercube H_d with 2^d nodes, two nodes i and j are connected if and only if the Hamming distance between them is $H(i, j) = 1$ (Figure 1). For a given number of nodes the hypercube architecture has the best communication possibilities, but the scalability of hypercube is constrained by the fact that the interconnection cost per node (node degree) increases with the total number of nodes. From the scalability point of view, torus is a more interesting type of interconnection topology.

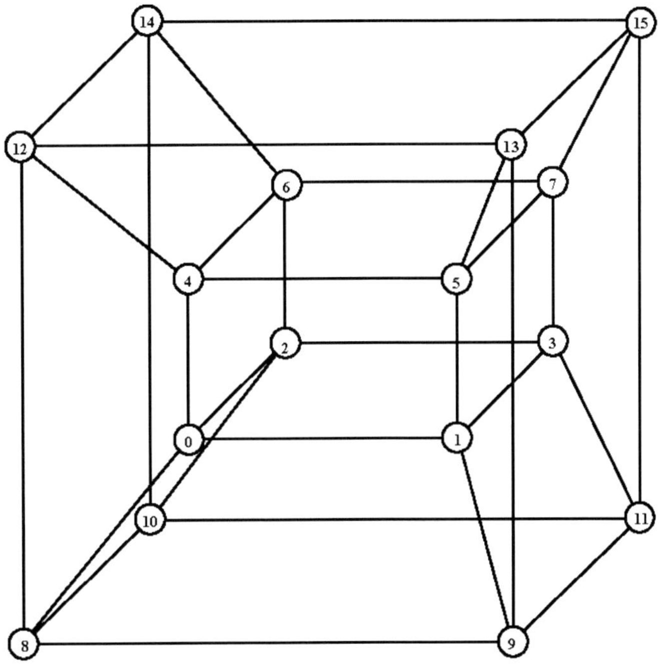

Figure 1. Example of hypercube ($d = 4$).

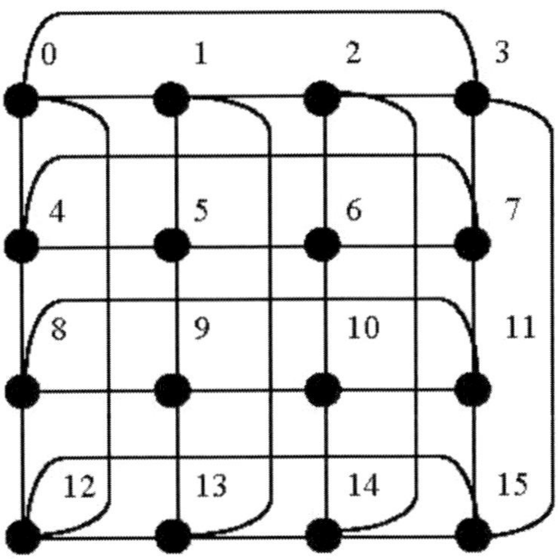

Figure 2. Example of two-dimensional torus.

Torus $E_n(k_1,...,k_n)$ with n dimensions has $N = k_1 \times k_2 \times ... \times k_n$ nodes and nodes i and j are connected if and only if $\exists l \in \{1,...,n\}$, $(i-j) \bmod k_l = 1$ (Figure 2).

The mapping data fragments onto processors must save their neighborhood. The consideration above shows that, for the low-level image processing, it is better to use the parallel program with a mesh structure because of a well-fitting torus. Actually, the two- or three-dimensional tori are produced accordingly from the two- or three-dimensional meshes by wrapping its columns and rows. Thus, the torus is a trade-off topology effectively used for low-level image processing. In modern supercomputer distributed systems the multidimensional tori are usually used as network graphs [15, 16].

A $p_1 \times p_2 \times \ldots \times p_n$ mesh is the nearest neighbor network where each node is labeled as $(a_1, a_2, \ldots, a_n)$, $a_i \in \{0, 1, \ldots, p_i - 1\}$, $i = 1, 2, \ldots, n$. Two nodes $(a_1, a_2, \ldots, a_n)$ and $(b_1, b_2, \ldots, b_n)$ are adjacent in the mesh if, for some i, $a_i = b_i \pm 1$ and for every $j \neq i$, $a_j = b_j$. Multidimensional tori are multidimensional meshes with a “wrap around”. That is a $p_1 \times p_2 \times \ldots \times p_n$ torus is a network of $p_1 \times p_2 \times \ldots \times p_n$ nodes where two nodes $(a_1, a_2, \ldots, a_n)$ and $(b_1, b_2, \ldots, b_n)$ are adjacent if, for some i, $a_i = b_i \pm 1 \mod p_i$ and for every $j \neq i$, $a_j = b_j$.

A parallel algorithm for DCS should be considered as a set of mutually interacting processes, where each process involves a sequential program and local data memory [18–21]. The processes interact by sending and receiving messages. The message transfer operation is asynchronous. Receiving operation of the communication is synchronous: it causes a blockage of the process up to receiving the message. In other words, a parallel algorithm for distributed CS will be considered as a distributed virtual CS and the interacting processes of a parallel algorithm as virtual processors (elementary computers) of such a system.

Methodology for designing parallel algorithm involves the following phases [18]:

- task decomposition to processes;
- synthesis of a graph of interactions between processes;
- merging processes;
- mapping processes to the processors of a computer system.

The interaction between the processes is called local if the process interacts with a small number of other processes called neighbors (the number of neighbors is significantly less than the total number of processes). An example of a neural network with local interactions is a cellular neural network. If the number of processes involved in the interaction is compared to the total number of processes, then the interaction is the global one (e.g., in computation of the sum of the vector components distributed over all the processes of the parallel program). Neural networks with global interactions are sigmoidal multilayer neural networks, Hopfield networks, Kohonen networks and others.

The algorithms with local interactions are easily mapped onto regular structures of parallel programs of types "line" or "mesh" (Figure 3). The algorithms with global interactions are mapped onto a hypercube which can then be embedded into tori of various dimensions (including the ring, i.e., one-dimensional torus).

3. Mapping Neural Networks with Local Interactions (Cellular Neural Networks)

In a cellular neural network (CNN) neurons are located in the mesh nodes (for example, see Figure 3a), or in the nodes of a regular graph. Each neuron has weighed connections with his neighbors. Such networks are useful for the realization of filtering operations [22], which are often described by the convolution $G(i, j)$ of the image $I(i, j)$ with a set of filter weights:

$$h(k,l,i,j),\quad k,l=-M,...,0,\ M,\quad i=1,...,N_1,\quad j=1,...,N_2:$$

$$G(i,j)=\sum_{k=-M}^{M}\sum_{l=-M}^{M}h(k,l,i,j)\cdot I(k+i,l+j)\,. \qquad (1)$$

Filtration (1) is usually preceded to other, more complex image transformations.

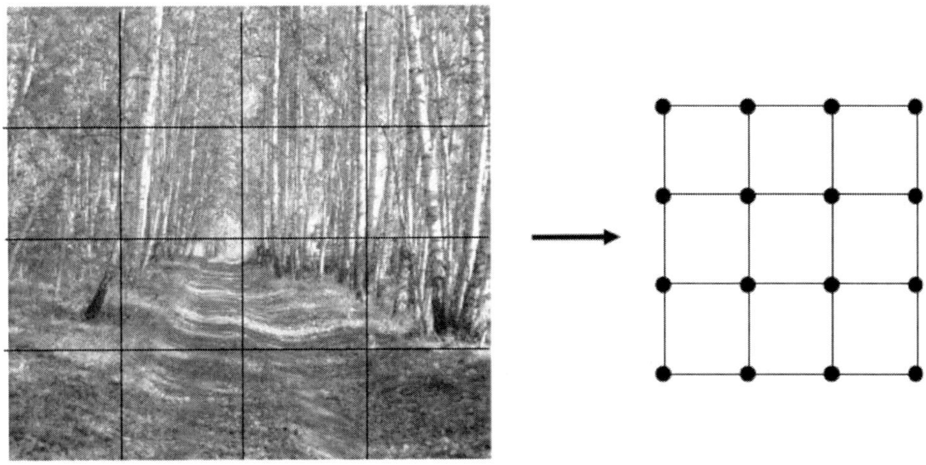

a) mapping onto mesh

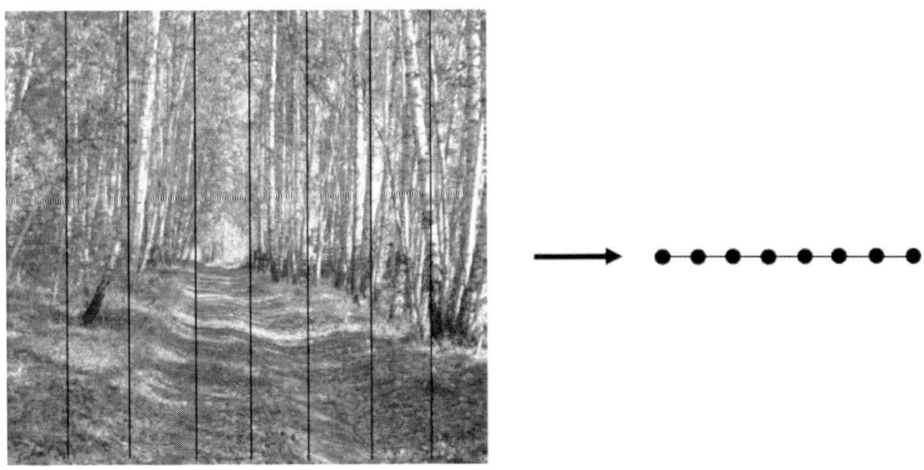

b) mapping onto line

Figure 3. Examples of mapping local algorithms of preliminary image processing onto regular structures of parallel programs.

In transformation (1) a rectangular window of size $(2M+1)\times(2M+1)$, $M \ll \min(N_1, N_2)$ is commonly used; so, the calculation of values in a point of the image is associated with the processing of a small neighborhood of this point, i.e., filtering algorithms of form (1) are local. From the locality of transformation (1) it follows that it should be used as a geometric parallelism, i.e.,

1) the neighborhood graph of processes in a parallel program must correspond to the neighborhood of image pixels;
2) the mapping of data fragments processed by the algorithms (1) onto the processes must preserve fragments neighborhood;
3) as a graph of parallel program, implementing image filtering, it is advisable to use the "mesh" (Figure 3a) or the “line” (Figure 3b).

In the limit, with a maximum parallelization, each process is in the one-to-one correspondence to a pixel.

The mesh and the line are well mapped onto hypercubic and toroidal structures of computer systems. Further we always assume that the image components are uniformly distributed throughout the computers of the system so that the neighboring pixels are always located in the same EC or in adjacent computers of the mesh or the line (geometric parallelism).

Computations of neuron activations in networks with global communications (sigmoid multilayer networks, Hopfield networks, Kohonen network, etc.) are usually reduced to the computation of the sum of data array components (scalar product of the neuron weight vector and the corresponding input vector of the neuron). The computation of this sum is one of the semigroup array operations.

4. Mapping Semigroup Array Operations onto Distributed Computer System with Torus Topology

Semigroup operation is a binary associative operation [19]. The examples of such operation are addition, multiplication, conjunction, disjunction, excluding OR and computation of minimum or maximum. In [19] the problem of implementation of semigroup operations on data arrays distributed on the mesh is solved so that the operation result is located in every processor. This solution can be easily translated onto the torus.

In this chapter we consider an alternative approach to mapping the semigroup operation onto computer systems with torus topology. This approach is based on using the butterfly scheme in parallel realization of semigroup operation and mapping the butterfly onto the hypercube with subsequent *XOR*-embedding [12] of the hypercube onto torus. We show that this approach gives more efficient parallel execution of the semigroup operation than the approach proposed in [19].

4.1. Semigroup Operations on Mesh and Torus Using Cyclic Intercomputer Data Shifts

Let array $x=(x_1,...,x_n)$ be initially mapped onto a 2D-mesh with $\sqrt{n}\times\sqrt{n}$ processors so that processor P_{ij} contains data element $x_{i\sqrt{n}+j}$, $i,j\in\{1,...,\sqrt{n}\}$. It is required to realize a semigroup operation $\otimes$ on x so that all processors would get the operation result.

In [19] an algorithm for implementation of semigroup operations on the processor mesh is proposed as a sequence of cyclic shifts with the execution of operation $\otimes$ after each shift:

1. to implement in parallel a cyclic data shift for each row i so that every processor in row gets the result $r_i=\otimes_{j=1}^{n^{1/2}} x_{i\sqrt{n}+j}$
2. to implement in parallel a cyclic data shift for each column j so that every processor in column gets the result $s=\otimes_{i=1}^{n^{1/2}} r_i$ which is equal to the required value $s=\otimes_{i=1}^{n^{1/2}} \otimes_{j=1}^{n^{1/2}} x_{i\sqrt{n}+j}$.

A cyclic shift in a row (or column) of the mesh is as follows: every data element moves from any processor to the right, while it does not come to the rightmost processor; after that the shift direction is changed to the contrary (the caterpillar's algorithm [19]) (see an example in Figure 4a).

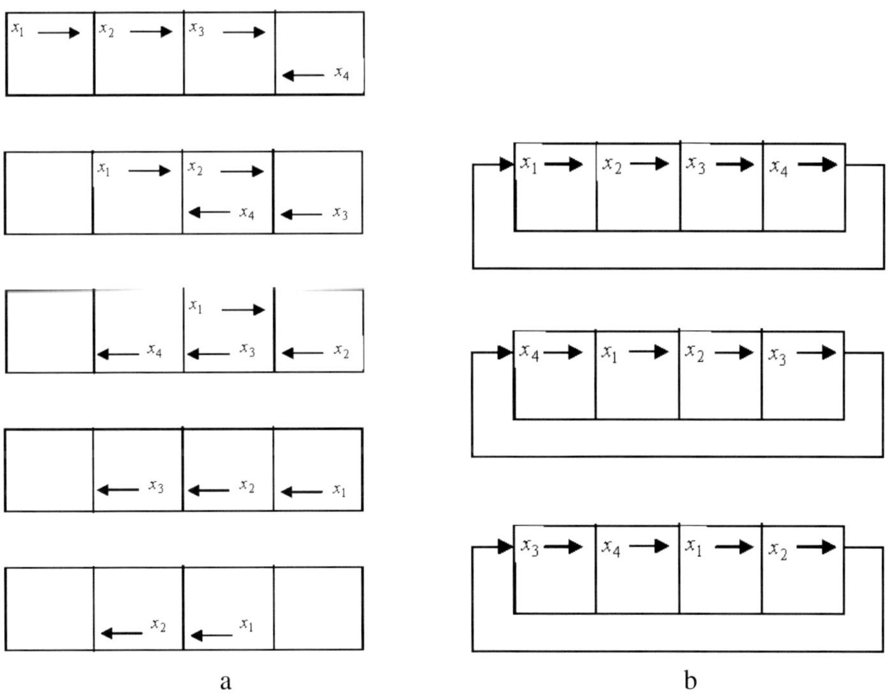

Figure 4. a) Caterpillar's algorithm of data exchanges in a mesh row (a column); b) Data shifts in a row (a column) of a torus (exchange of components of vector x in a ring of computers).

The shifts in the 2D-torus are different from those in the 2D-mesh in the following: the shift direction does not change because, in the 2D-torus, the rows and the columns are wrapped around (see Figure 4b). This algorithm is easily generalized to k -dimensional torus $E_k\left(2^{d_1},\ldots,2^{d_k}\right)$: the semigroup operation is implemented as a sequence of k steps with $2^{d_i}-1$ cyclic shifts on i -th step, $i=1,\ldots,k$.

4.2. Semigroup Operations in a Hypercube

The above algorithm of the semigroup operation realization on the torus is not optimal. This operation can be realized quicker by a system of parallel processes which is known as "butterfly" (see Figure 5: an example of sum evaluation on the butterfly). This system implements multiplication of computations with a maximum number of ⊗ operations executed simultaneously with different pairs of operands.

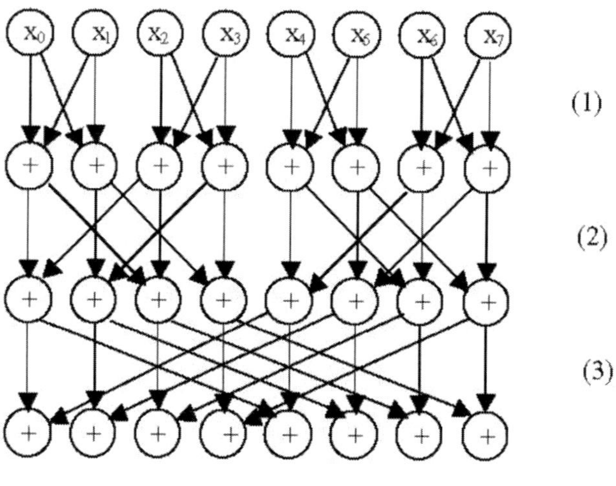

Figure 5. Sum evaluation on the butterfly.

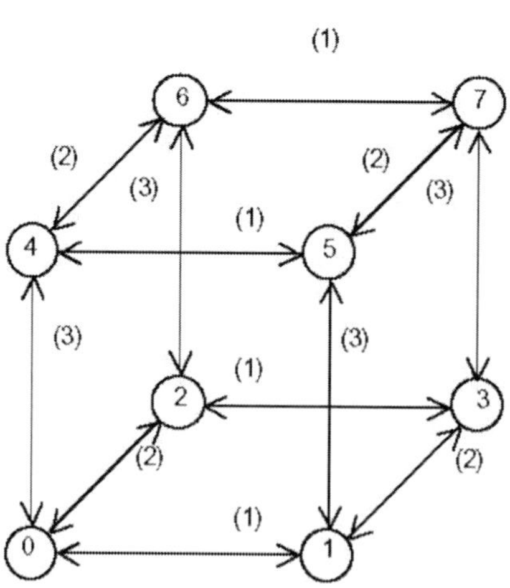

Figure 6. Hypercube obtained from the butterfly of Figure 5.

The butterfly is easily mapped onto the hypercube: the butterfly operations, which cannot be realized in parallel, are merged to the same process. In Figure 5 the united operations are on the same vertical line. The hypercube in Figure 6 is realized by merging the operations of Figure 5. Here the numbers in brackets are the summation step numbers.

4.3. Mapping Hypercube onto a Torus

The hypercube can be effectively mapped onto a torus. The method for mapping a hypercube onto a torus (XOR -embedding) is proposed in [12].

Embedding graph G into graph H is an injection f from the nodes of G to the nodes of H. If graph G is not isomorphic to some subgraph of H, then dilations of G edges are inevitable. The dilation of an edge (a,b) of G is the distance in H between nodes $f(a)$ and $f(b)$.

The XOR-embedding of a hypercube H_d onto k -dimensional torus $E_k\left(2^{d_1},\ldots,2^{d_k}\right)$, $\sum_{i=1}^{k} d_i = d$ is realized as follows. First, K_j are defined:

$$K_1 = 0,$$
$$K_j = \sum_{i=1}^{j-1} d_i,\ 1 < j \le k+1.$$

If G is hypercube H_d and T is the torus, then node v of G is mapped onto node $(m_1,\ldots,m_k) = f_{XOR}(v)$ in T as follows [12]:

$$m_j(i) = v(i+K_j), i \in \lfloor 0, d_j - 1 \rfloor,\ i \ne d_j - 2,$$
$$m_j(d_j - 2) = XOR\left(v\left(K_{j+1} - 1\right), v\left(K_{j+1} - 2\right)\right).$$

Here $x(i)$ is the ith bit of the binary representation of x. It is shown [12] that hypercube H_d can be embedded into torus $E_k\left(2^{d_1},\ldots,2^{d_k}\right)$, $\sum_{i=1}^{k} d_i = d$ with the average distance

$$D = \frac{\left(\sum_{i=1}^{k} 3\cdot 2^{d_i - 2}\right) - k}{d}. \tag{2}$$

The hypercube average edge dilations on two measured tori $E_2(2^m,2^m)$ with $m = 2,3,4,5,6$ are shown in Table 1.

As a result of mapping the hypercube onto the torus, we have paths in the torus instead of edges in the hypercube. The paths, in principle, can intersect each other; thus, besides dilations, the congestions on edges are possible. Congestions can increase communication latency.

Table 1. The hypercube edge dilations on the 2D-torus

n	16	64	256	1024	4096
D	1	1.667	2.75	4.6	7.833

Theorem 1. The XOR hypercube-onto-torus embedding does not produce congestions.

Proof.

1. Let us first consider one-dimensional torus (a ring) and arbitrary mapping hypercube onto torus i.e., arbitrary node enumeration. Let two arbitrary paths with different source and destination nodes are intersecting on the ring (i.e., have common edges) and both message transfers are beginning simultaneously.

If these two paths are oppositely oriented, then there are no congestions because every edge is used for simultaneous message transmissions as two oppositely oriented arcs (links).

If two paths are oriented the same way, then there are no congestions because of the beginning of a simultaneous transfer. When some input message comes to a node for translation, a suitable output arc is already free because an output message transfer across the arc is finished.

2. Let us consider a general case of the XOR embedding. Butterfly communication on d-dimensional hypercube is realized in d steps. At step

$$s \in \{1,2,...,d\} \tag{3}$$

node v communicates with node v' if $|v-v'| = 2^{s-1}$.

Consider the standard mapping d-dimensional hypercube onto torus $E_n(k_1, k_2, ..., k_n)$,

$$k_i = 2^{d_i}, \prod_{i=1}^{n} k_i = 2^d \tag{4}$$

as $f(v) = (p_1, p_2, ..., p_n)$ where

$$p_i = (v \bmod \prod_{j=1}^{i} k_j) div \prod_{j=1}^{i-1} k_j,\ i = 1,2,...,n. \tag{5}$$

Two different nodes v and v' lie on the m-th one-measured torus if

$$f(|v-v'|) = (\underbrace{0,...,0}_{m-1}, p_m, \underbrace{0,...,0}_{n-m}),\ p_m \neq 0.$$

Show that for $s \in \{1,2,...,d\}$, $\exists m \leq n$ is such that

$$f(|v-v'|)=f(2^{s-1})=(\underbrace{0,\ldots,0}_{m-1},2^{s-\sum_{i=1}^{m-1}d_i-1},\underbrace{0,\ldots,0}_{n-m}). \tag{6}$$

From (3) and (4) it follows that $\exists m \le n$ is such that

$$\prod_{i=1}^{m-1}2^{d_i} \le 2^{s-1} < \prod_{i=1}^{m}2^{d_i}. \tag{7}$$

From (7) it follows that:

- for $\forall i \in \{1,2,\ldots,m-1\}$ we have $2^{s-1} \bmod \prod_{j=1}^{i}2^{d_j}=0$. Then by (5) we have $p_i(2^{s-1})=0,\ i=1,2,\ldots,m-1$;
- $p_m(2^{s-1})=\dfrac{2^{s-1}}{\prod_{i=1}^{m-1}2^{d_i}}=2^{s-\sum_{i=1}^{m-1}d_i-1}$;
- for $\forall i \in \{m+1,\ldots,n\}$ we have $2^{s-1} \bmod \prod_{j=1}^{i}2^{d_j}=2^{s-1}$ and $2^{s-1}\,div\prod_{j=1}^{i-1}2^{d_j}=0$ because of $2^{s-1}<\prod_{j=1}^{i-1}2^{d_j}$ for $i>m$. Expression (6) is proved.

From (6) it follows that:

1. for the standard mapping any two communicated nodes belong to one-dimensional torus;
2. any two different pairs of communicated nodes either belong to the same one-dimensional torus or two different non-intersected tori. In both cases, in accordance with point 1 of the proof we have no congestions.
3. Consider the XOR embedding for the general case.

From (6) it follows that for any two communicated nodes v and v' the standard embeddings are as follows

$$f(v)=(p_1,\ldots,p_{m-1},p_m,p_{m+1},\ldots,p_n),$$
$$f(v')=(p_1,\ldots,p_{m-1},p_m \pm 2^{s-\sum_{i=1}^{m-1}d_i-1},p_{m+1},\ldots,p_n),$$

where s,m,n satisfy (3),(4),(7).

The *XOR* embedding changes the same bits in components of $f(v)$ and $f(v')$. Therefore, embeddings $f_{xor}(v)$ and $f_{xor}(v')$ are differentiated by the m-th component only.

Hence, these two nodes are on a one-dimensional torus and, for the *XOR* embedding, there are no congestions.

Theorem 1 is proved.

4.4. Time Analysis of Semigroup Operation Execution on Torus

Let t_w be the time for moving the data element between adjacent computers, t_o – the time of the semigroup operation execution on two arguments, T_C – the time of parallel execution of complete semigroup operation on a torus with the use of cyclic data shifts, and T_{HT} – the time of the same operation execution on the hypercube mapped onto a torus.

Theorem 2. $T_C > T_{HT}$.

Proof.

For arbitrary k, $\sum_{i=1}^{k} d_i = d$, the time of parallel execution of complete semigroup operation on the torus with the use of cyclic data shifts is

$$T_C = \sum_{i=1}^{k} \left(2^{d_i} - 1\right)\left(t_w + t_o\right).$$

The time for execution of the semigroup operation on the hypercube mapped onto the torus

$$T_{HT} = (Dt_w + t_o) \cdot d .$$

Taking into account equation (2) for D we have

$$T_{HT} = \left(\sum_{i=1}^{k} 3 \cdot 2^{d_i - 2} - k\right)t_w + dt_o .$$

Then

$$T_C - T_{HT} = \left[\sum_{i=1}^{k} \left(2^{d_i} - 1\right) - \sum_{i=1}^{k} 3 \cdot 2^{d_i - 2} + k\right] t_w + \left[\sum_{i=1}^{k} \left(2^{d_i} - 1\right) - d\right] t_o =$$
$$= t_w \cdot \frac{3}{4} \sum_{i=1}^{k} 2^{d_i} + t_o \cdot \sum_{i=1}^{k} \left(2^{d_i} - d_i - 1\right) > 0,$$

because $2^{d_i} - d_i - 1 \geq 0$ for $d_i \geq 1$. Theorem 2 is proved.

In particular, time values T_C and T_{HT} for k-dimensional torus with $\underbrace{\sqrt[k]{n}\times\sqrt[k]{n}\times\ldots\times\sqrt[k]{n}}_{k}$ computers are correspondingly equal to $T_C = k(\sqrt[k]{n}-1)\cdot(t_w+t_o)$ and

$$\begin{aligned}T_{HT} &= \log_2 n\cdot(t_o+Dt_w)= \\ &= \log_2 n\cdot t_o+\left(k\cdot\frac{3}{4}\sqrt[k]{n}-2\right)t_w\end{aligned}.$$

From here we have

$$\begin{aligned}T_C - T_{HT} &= \left[k\left(\frac{\sqrt[k]{n}}{4}-1\right)+2\right]t_w + \\ &+\left[k\left(\sqrt[k]{n}-1\right)-\log_2 n\right]t_o,\end{aligned} \tag{8}$$

where $k\left(\sqrt[k]{n}-1\right)-\log_2 n\geq 0$ for $n\geq 2^k$. From (2) for $n\to\infty$ we get the following asymptotical equation

$$T_C - T_{HT} = O\left(\sqrt[k]{n}\right)\cdot\left(t_w+t_o\right).$$

So, the algorithms for mapping semigroup (binary associative) array operations onto distributed computer systems with torus topology are analyzed. The first algorithm is based on the cyclic data shifts in rows and columns of the torus. The second algorithm is based on the use of the butterfly scheme mapped onto the hypercube with subsequent XOR– mapping of the hypercube onto the torus. It is shown that, in spite of the hypercube edges dilation on the torus, the hypercube-onto-torus mapping algorithm provides the time of the semigroup operation execution on the torus less than the time provided by the cyclic-data-shift algorithm.

5. Mapping Neural Networks with Global Connections onto Hypercubic Computer Systems

The neural network element (neuron) implements transformation of the form

$$y = f(w,x)$$

where x is a vector of input signals, w is a vector of the neuron weight coefficients, y is an output signal of the neuron. Each weight coefficient corresponds to one input (synapse) of the neuron. A set of neurons, processing the same input vector x, forms a layer of neurons. The layer operation is described by the formula:

$$Y = f(W, x), \tag{9}$$

where W is a matrix with neuron weight vectors of the layer as rows, Y is a vector of the layer output signals.

The bulk of the computations in the neural networks [23, 24] form semigroup operations on the rows of matrix W of weight coefficients of the neuron layer and vector x whose elements correspond to the pixels of the processed image. It leads to a large volume of computations and the need to use highly parallel computer systems [21]. The maximum achievable degree of parallelism is equal to the number of the image pixels.

The method for interprocess exchange organization in parallel implementation of operation (9) is determined by the distribution of coefficients of the weight matrix W to the processes. At present, there are many methods of mapping neural networks onto parallel computer systems [2–7], but these methods do not use mapping semigroup operations onto the hypercube with subsequent embedding in the torus, which provides less time for performing calculations in comparison with other methods. This mapping is used here.

Let image (or signal) x contains $N = 2^q$ pixels (indications). These pixels can be mapped into vertices of the hypercube of dimension q. The number N of the hypercube vertices can be reduced 2^r times, $r \leq q$, by multiple merging vertices for the corresponding coordinates $i \in \{1, 2, ..., q\}$.

Consider a layer of neurons in which operation (9) takes the form

$$Y = f(W \cdot x) \tag{10}$$

where $W \cdot x$ is a product of the weight matrix W of the layer on the vector x composed of pixels of the image, the fragments of which are evenly distributed among the computers of the mesh (see Fig. 3), f is the neuron activation function. Formula (10) describes the computations in the layers of multilayer backpropagation networks and Hopfield networks.

Consider two ways of embedding layers of neurons onto the structure of distributed CS:

- placement of the rows of weight matrix W onto computers of CS (parallelism of neurons);
- placement of the columns of weight matrix W onto computers of CS (parallelism of synapsis).

5.1. Placement of the Weight Matrix Rows to Hypercube Nodes

Consider the organization of intercomputer exchanges in the distribution of the rows of weight matrix W onto the hypercube nodes. Since each row of the weight matrix corresponds to one network neuron, then the rows distribution describes the placement of the neurons. To perform calculations for all neurons according to formula (10), it is necessary to collect all pixels of image x at each vertex, i.e., to perform all–to–all exchange of the vector x components. Further weight matrix rows multiplication on this vector can be made in all processes in parallel (number of concurrent multiplications of vectors pairs is the hypercube vertices number).

An all-to-all data exchange in the q-dimensional hypercube reduces to sequential implementation of bidirectional point-to-point exchanges across dimensions $i = 1, 2, ..., q$ of the hypercube that corresponds to sequential executions of the butterfly stages. At each stage, all the bidirectional exchanges are performed simultaneously. After each stage the amount of data doubles in each process. Upon completion of q stages each process contains all the vector x data. Figure 6 shows an example of organizing intercomputer exchanges on a hypercube for $q = 3$. The numbers in brackets are the exchange step numbers.

Suppose that N is the image pixels number, m is the neurons number in layer, $n = 2^q$ is the processes number in the parallel program (CPUs in the system), t_o is the execution time of one arithmetic operation, t_w is the transmission time of one data item. Then the time of exchanges in the hypercube is

$$T_{ex} = \frac{N}{n} t_w \sum_{i=0}^{q-1} 2^i = N\left(1 - \frac{1}{n}\right) t_w .$$

So, we have

Theorem 3. Time T_{ex} of all-to-all data exchange in the hypercube is equal to

$$T_{ex} = N\left(1 - \frac{1}{n}\right) t_w . \tag{11}$$

Since the pixels number in the image is $N >> 1$, we get the time of sequential implementation of multiplication operation $W \cdot x$ in the layer:

$$T_{seq} \approx 2m \cdot N \cdot t_o .$$

Let the neurons number m and the pixels number N in the image are multiples of the number of processes n of a parallel program. Consider the case where the layer neurons are evenly distributed over the processes. Under the assumption that the parallel program (computer system) has a hypercube topology of $n = 2^q$ processes (processors), we obtain the computation time of the parallel computations implementation in the layer (due to $N >> 1$ the time of computing activation function is neglected):

$$T_r = \frac{T_{seq}}{n} + T_{ex} = \frac{2mN}{n} t_0 + N\left(1 - \frac{1}{n}\right) t_w .$$

From here we have the speedup coefficient

$$S_r = \frac{T_{seq}}{T_r} = \frac{2mNt_o}{\frac{2mNt_o}{n} + N\left(1 - \frac{1}{n}\right)t_w} = n\frac{1}{1 + \frac{(n-1)t_w}{2mt_o}}.$$

Thus, we have proved the theorem.

Theorem 4. In allocating the rows of matrix W to computers (parallelism of neurons) the speedup coefficient does not depend on the number of pixels in the image and is equal to

$$S_r = \frac{T_{seq}}{T_r} = n\frac{1}{1 + \frac{(n-1)t_w}{2mt_o}}. \quad (12)$$

5.2. Placement of the Weight Matrix Columns to Hypercube Nodes

When placing the columns of weight matrix W on the processes, the parallel computation of product $W \cdot x$ can be organized as follows:

a) Matrix W coefficients are multiplied to the corresponding components of vector x in parallel and, for each neuron, the summation of the resulting products is performed. When $N = 2^d$ is multiple to x, partial sums are computed in parallel in all processes.

b) To calculate the total sum for each neuron, it is necessary to make interprocess data exchanges using a binary tree of interprocess communications embedded in the graph of the computer system. A number of computed sums is equal to number m of the neurons which may be arbitrary and, in particular, times of the number of processes.

The time of multiplying the corresponding components of the weights vector and the image vector is equal to

$$T_{mult} = \frac{mN}{n}t_o.$$

The time of summing the resulting products:

$$T_{add} = m\left(\frac{N}{n} - 1\right)t_o.$$

Then the computation time of all partial sums in the computers working in parallel is equal to

$$T_{ps} = T_{mult} + T_{add} = \frac{mN}{n}t_o + m\left(\frac{N}{n} - 1\right)t_o = m\left(\frac{2N}{n} - 1\right)t_o. \quad (13)$$

Next, the full sums are calculated for each of m neurons on the hypercube of n processes in $\log_2 n$ steps. At each of these steps, a summing operation can be performed for no more than two neurons. Since, during the transition from step to step, the number of terms is half-reduced, and the minimum possible number of sums computed at each step is 1, the time of calculation of all complete sums for m neurons equals to

$$T_{cs} = (t_w + t_o) \sum_{i=1}^{\log_2 n} \max\left(1, \frac{m}{2^i}\right). \tag{14}$$

Full-time of parallel implementation:

$$T_c = T_{ps} + T_{cs} = m\left(\frac{2N}{n} - 1\right)t_o + (t_w + t_o) \sum_{i=1}^{\log_2 n} \max\left(1, \frac{m}{2^i}\right). \tag{15}$$

For m multiple n from (14) we have:

$$T_{cs} = m(t_w + t_o) \sum_{i=1}^{\log_2 n} \frac{1}{2^i} = m\frac{n-1}{n}(t_w + t_o). \tag{16}$$

From formulas (13) – (16) it follows:

$$T_c = T_{ps} + T_{cs} = m\left(\frac{2N}{n} - 1\right)t_o + m\frac{n-1}{n}(t_w + t_o) =$$
$$= \frac{m}{n}\left[(2N-1)t_o + (n-1)t_w\right] .$$

The speedup is

$$S_c = \frac{T_{seq}}{T_c} = \frac{2mNt_o}{\frac{m}{n}\left[(2N-1)t_o + (n-1)t_w\right]} = n\frac{1}{\frac{2N-1}{2N} + \frac{(n-1)t_w}{2Nt_o}}. \tag{17}$$

For $N >> 1$ from (17) we have

Theorem 5. In the allocation of the matrix W columns to computers (parallelism of synapses) speedup S_c does not depend on number m of neurons in the layer and is

$$S_c = n\frac{1}{1+\frac{(n-1)t_w}{2Nt_o}}. \tag{18}$$

From (12) and (18) it follows

Theorem 6. If $m > N$, then $S_r > S_c$, else $S_r \leq S_c$, i.e., if the neurons number m is more than the synapses number N of the neuron (image pixels), then the matrix W rows distribution to computers (parallelism of neurons) is more efficient than the distribution of its columns (parallelism of synapses), and vice versa.

5.3. Mapping the Hopfield Network

In the Hopfield neural network, weight matrix W is square, i.e., the number of neurons m is equal to synapses number N (number of pixels in the image). From this and (12), and (18) we obtain:

$$S_r = S_c = n\frac{1}{1+\frac{(n-1)t_w}{2Nt_o}},$$

i.e., the following theorem is correct.

Theorem 7. For all values of the image parameters and computer system parameters, the neuron parallelization efficiency is equivalent to synapses parallelization efficiency for mapping the Hopfield network onto the hypercube.

5.4. Mapping the Kohonen Network

In the analysis of mapping the Kohonen network onto the hypercubic DCS, we should note that, instead of the scalar product of the vector w^i of neuron weights to input vector x of the signal (image), the measure of proximity ("distance") between these vectors is calculated. For the distance we may use the value:

$$d(w^i, x) = \sqrt{\sum_{j=1}^{N}(w_j^i - x_j)^2}. \tag{19}$$

For $N >> 1$, the time of sequential computation of all distances for m neurons is equal to

$$T_{seq} \approx 3mNt_o. \tag{20}$$

The analysis, similar to the above-mentioned, shows that, for parallel distances computations, we have the equalities:

$$S_r = n\frac{1}{1+\frac{(n-1)t_w}{3mt_o}} \tag{21}$$

and

$$S_c = n\frac{1}{1+\frac{(n-1)t_w}{3Nt_o}} . \tag{22}$$

From (21) and (22) we obtain theorem 7 for the Kohonen network.

The time of the sequential choise of value $d_{\min} = \min\limits_{i=1,\dots,m} d(w^i, x)$ is equal to

$$T_{\min} = t_o \cdot (m-1) . \tag{23}$$

The parallel choise of minimum distanse $d_{\min}$ among distances $d(w^i, x)$ is realized in two steps:

1. In the first step, in each s -th computer the minimum $d^s_{\min}$, $s = 1,2,\dots,n$ is searched.
2. In the second step of the search of $d_{\min} = \min(d^0_{\min}, d^1_{\min}, \dots, d^{n-1}_{\min})$, using a hypercube, the butterfly is used, where the addition operation is replaced by an operation of selecting the minimum of the two values.

As a result, each computer will have the value $d_{\min}$.

The time of parallel search of $d_{\min}$ is equal to

$$T_{par\min} = t_o\left(\frac{m}{n} - 1\right) + (t_w + t_o)\log_2 n . \tag{24}$$

From (23) and (24) we get the search speedup

$$S_{par\min} = \frac{T_{\min}}{T_{par\min}} = n\frac{m-1}{m-n+\frac{(t_w+t_o)}{t_o}n\log_2 n} . \tag{25}$$

For $m >> n$ from (25) we get

$$S_{par\min} \approx n \frac{1}{1+\frac{(t_w+t_o)}{t_o}\frac{n\log_2 n}{m}}, \tag{26}$$

and for $m >> n\log_2 n$ and $\frac{t_w+t_o}{t_o} = O(1)$ from (26) we have

$$S_{par\min} \approx n . \tag{27}$$

Formula (27) informs us about the possibility of having effective parallelization of the search of value $d_{\min}$ for a big number m of neurons (relative to the number of computers n).

6. Mapping Neural Networks with Global Connections onto Toroidal Computer Systems

In modern DCS the multidimensional torus [15, 16] is most commonly used as a graph of intercomputer connections.

6.1. Placement of the Weight Matrix Rows to Torus Nodes

An all-to-all exchange in the *k*-dimensional torus is reduced to implementation of all-to-all exchanges in the torus rings, i.e., in the structures described by cyclic subgroups. In each ring the exchanges are performed as shown in Figure 5.

Every computer M_j, $j=1,...,n_i$, $i=1,...,k$ transmits its pixel array to the computer $M_{(j-1)\bmod n_i}$, $j=1,...,n_i$ and receives an array from the computer $M_{(j+1)\bmod n_i}$, $j=1,...,n_i$. It is assumed that the links of the ring are operated simultaneously.

These steps continue until each computer of the ring receives all the pixels distributed over the computers. The exchanges are performed in parallel for all the rings of dimension i and successively across all dimensions $i=1,2,...,k$. For a two-dimensional torus (Fig. 2), the exchanges, for example, can be executed in parallel in all horizontal rings, and then in parallel for all the vertical rings.

Upon completion of the l -th step of an exchange, $l \in 1,2,...,k$, each computer comprises $\frac{N}{n}\prod_{i=1}^{l} n_i$ data elements and, after k steps, it contains N elements, respectively, because $\prod_{i=1}^{k} n_i = n$. The time of performing l exchange steps is

$$T_e(l) = \frac{N}{n}\left[(n_1-1)+\sum_{i=2}^{l}(n_i-1)\prod_{j=1}^{i-1} n_j\right]t_w . \tag{28}$$

For $l = k$, transforming formula (28), we obtain:

Theorem 8. When distributing the weight matrix W rows to the torus computers, the time $T_{ex} = T_e(k)$ of all-to-all data exchange does not depend on torus dimension k and is equal to

$$T_{ex} = N\left(1 - \frac{1}{n}\right)t_w . \tag{29}$$

From (11) and (29) it follows that the times of all-to-all communication on the hypercube and torus are the same. Given the fact that, after the exchange, all the calculations are performed in parallel, we obtain for the torus the following:

Theorem 9. In allocating the matrix W rows (parallelism of neurons) to the torus computers, the speedup does not depend on the number of pixels in the image and is equal to the speedup (12) for the hypercube.

6.2. Placement of the Weight Matrix Columns to Torus Nodes

The hypercube, resulted by merging the butterfly processes, can be embedded into a torus (XOR- embedding) [12]. When placing the matrix W columns to computers, the computation time of all partial sums in computers, working in parallel, is given in (13). Next, the complete sums are calculated in $\log_2 n$ steps for each of m neurons on the hypercube with n nodes (computers) embedded in a torus. At each of these steps the summing operations can be performed for no more than two neurons. Similar to calculations (14) – (18), subject to dilation D of the hypercube edges on the torus for $N >> 1$, we get

Theorem 10. In allocating the matrix W columns (parallelism of synapses) to the torus computers, speedup S_c does not depend on the number of m neurons in a layer and is equal to

$$S_c = n\frac{1}{1 + \dfrac{(n-1)Dt_w}{2Nt_o}} . \tag{30}$$

From (18) and (30) we have the following:

Theorem 11. If $m > \dfrac{N}{D}$ then $S_r > S_c$ else $S_r \le S_c$, i.e., if the neurons number m is greater than the ratio of the neuron synapses number N (image pixels) to the middle dilation D of the hypercube edges on the torus, then the distribution of the weight matrix W rows (parallelism of neurons) to computers is more efficient than its columns distribution (parallelism of synapses), and vice versa.

Table 2. Speedup coefficient S_r with respect neurons number m

m	1024	2048	4096	8192	16384	32768	65536
S_r	171	293	455	630	780	885	949

To obtain the numerical values of the speedup we use the parameters of computer Cray T3E [25]: CPU performance (1200 Mflops) and communication bandwidth (480 Mb/sec). Assume that the data element size is 4 bytes. Then we have $t_o = \dfrac{1}{1,2\cdot 10^9} \approx 0,83\cdot 10^{-9}$ seconds and $t_w = \dfrac{4}{480\cdot 10^6} \approx 8,3\cdot 10^{-9}$ seconds. Considering $n = 1024$, from the above formulas, we obtain the speedup coefficients $S_c = 753$ and S_r shown in Table 2. From Table 2 it follows that for a large number of neurons in the layer ($m = 16384,\ 32768,\ 65536$), it is profitable to obtain parallelization through neurons and, when $m \le 8192$, it is appropriate to realize the parallelization by synapses.

6.3. Mapping Hopfield Network and Kohonen Network onto the Torus

For the Hopfield network with $m = N$ from (18) and (30), we obtain the following:

Theorem 12. In mapping the Hopfield network onto the torus for $D > 1$ and any parameter values of the image and computer system, the neurons parallelization is more efficient than synapses parallelization, i.e.

$$S_r > S_c .$$

It is easy to see that, for mapping the Kohonen network onto the torus when placing rows of the weight matrix on computers, formula (21) is correct for speedup S_r, while for placing the columns the speedup is

$$S_c = n\frac{1}{1+\dfrac{(n-1)Dt_w}{3Nt_o}} . \tag{31}$$

Comparing (21) and (31), we see that, for the Kohonen network, theorem 12 is correct.

In higher-order Hopfield networks [26], the neurons data inputs are the products of pixel intensities, the choice of which for multiplication is determined by the objects configuration to be recognized and, therefore, it can be arbitrary. In this respect, the efficient parallelization in such networks can be achieved by neurons parallelism when the all-to-all exchange is prior to computing, when each process obtains the whole image. At the same time, the synapses parallelism cannot be used because the multiplication of the pixel values, distributed over different processes, involves a large number of interprocess communication.

6.4. Mapping Multilayer Neural Networks

Consider a two-layer sigmoid neural network with m neurons in the hidden layer and k neurons in the output layer. When processing data arrays (images, for example) with N elements, the following relations are usually performed:

$$m << N,\ k << N.$$

Let the neural network is mapped onto DCS with the structure of a hypercube or torus with the number of computers $n \le m << N$. According to Theorem 6 for $m < N$ the weights matrix of the hidden layer should be placed on processors by columns (parallelism of synapses).

For the output neural network layer, we obtain the parallelization coefficients:

a) for the hypercube

$$S_r = \frac{n}{1+\dfrac{(n-1)t_w}{2kt_o}},\ S_c = \frac{n}{1+\dfrac{(n-1)t_w}{2mt_o}};$$

b) for the torus

$$S_r = \frac{n}{1+\dfrac{(n-1)Dt_w}{2kt_o}},\ S_c = \frac{n}{1+\dfrac{(n-1)Dt_w}{2mt_o}}.$$

Hence, when $k > m$, we see $S_r > S_c$; otherwise $S_c > S_r$, i.e., for image (or signal) compression problems ($k > m$) in the output layer, we should use neurons parallelism, and, for classification tasks (recognition) ($m > k$), we should use synapses parallelism.

7. Training Neural Networks on Distributed Computer Systems

7.1. Training Hopfield Networks

7.1.1. Training Hopfield Network According to Hebb Rule

According to Hebb rule [1], the matrix of the Hopfield network weight coefficients is evaluated as

$$W = \sum_{p=1}^{n} X^p X^{pT}, \tag{32}$$

where X^p is a reference vector, $p = 1,...,n$, n is a number of reference vectors.

The components of vector X^p are distributed to m computers (processors) of the computer system. According to (32), each vector X^p needs the pairwise multiplication of all its components. For parallel execution of this multiplication it is necessary to:

1. Perform all-to-all exchange of the vector X^p components among the computers to obtain the vector X^p entirely in each processor.
2. Multiply the corresponding share of N/m components of the vector X^p by all components of the same vector in each processor.

As a result, we have N/m rows of matrix W in each computer.

7.1.2. Training Hopfield Network According to Projection Method

This training is based on the formulas [2]:

1. $W^0 = 0$.

2. $$\begin{cases} Y^p = \left(W^{p-1} - E\right) X^p, \\ W^p = W^{p-1} + \dfrac{Y^p Y^{pT}}{Y^{pT} Y^p}, \ p = 1,...,n, \end{cases}$$

where E is the identity matrix.

For each vector X^p, $p = 1,...,n$ we need to perform the following steps:

1) all-to-all exchange of the vector X^p components among the computers to obtain the vector X^p entirely in each processor;
2) parallel multiplication of matrix $W^{p-1} - E$ bands by vector X^p to obtain vector Y^p fragments;
3) all-to-all exchange of vector Y^p components among the computers to obtain the vector Y^p entirely in each computer;
4) inner product $Y^{pT} Y^p$ computation: vector Y^p components parallel multiplication, using the doubling scheme with mapping it onto hypercube to calculate the sum of the products;
5) outer product $Y^p Y^{pT}$ computation: parallel multiplication of column vector Y^p fragments to row vector Y^{pT};
6) parallel computation of matrix W^p bands.

7.2. Training Two-Layer Sigmoidal Neural Network on a Hypercube

Consider the backpropagation algorithm [1] which calculates the weight corrections for the output and hidden layers. Let a two-layer sigmoidal neural network processes a vector $x = (x_1, x_2, ..., x_N)$. The outputs of the neurons in the hidden layer are calculated by the formula

$$u_j = f\left(a_j^{(1)}\right),\ a_j^{(1)} = \sum_{i=0}^{N} w_{ji}^{(1)} x_i,\ j = 1,...,n\ ,$$

where n is a neurons number in the hidden layer, $a_j^{(1)}$ is the activation of the j-th neuron of the hidden layer, $w_{ji}^{(1)},\ i = 0,1,...,N,\ j = 1,...,n$ are this neuron weights, f is the neuron activation function. The network outputs (the neurons output in the output layer) are

$$y_k = f\left(a_k^{(2)}\right),\ a_k^{(2)} = \sum_{j=0}^{n} w_{kj}^{(2)} u_j, k = 1,...,m\ ,$$

where m is a neurons number in the output layer, $a_k^{(2)}$ is the k-th neuron activation of the output layer, $w_{kj}^{(2)},\ k = 1,...,m,\ j = 1,...,n$ are this neuron weights.

7.2.1. Training Neurons in the Output Layer Is Carried Out by the Formulas

$$\Delta w_{kj}^{(2)} = -\alpha \delta_k u_j,\ \delta_k = \left(y_k - d_k\right) \frac{\partial f(a_k^{(2)})}{\partial a_k^{(2)}}, \tag{33}$$

$$w_{kj}^{(2)}(t+1) = w_{kj}^{(2)}(t) + \Delta w_{kj}^{(2)}(t), \tag{34}$$

where d_k is a desired k-th neuron output of the output layer, t is a number of the current training iteration.

Values $\delta_k, k = 1,...,m$ and $u_j,\ j = 1,...,n$ are distributed on computers, as well as the neurons of the output and hidden layers, respectively. Formula (33) implies the need for computing products $\delta_k u_j, k = 1,...,m,\ j = 1,...,n$. Therefore, before you perform calculations using formulas (33)−(34), you must perform an all-to-all intercomputer exchange of quantities $\delta_k, k = 1,...,m$ or values $u_j,\ j = 1,...,n$, depending on the method of matrix $w^{(2)}(t)$ elements distribution on computers.

If the matrix $w^{(2)}(t)$ rows are distributed on computers (neurons parallelism), it is necessary to make an all-to-all exchange of the signal $u_j,\ j = 1,...,n$ values and then perform parallel computations using formulas (33)−(34). In each computer signals $u_j,\ j = 1,...,n$ are multiplied by the elements $\delta_k, k = 1,...,m$ that are located on this computer.

If the matrix $w^{(2)}(t)$ columns are distributed on computers (synapses parallelism), there must first be an all-to-all exchange by values $\delta_k, k=1,...,m$ and then one should perform parallel computations by formulas (33) – (34). So, to complete the step of training the neural network output layer, it is necessary to carry out:

- an all-to-all intercomputer data exchange;
- parallel computations of products $\delta_k u_j, k=1,...,m,\ j=1,...,n$.

7.2.2. Training the Hidden Layer Is Carried Out by the Equations

$$\Delta w_{ji}^{(1)} = -\alpha\sigma_j x_i,\ \sigma_j = \frac{\partial f(a_j^{(1)})}{\partial a_j^{(1)}} \sum_{k=1}^{m} \delta_k w_{kj}^{(2)},$$

$$w_{ji}^{(1)}(t+1) = w_{ji}^{(1)}(t) + \Delta w_{ji}^{(1)}(t) .$$

The basic operation here is to calculate quantities $\sigma_j,\ j=1,...,n$. The method of σ_j parallel computing depends on the distribution of the matrix $w^{(2)}$ elements on computers.

If the matrix $w^{(2)}(t)$ rows are distributed on computers (neurons parallelism of the output layer), then it is necessary:

1) to multiply the elements δ_k disposed therein to their respective rows $w_k^{(2)},\ k \in \{1,...,m\}$ (parallel operation of all computers) in every computer;
2) to sum products $\delta_k w_{kj}^{(2)}$ for all values $j=1,...,n$ using a doubling scheme;
3) to multiply the sums obtained for the corresponding derivatives $\frac{\partial f(a_j^{(1)})}{\partial a_j^{(1)}},\ j=1,...,n$ (parallel operation of all computers).

If the matrix $w^{(2)}(t)$ columns are distributed on computers (synapses parallelism of the output layer neurons), then it is necessary:

- to carry out an all-to-all intercomputer exchange of values $\delta_k, k=1,...,m$;
- to calculate values $\sigma_j,\ j=1,...,n$ in parallel for all the computers of the system.

The method of calculating values $\Delta w_{ji}^{(1)} = -\alpha\sigma_j x_i$ is similar to calculating values $\Delta w_{kj}^{(2)} = -\alpha\delta_k u_j$. It is determined by the type of distribution on computers of the weight matrix $w^{(1)}$ elements of the hidden layer.

Conclusion

The methods for efficient mapping data processing neural networks onto robust distributed computer systems (DCS) are proposed. The cellular neural networks are mapped onto the graphs of parallel programs with structures "mesh" and "line". The efficiency of the proposed methods for neural networks with global connections (Hopfield network, Kohonen network and multilayer perceptron) is based on a butterfly scheme and doubling scheme, and mapping these schemes onto a hypercube with a subsequent hypercube embedding onto the torus. These networks are mapped onto regular graphs of parallel programs ("line", "ring", "mesh", "hypercube", "torus"), intended for their implementation on DCS.

The method for mapping a neuron layer (for multilayer feedforward networks, Hopfield network or Kohonen network) depends on the ratio of the neurons number in the layer and the number of neuron weight coefficients (image pixels number) : if the neurons number is relatively small, it is a more efficient method of distributing the layer weight matrix columns (synapses parallelism). Otherwise the distribution of the weight matrix rows (neurons parallelism) is more efficient. In particular, for mapping the Hopfield network onto the torus, the rows distribution gives the best result. On the hypercube, for the Hopfield network, both weights distribution methods give the same result.

The proposed mapping techniques provide a uniform distribution of the results of image transformation by the neurons layer on the processes of the parallel program with a toroidal structure. Hence, the mapping of the weight matrix of the second neurons layer can be realized similar to the the first layer mapping. The mapping method (by rows or columns) is also determined by the ratio of the neurons number of the second layer to its input signals number.

So, we found that the neural network layers mapping onto a distributed computing system, during the network operation and during the training phase, is reduced to the following types of distributed computing schemes:

1) parallel (independent) computations in elementary computers of the system;
2) an all-to-all intercomputer data exchange;
3) sums computation by a doubling scheme with the mapping of this scheme onto a hypercube with a subsequent embedding of the hypercube into the torus (implementation of semigroup array operations on the hypercube and torus).

The proposed methods lead to the parallel programs generation with the following regular structures: line, mesh, binary tree, hypercube and toroidal structures of different dimensions (in particular, the ring).

References

[1] Haykin, S., (1999). *Neural Networks. A Comprehensive Foundation*, Prentice Hall Inc.

[2] Michel, A., Farrel, J, (1990). Associative memories via artificial neural networks, *IEEE Control System Magazine*. 10, 6-16.

[3] Sundararajan, N., Saratchandran, P., (1988). *Parallel Architectures for Artificial Neural Networks. Paradigms and Implementations*. IEEE Computer Society.

[4] Ayoubi, R.A., Bayoumi, M.A., (2003). Efficient Mapping Algorithm of Multilayer Neural Network on Torus Architecture. *IEEE Trans. on Parallel and Distributed Systems*. 14, 932-943.

[5] Lin, W.-M., Prasanna, V.K., Prjitula, K.W., (1991). Algorithmic Mapping of Neural Network Models onto Parallel SIMD Machines. *IEEE Trans. on Computers*. 40, 1390-1401.

[6] Mahapatra, R.N., Mahapatra, S., (1996). Mapping of neural network models onto two-dimensional processor arrays. *Parallel Computing*. 22, 1345-1357.

[7] Mahapatra, S., Mahapatra, R.N., Chatterji, B.N., (1997). A parallel formulation of back-propagation learning on distributed memory multiprocessors. *Parallel Computing*. 22, 1661-1675.

[8] Fujimoto, Y., Fukuda, N., Akabane, T., (1992). Massively Parallel Architectures for Large Scale Neural Network Simulations. *IEEE Trans. on Neural Networks*. 3, 876-888.

[9] Tarkov, M.S., Mun, Y., Choi, J., Choi, H.–I., (2002). Mapping Adaptive Fuzzy Kohonen Clustering Network onto Distributed Image Processing System. *Parallel Computing*. 28, 1239–1256.

[10] Wolf, W., Jerraya, A.A., Martin, G. Multiprocessor System-on-Chip (MPSoC) Technology., (2008). *IEEE Trans. On Computer-Aided Design Of Integrated Circuits And Systems*, 27, 1701-1713.

[11] Pham, P.-H., Jelaca, D., Farabet, C., Martini, B., LeCun, Y., Culurcielo, E., (2012). NeuFlow: Dataflow Vision Processing System-on-a-Chip. *IEEE 55th International Midwest Symposium on Circuits and Systems* (*MWSCAS*). 1044 – 1047.

[12] Gonzalez, A., Valero-Garcia, M., Diaz de Cerio, L., (1995). Executing Algorithms with Hypercube Topology on Torus Multicomputers. *IEEE Trans. on Parallel and Distributed Systems*. 6, 803–814.

[13] Lakshmivarahan, S., Dhall, S.K., (1999). Ring, torus and hypercube architectures/algorithms for parallel computing. *Parallel Computing*. 25, 1877-1906.

[14] Tarkov, M.S., (2011). Mapping semigroup array operations onto multicomputer with torus topology. *Proc. of the 5th Int. Conf. on Ubiquitous Information Management and Communication*. Article No. 135.

[15] Yu, H., Chung, I-Hsin, Moreira, J., (2006). Topology Mapping for Blue Gene/L Supercomputer. *Proc. of the ACM/IEEE SC2006 Conf. on High Performance Networking and Computing*. ACM Press, 52–64.

[16] Balaji, P.; Gupta, R.; Vishnu, A. & Beckman, P. (2011). Mapping Communication Layouts to Network Hardware Characteristics on Massive-Scale Blue Gene Systems, *Comput. Sci. Res. Dev*. 26, 247–256.

[17] Palmer, J.E., (1986). The NCUBE family of parallel supercomputers. *Proc. of the International Conference on Computer Design*. IEEE.

[18] Foster, I. *Designing and Building Parallel Programs*, Available at: http://www-unix.mcs.anl.gov/dbpp

[19] Miller, R., Boxer, L., (2000). *Algorithms Sequential and Parallel: A Unified Approach*. Prentice Hall.

[20] Ortega, J.M. (1988). *Introduction to Parallel and Vector Solution of Linear Systems*, New York: Plenum.

[21] Parhami, B. (2002). *Introduction to Parallel Processing. Algorithms and Architectures*, New York: Kluwer Academic Publishers.

[22] Gonzalez, R.C., Woods, R. E., (2008). *Digital Image Processing*. Prentice Hall.

[23] de Ridder, D., Duin, R.P.W., Verbeek, P.W., van Vliet, L.J., (1999). The Applicability of Neural Networks to Non-linear Image Processing. *Pattern Analysis & Applications*. 2, 111-128.

[24] Egmont-Petersen, M., de Ridder, D., Handels, H., (2002). Image processing with neural networks—a review, *Pattern Recognition*. 35, 2279–2301.

[25] *The Cray T3E*, Available at: http://www.cray-cyber.org/systems/t3e.php

[26] Spirkovska, L., Reid, M.B., (1994). Higher-Order Neural Networks Applied to 2D and 3D Object Recognition, *Machine Learning*, 15, 169-199.

In: Parallel Programming
Editor: Mikhail S. Tarkov
ISBN: 978-1-63321-957-1

Chapter 2

MAPPING PARALLEL PROGRAM GRAPHS ONTO GRAPHS OF DISTRIBUTED COMPUTER SYSTEMS BY NEURAL NETWORK ALGORITHMS

Mikhail S. Tarkov *
Institute of Semiconductor Physics SB RAS, Novosibirsk, Russia

Abstract

The problem of mapping a parallel program with weighed vertices (processes) and edges (interprocess exchanges) onto a weighed graph of the distributed computer system is considered. An algorithm for solving this problem based on the use of Hopfield networks is proposed. The algorithm is tested on mapping a number of graphs of parallel programs onto a multicore computer. Experiments have shown that the proposed algorithm provides well-balanced sub-optimal mappings. Optimal solutions are found for mapping a "line"-graph onto a two-dimensional torus. To increase the probability of finding an optimal mapping, a method for splitting the mapping is proposed. The method's essence is reducing the solution matrix to a block-diagonal form. The Wang recurrent neural network is used to exclude incorrect solutions of the problem of mapping the line-graph onto a three-dimensional torus. An algorithm based on a recurrent neural Wang network and the WTA ("Winner takes all") principle is proposed for the construction of Hamiltonian cycles in graphs of distributed computer systems.

Keywords: mapping, graphs of parallel programs, multicore systems, load balancing, neuron, Hopfield networks

1. Introduction

Due to the ever increasing power of computers it is possible to create high-performance multicomputer systems [1]. Such a system, in general, is a unified, by communication lines, set of computing nodes, which has a high isolation degree, i.e., each node has its own

* E-mail address: tarkov@isp.nsc.ru

processor, often multicore, the memory, perhaps, own hard drive and a way to communicate with other nodes (network card, modem, etc.). Nodes of the computer system can have a different performance and different communication capabilities. In general, the structure of a computer system is arbitrary and depends on several factors, such as, for example, the hardware capabilities, the purpose for which the system is created, the financial constraints.

Unlike systems with shared memory, in multicomputer systems, a more urgent issue is reducing the amount of intercomputer interactions, since the capacity of the network is low. We must, therefore, allocate the processes of a parallel program to available computing nodes to minimize the execution time of a parallel program. To make this, we must download the processors according to their performance (the higher the performance, the higher the load is) and minimize the interaction between the processes at different nodes, which can reduce the CPU idle time, reducing the efficiency of the computer system.

In general, this problem is reduced to the mapping of the graph of the parallel program onto the graph of the computer system [2-6]. The purpose of the mapping is to minimize the execution time of the program. Due to the complexity of the mapping problem (it is NP-complete), various heuristics are widely used to find the best mappings. Currently, popular methods are based on the analogies with physics and biology, such as the method of simulated annealing, genetic algorithms and neural networks [7]. The latter include the Hopfield network [8, 9].

2. Mapping Problem

The purpose of optimal allocation of parallel program processes (branches) to the system processors is to minimize the execution time of the program, which is equivalent to minimizing the downtime of each processor involved in the task and, at the same time, minimizing the cost of communications among the processes placed in different processors.

Let

$G_p(V_p, E_p)$ is a graph of a parallel program;

V_p is a set of the program branches, $n = |V_p|$;

E_p is a set of logical (virtual) channels, each channel implements an interaction between two branches;

$G_s(V_s, E_s)$ is a graph of the computer system;

V_s is a set of processors (processor cores – CPUs), $m = |V_s|$, $m \le n$;

E_s is a set of connections between processors;

w_x is a weight (computational complexity) of branch $x \in V_p$;

ϑ_i is a performance of processor $i \in V_s$;

$\tau_{xi} = \dfrac{w_x}{\vartheta_i}$ is a run-time of branch $x \in V_p$ on CPU $i \in V_s$;

c_{xy} is a weight of edge $(x, y) \in E_p$, equal to the number of information units transmitted between branches x and y;

d_{ij} is a time of information unit transmission between processors (cores) i and j.

Let $f_m : G_p \to G_s$ is a mapping of program graph $G_p(V_p, E_p)$ onto graph $G_s(V_s, E_s)$ of the computer system. The mapping f_m quality will be estimated by the objective function

$$H_g(f_m) = H_{gc}(f_m) + H_{gt}(f_m),$$

where $H_{gc}(f_m)$ is an estimate of the computational load imbalance, $H_{gt}(f_m)$ is an estimate of the total interprocessor communications time.

For mapping f_m, the full time of i-th CPU computations is equal to

$$T_i = \sum_{f_m(x)=i} \tau_{xi} .$$

From here we have

$$H_{gc}(f_m) = \sum_{i=1}^{m} (T_i - T_{\min})^2 ,$$

where $T_{\min} = \dfrac{\sum_x w_x}{\sum_i \vartheta_i}$ is the minimum possible (ideal) execution time of the parallel program (run time of the program on a single processor with a capacity equal to the total performance of the system at no cost of the interactions between the program branches).

The interaction cost is estimated by the function

$$H_{gt}(f_m) = \sum_{x \neq y, i=f_m(x), j=f_m(y)} c_{xy} d_{ij},$$

where the summation is realized over all pairs (x, y) of interacting branches of the parallel program.

3. Hopfield Network for the Mapping Problem

Consider the neuron states matrix v with size $n \times m$. Each row of the matrix corresponds to the branch of a parallel program, each column corresponds to the processor (core). Each row of matrix v must contain one and only one non-zero element equal to one; the other elements are zero (the branch of a parallel program can not be mapped simultaneously onto several processors). Each column can contain any number of elements equal to one (including zero), but the total number of unique elements must be equal to the number of branches of the parallel program. We call matrix v satisfying these restrictions the permissible (correct) solution of the mapping problem.

The corresponding Hopfield neural network energy is described by the Lyapunov function

$$H = \frac{A}{2}H_c + \frac{B}{2}H_g. \tag{1}$$

Here A and B are the Lyapunov function parameters. The H_c minimum ensures the above restrictions on the elements of matrix v; H_g is the objective function.

$$H_c = H_{c1} + H_{c2},\ H_{c1} = \left(\sum_x \sum_i v_{xi} - n\right)^2,\ H_{c2} = \sum_x \left(\sum_i v_{xi} - 1\right)^2. \tag{2}$$

The H_{c1} minimum ensures n units in the matrix v exactly. The H_{c2} minimum provides exactly one unit in each matrix v row.

$$\begin{gathered} H_g = H_{gc} + H_{gt},\ H_{gc} = \sum_i \left(\sum_x v_{xi}\tau_{xi} - T_{\min}\right)^2, \\ H_{gt} = \sum_x \sum_i v_{xi} \sum_y \sum_j v_{yj} c_{xy} d_{ij}. \end{gathered} \tag{3}$$

Here v_{xi} is the state of the neuron in row x and column i of matrix v.

The Hopfield network dynamics, minimizing function (1), is described by the system of equations

$$\frac{\partial u_{xi}}{\partial t} = -\frac{\partial H}{\partial v_{xi}}, \tag{4}$$

where u_{xi} is activation of the neuron with indexes x,i, $x,i = 1,\dots,n$, $v_{xi} = \dfrac{1}{1+\exp(-\beta u_{xi})}$ is the state (output signal) of the neuron, β is the activation function parameter.

From (1)-(4) we have

$$\begin{gathered} \frac{\partial u_{xi}}{\partial t} = -A\left(\sum_y \sum_j v_{yj} + \sum_j v_{xj} - n - 1\right) - \\ -B\left[\left(\sum_y v_{yi}\tau_{yi} - t_{\min}\right)\cdot \tau_{xi} + \sum_y \sum_j v_{yj} c_{xy} d_{ij}\right]. \end{gathered} \tag{5}$$

The corresponding (5) difference equation is (t is the number of the current iteration, Δt is the time step value):

$$u_{xi}^{t+1} = u_{xi}^{t} - \Delta t \cdot \{A\left(\sum_{y}\sum_{j} v_{yj} + \sum_{j} v_{xj} - n - 1\right) + \\ +B\left[\left(\sum_{y} v_{yi}\tau_{yi} - t_{\min}\right) \cdot \tau_{xi} + \sum_{y}\sum_{j} v_{yj} c_{xy} d_{ij}\right]\}. \tag{6}$$

In order to accelerate the convergence, the Hopfield network (6) is transformed into the Wang network [10, 11] by multiplying the objective function of the optimization problem to $\exp(-t/\eta)$, where η is a parameter:

$$u_{xi}^{t+1} = u_{xi}^{t} - \Delta t \cdot \{A\left(\sum_{y}\sum_{j} v_{yj} + \sum_{j} v_{xj} - n - 1\right) + \\ +B\left[\left(\sum_{y} v_{yi}\tau_{yi} - t_{\min}\right) \cdot \tau_{xi} + \sum_{y}\sum_{j} v_{yj} c_{xy} d_{ij}\right] \cdot \exp(-t/\eta)\}. \tag{7}$$

The new value of v_{xi}^{t+1} is calculated immediately after finding the corresponding value of u_{xi}^{t+1} (Gauss–Seidel method).

4. Mapping Parallel Programs onto Multicore Computers

In experiments, the mappings onto the computer with $m = 2,4,8$ cores are investigated for the following types of the parallel program with the same weights $w_x = 1, x = 0,...,n-1$ of nodes (branches) and weights $c_{xy} = 0$ (there is no edge (x, y)) or $c_{xy} = 1$ (there is an edge (x, y)), $x, y = 0,...,n-1$, $x \neq y$ of the program graph edges:

1. a set of independent branches (no data exchanges between branches, i.e., $c_{xy} = 0$ for any edge (x, y)),
2. typical graphs of parallel programs (line, ring and mesh) (Figure 1), $c_{xy} = 1$ to adjacent vertices x and y of the program graph,
3. irregular grids with identical edges: $c_{xy} = 1$ for adjacent vertices x and y.

The computer system parameters:
core performance $\vartheta_i = 1$, $i = 0,...,m-1$;

$$d_{ij} = \begin{cases} 0, & i = j, \\ 1, & i \neq j. \end{cases} \quad (8)$$

According to (8), we consider the cost of data exchanges between the branches of the program within the core to be negligible with respect to the intercore exchanges. In other words, the data in the core are considered as arrays processed by one branch.

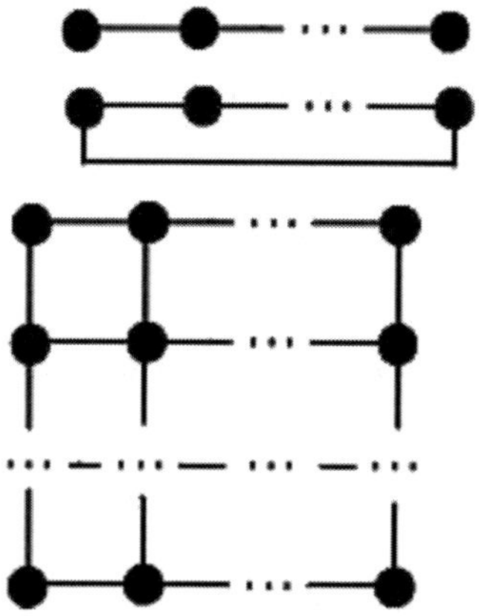

Figure 1. Typical graphs of parallel programs (line, ring and mesh).

For $w_x = 1$ and $\vartheta_i = 1$ we have $\tau_{xi} = 1$, $x = 1,...,n,\ i = 1,...,m$. The neural network parameters are equal to $A = 1000,\ B = 100,\ \Delta t = 1, \beta = 1,\ \eta = 100$. The mapping procedure is as follows:

```
do
{ initialize();
do
{ iterate(); iter = iter + 1;
 δ = nobalance();
} while ( δ >0 && iter < maxiter);
} while ( δ >maxnb || noncorrect());
```

Here

initialize sets the initial value of matrix u^0 (and, respectively v^0) elements using a random number generator ;

iterate performs a step of the iterative process (7), calculating new values of the elements of matrices u^{t+1} and v^{t+1} ;

nobalance calculates the load imbalance by the formula

$$\delta = \frac{\sqrt{\sum_{i=0}^{m-1} \left(T_i - T_{\min}\right)^2}}{m \cdot T_{\min}};$$

noncorrect verifies conditions (2) of solution v^{t+1} correctness.

Iterative process (7) continues until the load balance is obtained ($\delta = 0$) or the maximum number of iterations $maxiter = 1000$ is reached. If under these conditions the iterative process is completed, the correctness of solution v^{t+1} is verified. If solution v^{t+1} is incorrect or the load imbalance exceeds the allowable maximum maxnb, then we set new initial conditions and the iteration process is repeated (the algorithm is restarted).

Tables 1-4 show the following results obtained on the CPU Pentium (R) Dual-Core CPU E 52000, 2,5 GHz in the series of 100 tests of the algorithm for mapping the program graphs onto a computer with four cores ($m = 4$):

I_a is the average number of iterations to 100 tests;

I_m is the maximum number of iterations;

t_a is the average running time of the mapping algorithm (in seconds);

t_m is the maximum running time of the mapping algorithm (in seconds);

N_a is the average number of restarts of the algorithm if condition δ >maxnb || noncorrect() is not satisfied;

N_m is the maximum number of restarts of the algorithm if condition δ >maxnb || noncorrect() is not satisfied;

C_a is the average total amount of data transferred between the cores for the evaluated mapping;

C_m is the maximum total amount of data transferred between the cores for the evaluated mapping.

Note that under the above weights c_{xy}, values C_a and C_m specify the number of the program graph $G_p(V_p, E_p)$ edges connecting the graph vertices mapped onto different computer cores.

Table 1. Independent tasks

n	4	8	16	32	64
I_a	61	50	50	57	70
I_m	374	265	275	356	222
t_a	0,0084	0,026	0,05	0,066	0,441
t_m	0,109	0,235	0,579	0,781	2,92
N_a	0,51	0,59	0,41	0,28	0,82
N_m	6	5	7	3	5

Table 2. Line

n	4	8	16	32	64
I_a	75	68	70	83	112
I_m	312	423	515	285	529
t_a	0,0027	0,003	0,014	0,046	0,334
t_m	0,032	0,062	0,156	0,454	2,985
N_a	0,19	0,05	0,17	0,21	0,47
N_m	2	2	3	2	4
C_a	3	4,23	5,13	7,24	11,17
C_m	3	7	10	13	17

Table 3. Ring

n	4	8	16	32	64
I_a	110	71	59	74	97
I_m	348	243	213	273	216
t_a	0,0061	0,0044	0,0078	0,0055	0,336
t_m	0,047	0,047	0,141	0,796	5,93
N_a	0,37	0,12	0,07	0,26	0,43
N_m	3	2	2	2	5
C_a	4	4,86	5,53	7,82	11,68
C_m	4	7	10	15	19

Table 4. Mesh

n	16	64	256
I_a	60	89	571
I_m	166	306	1000
t_a	0,0097	0,283	15,8
t_m	0,032	1,77	99,7
N_a	0,24	0,62	1,28
N_m	2	4	15
C_a	11,41	29,82	92,32
C_m	17	40	123

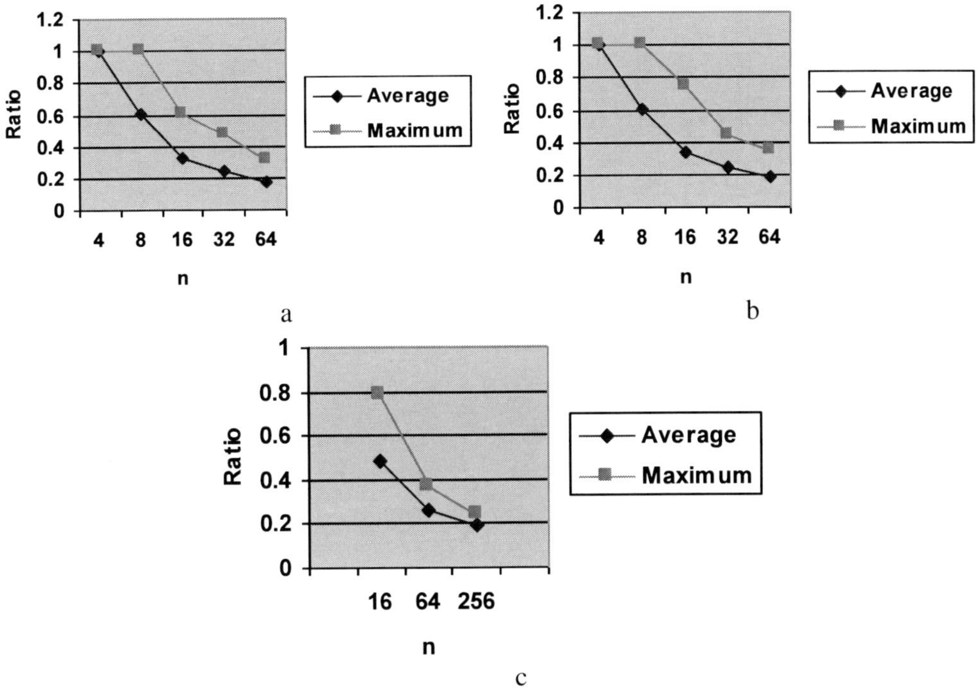

Figure 2. Ratio of numbers C_a (Average) and C_m (Maximum) to number $C_{\max}$ of the edges in the program: a) line; b) ring; c) mesh.

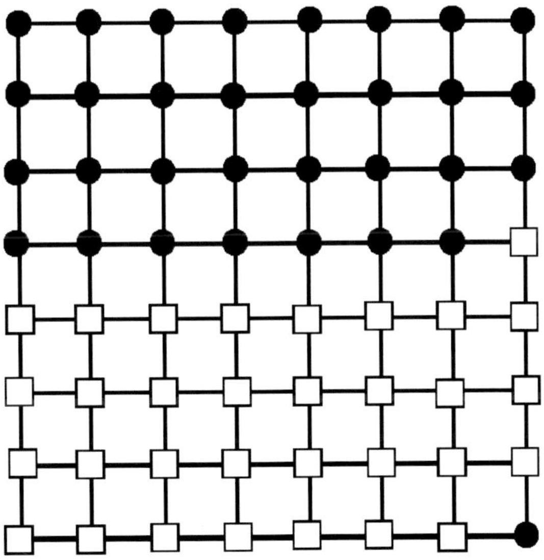

Figure 3. Example of the mapping mesh with 8×8 vertices onto the system with two cores.

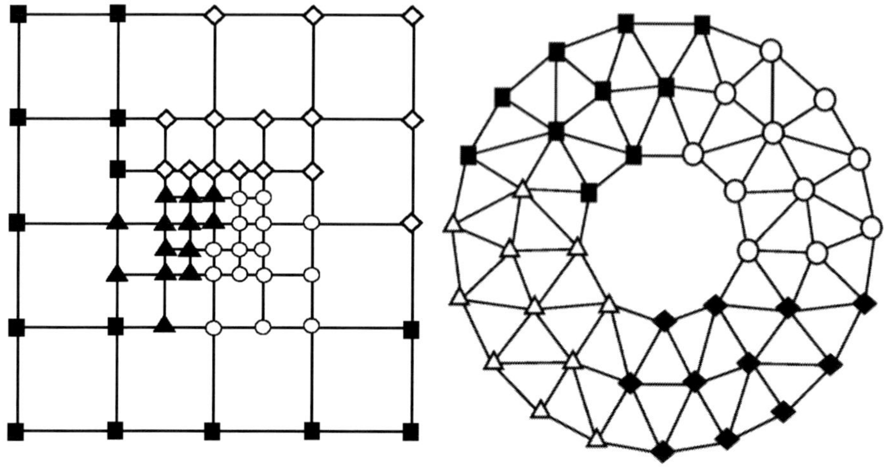

a b

Figure 4. Examples of mapping irregular grids onto the system with 4 cores: a) rectangular grid ($n=57$), b) triangular grid ($n=43$).

In all cases listed in Tables 1-4, the completely balanced mappings ($\delta=0$) are obtained except for the mapping mesh with the number 256=16×16 of vertices where $0<\delta<0{,}01$. The meshes with $n=k\times k$ vertices, $k=4, 8, 16$ are considered (for $k=2$ a mesh degenerates into a ring).

In Figure 2, the curves are presented for the ratio of numbers C_a and C_m to number $C_{\max}$ of the edges of the program graph for a line ($C_{\max}=n-1$), a ring ($C_{\max}=n$) and a square mesh ($C_{\max}=2\sqrt{n}(\sqrt{n}-1)$), respectively. The curves show that, despite the increase of size of the data transferred between the cores of the system, the relative fraction of edges falling on intercore interactions is significantly reduced when number n of the program vertices is increased. In Figures 3 and 4, examples of mapping the mesh (Figure 3) and the irregular grids (Figure 4) are shown. The same signs marked the program graph vertices mapped onto the same core. Figures 3 and 4 indicate suboptimality of the obtained mappings.

Table 5. Line ($n=32$)

m	2	4	8
I_a	14	83	177
I_m	81	285	375
t_a	0,0026	0,046	2,85
t_m	0,031	0,454	27,39
N_a	0,58	0,21	2,28
N_m	6	2	23
C_a	5,69	7,24	10,79
C_m	13	13	18

Table 5 shows ($n = 32$) that for cores numbers $m = 2,4$, times t_a and t_m of the mapping algorithm implementation, and numbers N_a and N_m of the algorithm restarts are small, but, with the cores number increasing to $m = 8$, these values are sharply increased.

The experiments have shown that the proposed mapping algorithm, based on a network of Wang [10, 11], for the computer with the number of cores $m = 2,4,8$ gives:

1) full balance of the computational load (the load is distributed evenly) for typical graphs of parallel programs (empty graph, line, grid, ring, mesh) with the number of vertices $n \in \{2,4,8,16,32,64\}$, $m \le n$;
2) suboptimal mappings for irregular grids with dozens of nodes (imbalance of load does not exceed 5%).
3) significant decline in the proportion of program edges accounted for intercore exchanges with an increase of the vertices number of the program graph.

The case of a large number of nodes of a program graph ($10^3 \div 10^6$) and a system graph ($10^2 \div 10^6$) can be reduced to the above-mentioned using the Karypis-Kumar methodology [4] of coarsening the program graph.

5. Mapping Problem for Uniform Graphs

For distributed computer systems (CS), the graph of a parallel program $G_p(V_p, E_p)$ is usually determined as a set V_p of the program branches (virtual elementary computers) interacting with each other by the point–to–point principle through transferring messages via logical (virtual) channels (which may be unidirectional or bidirectional ones) of the set $E_p = V_p \times V_p$. Interactions between the processing modules are ordered in time and regular in space for most parallel applications (line, ring, mesh, etc.) (Figure 1).

For this reason, the maximum efficiency of information interactions in advanced high-performance CSs is obtained using regular graphs $G_s(V_s, E_s)$ of connections between individual computers (hypercube, 2D-torus, or 3D-torus) [5, 6]. The hypercube structure is described by a graph known as a m-dimensional Boolean cube with a number of nodes $n = 2^m$. Toroidal structures are m-dimensional Euclidean meshes with closed boundaries. The group of automorphisms E_m of such a structure is a direct product of cyclic subgroups C_{N_k} : $E_m = \bigotimes_{k=1}^{m} C_{N_k}$, where N_k is the order of the subgroup and $\otimes$ is the symbol of the direct product. For m = 2, we obtain a two-dimensional torus (2D-torus); for m = 3, we obtain a 3D-torus.

In many cases of parallel programming practice the weights of all nodes (and all edges) may be defined as equal to each other. In these cases the problem of mapping parallel program structure onto the structure of distributed CS can be described as follows [2].

Due to the fact that elementary computers and intercomputer connections are not completely reliable, a regular structure of CS can be violated as a result of a failure of its elements. Therefore, there is a need to develop algorithms for embedding program graphs in arbitrary CS graphs.

Graph $G_p(V_p, E_p)$ of a parallel program is considered as a set V_p of nodes (the program branches) and a function

$$G_p : V_p \times V_p \to \{0,1\},$$

such that

$$G_p(x,y) = G_p(y,x),\ G_p(x,x) = 0$$

for all $x, y \in V_p$. Equality $G_p(x,y) = 1$ is taken to indicate that there is an edge between x and y, i.e., $(x,y) \in E_p$.

Analogously, the graph of distributed CS $G_s = (V_s, E_s)$ is defined as a set of nodes (elementary computers – ECs) V_s and a function

$$G_s : V_s \times V_s \to \{0,1\}.$$

Here E_s is a set of edges (connections between ECs).

Let $|V_p| = |V_s| = n$. Let us denote a mapping of parallel program branches onto computers by one-to-one function $f_m : V_p \to V_s$. The mapping quality we can define as a number of the program graph edges coincided with the edges of the CS graph. We call this number cardinality $|f_m|$ of mapping f_m and define it by the following expression [2] (maximum criterion of the mapping quality):

$$|f_m| = (1/2) \sum_{x \in V_p, y \in V_p} G_p(x,y) G_s(f_m(x), f_m(y)). \tag{9}$$

In accordance to (9), criterion $|f_m|$ is equal to the number of the program graph G_p edges coinciding with the edges of computer system graph G_s.

The minimum mapping criterion is

$$|f_m| = (1/2) \sum_{x \in V_p, y \in V_p} G_p(x,y) L_s(f_m(x), f_m(y)). \tag{10}$$

Here $L_s(f_m(x), f_m(y))$ is equal to the distance between nodes $f_m(x)$ and $f_m(y)$ on graph G_s.

In this section, we consider a problem of mapping graph $G_p(V_p, E_p)$ of a parallel program onto graph $G_s(V_s, E_s)$ of a distributed CS, where $n = |V_p| = |V_s|$ is a number of program branches (of computers). The mapping objective is to map the nodes of program graph G_p onto the nodes of system graph G_s one-to-one to realize the coincidence of G_p edges with the edges of G_s (to establish an isomorphism between program graph G_p and a spanning subgraph of system graph G_s).

The recurrent neural networks [10, 11] are the most interesting tool for the solution of discrete optimization problems. A model of a globally converged recurrent Hopfield neural network is in good accordance with Dijkstra's self-stabilization paradigm [12]. This signifies that the mappings of parallel program graphs onto graphs of distributed computer systems, realized by Hopfield networks, are self-stabilizing. The importance of the use of self-stabilizing mappings is caused by a possibility of breaking the CS graph regularity by the failures of ECs and intercomputer connections.

5.1. Hopfield Network for the Uniform Mapping Problem

Let us consider neurons matrix v with size $n \times n$; each row of the matrix corresponds to some branch of a parallel program and every column of the matrix corresponds to some EC. Each row and every column of matrix v must contain only one nonzero entry equal to one, another entries must be equal to zero. The corresponding Hopfield network energy is described by the Lyapunov function

$$E = \frac{C}{2}\left[\sum_x \left(\sum_j v_{xj} - 1\right)^2 + \sum_i \left(\sum_y v_{yi} - 1\right)^2\right] + \\ + \frac{D}{2}\sum_x \sum_i \sum_{y \in Nb_p(x)} \sum_{j \neq i} v_{xi} v_{yj} d_{ij} . \qquad (11)$$

Here v_{xi} is a neuron state in row x and column i of matrix v, C and D are the Lyapunov function parameters. In square brackets, the first term is minimal when each row of v contains only one unity entry, and the second term is minimal when every column has only one unity entry (all another entries are zero). Such matrix v is a correct solution of the mapping problem. The third term's minimum provides a minimum of the sum of distances between adjacent G_p nodes mapped onto the nodes of system graph G_s. Here d_{ij} is a distance between nodes i and j of the system graph corresponding to the adjacent nodes of the program graph (a "dilation" of the edge of the program graph on the system graph), $Nb_p(x)$ is a set of the program graph nodes adjacent to x.

The Hopfield network minimizing function (11) is described by the equation

$$\frac{\partial u_{xi}}{\partial t} = -\frac{\partial E}{\partial v_{xi}}, \tag{12}$$

where u_{xi} is neuron activation with indices x,i, $x,i = 1,\dots,n$, $v_{xi} = \frac{1}{1+\exp(-\beta u_{xi})}$ is the neuron state (output signal), β is the activation parameter. From (11) and (12) we have

$$\frac{\partial u_{xi}}{\partial t} = -C\left(\sum_j v_{xj} + \sum_y v_{yi} - 2\right) - D \sum_{y\in Nb_p(x)} \sum_{j\neq i} v_{yj} d_{ij}. \tag{13}$$

The difference approximation of equation (13) is

$$u_{xi}^{t+1} = u_{xi}^{t} - \Delta t \cdot \left[C\left(\sum_j v_{xj} + \sum_y v_{yi} - 2\right) + D \sum_{y\in Nb_p(x)} \sum_{j\neq i} v_{yj} d_{ij} \right], \tag{14}$$

where Δt is a temporal step. The initial values u_{xi}^0, $x,i = 1,\dots,n$ are stated randomly.

The choice of parameters $\beta,\ \Delta t,\ C,\ D$ [10-13] determines the quality of solution v of equation (14). In accordance with [13] for the problem (11) − (14), the necessary condition of convergence is

$$C > D\frac{f_{\min}}{2(1-\alpha)}, \tag{15}$$

where $f_{\min} = \min\left\{ \sum_{y\in Nb_p(x)} \sum_{j\neq i} v_{yj} d_{ij} \right\}$, $\alpha \in [0,1)$ and α being a value close to 1. For a parallel program graph of a line type, we have $f_{\min} = 1$. For example, taking $\alpha = 0.995$ for the line we have

$$C > 100 \cdot D.$$

From (14) and (15) it follows that parameters Δt and D are equally influenced on the solution of equation (4). Therefore, we state $\Delta t = 1$ and have the equation

$$u_{xi}^{t+1} = u_{xi}^{t} - C\cdot\left(\sum_j v_{xj} + \sum_y v_{yi} - 2\right) - D\cdot \sum_{y\in Nb_p(x)} \sum_{j\neq i} v_{yj} d_{ij}. \tag{16}$$

Let $\beta = 0.1$ (this value was stated in [9]). We will try to choose value D to provide the absence of incorrect solutions.

5.2. Mapping Program by the Hopfield Network

Let us evaluate the mapping quality by a number of coincidences of the program edges with the edges of the system graph. We call this number a mapping rank. The mapping rank is an approximate evaluation of the mapping quality because the mappings with different dilations of the program graph edges may have the same mapping rank. Nevertheless, the maximum rank value, which equals to the number $|E_p|$ of program graph edges, corresponds to optimal mapping, i.e., to the global minimum of the sum $S_d = \sum_x \sum_i \sum_{y \in Nb_p(x)} \sum_{j \neq i} v_{xi} v_{yj} d_{ij}$ in (11). Our objective is to determine the mapping algorithm parameters providing maximum probability of the optimal mapping. As an example of the investigation of the mapping algorithm, we consider the mapping of a line-type program graph onto a 2D-torus (two-dimensional torus). The maximal value of the mapping rank for a line with n nodes is obviously equal to $n-1$.

For experimental investigation of the mapping quality, the histograms of the mapping rank frequencies are used for a number of experiments equal to 100. The experiments for mapping the line to the 2D-torus with the number of nodes $n = l^2$, $l = 3, 4$, where l is the cyclic subgroup order, are realized.

For $D \geq 8$, the correct solutions are obtained for $n = 9$ and $n = 16$, but, as follows from Figure 5a ($n = 9$) and Figure 5b ($n = 16$) for $D = 8$, the number of solutions with optimal mapping, corresponding to the maximal mapping rank, is small.

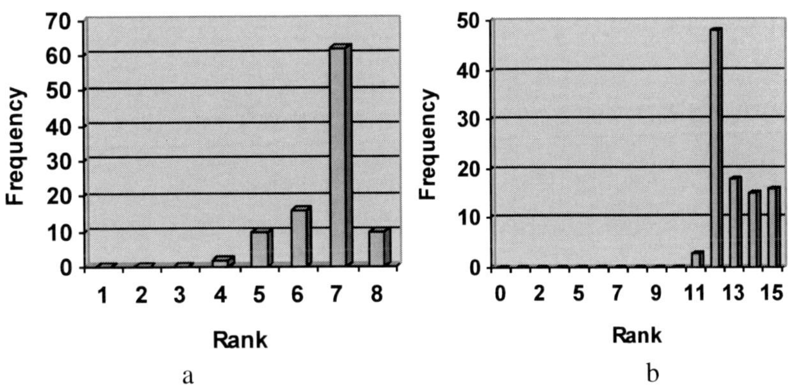

Figure 5. Histograms of neural network (16) mappings.

To increase the frequency of optimal solutions of equation (16) we replace distance values d_{ij} by values

$$c_{ij} = \begin{cases} d_{ij}, & d_{ij} = 1, \\ p \cdot d_{ij}, & d_{ij} > 1, \end{cases} \tag{17}$$

where p is a penalty coefficient for the distance d_{ij} exceeding the value of 1, i.e., for non-coincidence of the program graph edge with the system graph edge. So, we obtain the equation

$$u_{xi}^{t+1} = u_{xi}^{t} - C \cdot \left(\sum_j v_{xj} + \sum_y v_{yi} - 2 \right) - D \cdot \sum_{y \in Nb_p(x)} \sum_{j \neq i} v_{yj} c_{ij}. \qquad (18)$$

For the above mappings with $p = n$, we obtain the histograms shown in Figure 6 a ($n = 9$) and Figure 6 b ($n = 16$). These histograms indicate the improvement of the mapping quality, but, for $n = 16$, the suboptimal solutions with rank 13 have the maximal frequency.

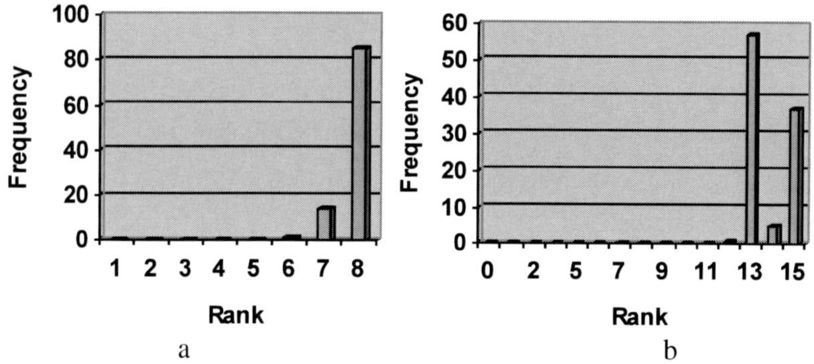

Figure 6. Histograms of neural network (18) mappings.

5.3. Splitting Method

To decrease a number of local extremums of function (11), we partition the set $\{1,2,...,n\}$ of subscripts x and i of variables v_{xi} to K sets $I_k = \{(k-1)q,\ (k-1)q+1,...,k \cdot q\}$, $q = n/K$, $k = 1,2,...,K$, and map subscripts $x \in I_k$ only to subscripts $i \in I_k$, i.e., we reduce solution matrix v to a block-diagonal form. Then, taking into account expression (17), the Lyapunov function (11) is transformed to

$$E = \frac{C}{2} \sum_{k=1}^{K} \left[\sum_{x \in I_k} \left(\sum_{j \in I_k} v_{xj} - 1 \right)^2 + \sum_{i \in I_k} \left(\sum_{y \in I_k} v_{yi} - 1 \right)^2 \right] +$$

$$+ \frac{D}{2} \sum_{k=1}^{K} \sum_{x \in I_k} \sum_{i \in I_k} \sum_{y \in Nb_p(x)} \sum_{j \neq i} v_{xi} v_{yj} c_{ij},$$

and the Hopfield network is described by the equation

$$u_{xi}^{t+1} = u_{xi}^{t} - C \cdot \left(\sum_{j \in I_k} v_{xj} + \sum_{y \in I_k} v_{yi} - 2 \right) - D \cdot \sum_{y \in Nb_p(x)} \sum_{j \neq i} v_{yj} c_{ij},$$
$$v_{xi} = \frac{1}{1 + \exp(-\beta u_{xi})}, \quad x, i \in I_k, \ k = 1, 2, ..., K. \tag{19}$$

In this case $v_{xi} = 0$ for $x \in I_k, i \notin I_k, k = 1,2,...,n.$

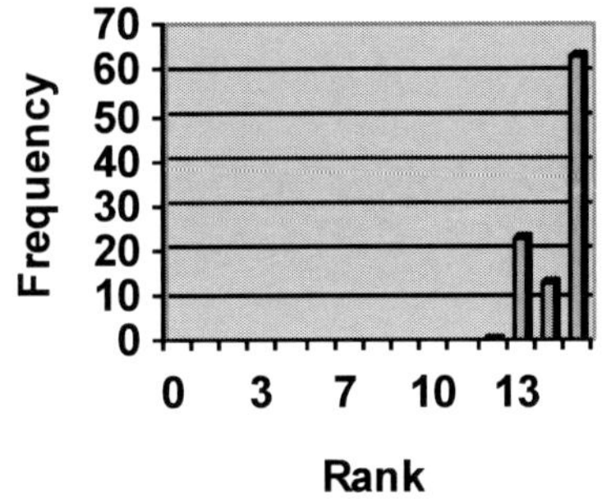

a) $n = 16$, $K = 2$, $D = 8$.

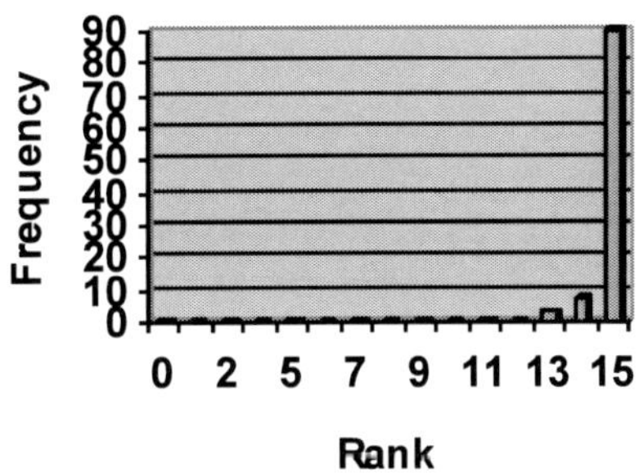

b) $n = 16$, $K = 2$, $D = 32$.

Figure 7. Histograms of neural network (19) mappings.

In this approach, which we call splitting, for a mapping line with the number of nodes $n = 16$ onto a 2D-torus, for $K = 2$ we have the histogram presented in Figure 7 a. From Figures 4 b and 7 a we see that the splitting method essentially increases the frequency of optimal mappings. The increase of parameter D up to value $D = 32$ results in an additional increase of the optimal mappings frequency (Figure 7b).

5.4. Mapping Program by the Wang Network

In a recurrent Wang neural network [10, 11], the sum $S_d = \sum_x \sum_i \sum_{y \in Nb_p(x)} \sum_{j \neq i} v_{xi} v_{yj} d_{ij}$ in expression (11) is multiplied by value $\exp\left(-\frac{t}{\tau}\right)$ where τ is a parameter. For the Wang network, equation (19) is modified into

$$u_{xi}^{t+1} = u_{xi}^{t} - C \cdot \left(\sum_{j \in I_k} v_{xj} + \sum_{y \in I_k} v_{yi} - 2 \right) - D \cdot \sum_{y \in Nb_p(x)} \sum_{j \neq i} v_{yj} c_{ij} \exp\left(-\frac{t}{\tau} \right),$$
$$v_{xi} = \frac{1}{1+\exp(-\beta u_{xi})}, \quad x, i \in I_k, \;\; k = 1, 2, ..., K. \tag{20}$$

We note that, in the experiments we frequently have incorrect solutions if, for a given maximal number of iterations $t_{\max}$ (for example, $t_{\max} = 10000$), the condition of convergence $\sum_{x,i} \left| u_{xi}^{t} - u_{xi}^{t-1} \right| < \varepsilon$, $\varepsilon = 0{,}01$ is not satisfied. The factor of $\exp\left(-\frac{t}{\tau} \right)$ introduction accelerates the recurrent neural network convergence and the number of incorrect solutions is reduced.

So, for the three-dimensional torus with $n = 3^3 = 27$ nodes and $p = n$, $K = 3$, $D = 4096$, $\beta = 0{,}1$ in 100 experiments, we have the following results:

1. On the Hopfield network we have 23 incorrect solutions, 43 solutions with rank 25 and 34 optimal solutions (with rank 26) (Figure 8 a).
2. On the Wang network with the same parameters and $\tau = 500$, we have all (100) correct solutions, where 27 solutions have rank 25 and 73 solutions are optimal (with rank 26) (Figure 8 b).

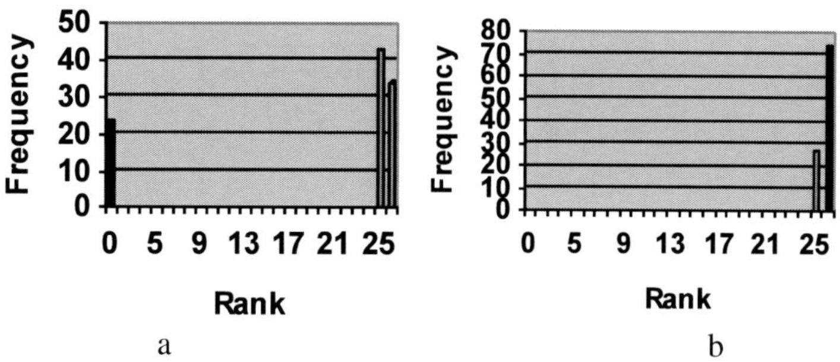

Figure 8. Histograms of mappings ($n = 3^3 = 27$): a) for Hopfield network; b) for Wang network.

So, in this section, a problem of mapping graphs of parallel programs onto distributed computer systems graphs by recurrent neural networks is formulated for uniform graphs with equal amounts of nodes. The parameter values providing the absence of incorrect solutions are experimentally determined.

For mapping a line-type graph of parallel program onto a two-dimensional torus with the same number of nodes it is shown that when a penalty parameter is introduced to the Lyapunov function for the program graph edges non-coincided with the edges of the system graph, we obtain optimal solutions for a number of nodes $n \in \{9, 16\}$. To increase the probability (the frequency) of optimal mappings, we propose to use:

1) a splitting method reducing the solution matrix to the block-diagonal form;
2) the Wang recurrent network which is converged more rapidly than the Hopfield network.

As a result, we have a high frequency of optimal solutions (for 100 experiments):

1) more than 80 for two-dimensional tori ($n=3^2=9$ and $n=4^2=16$);
2) more than 70 for a three-dimensional torus $(n=3^3=27)$.

Further investigations must be directed to increasing the probability of getting optimal solutions of the mapping problem when the number of parallel program nodes is increased.

6. On the Efficient Construction of Hamilton Cycles in Distributed Computer Systems by Recurrent Neural Networks

The ring structure of the parallel program is one of the most fundamental structures for parallel and distributed computing. These parallel applications, as processing signals and images, tend to have a ring architecture [14] prompted many simple and effective ring algorithms for solving various algebraic and graph-theoretical problems [15, 16]. It is, therefore, important to have an effective mapping of the ring onto the structure of the distributed computer system.

Here we present the neural network algorithms for mapping the ring structures of parallel programs onto the structures of distributed CS when $|V_p|=|V_s|=n$. Such a mapping is reduced to the construction of a Hamiltonian cycle in the CS graph. The mapping is based on the solution of the traveling salesman problem using a matrix of the distances between the vertices of the CS graph with the unit distance between adjacent vertices. We propose a method of partial sums to reduce the time to solve the system of differential equations describing the neural network from $O(n^3)$ to $O(n^2)$ and show that the neural network algorithm, using the method of partial sums for the cycle construction, is not inferior than the known permutation methods [2, 17-19] in the run-time.

6.1. On Solving the Traveling Salesman Problem by Recurrent Neural Networks

Many papers are devoted to the solution of combinatorial optimization problems by neural networks [8]. The most popular in this respect are the Hopfield networks [20], but their use is limited by high computational complexity $O(n^4)$. The situation can be simplified by the following approach.

The traveling salesman problem can be formulated as an assignment problem [21]:

$$\min \sum_{i=1}^{n} \sum_{j \neq i} C_{ij} v_{ij} \tag{21}$$

under the constraints

$$\begin{aligned} & v_{ij} \in \{0,1\}, \\ & \sum_{i=1}^{n} v_{ij} = 1,\ j = 1,2,\dots,n, \\ & \sum_{j=1}^{n} v_{ij} = 1,\ i = 1,2,\dots,n, \\ & v \text{ forms a Hamiltonian cycle.} \end{aligned} \tag{22}$$

Here C_{ij}, $i \neq j$, is the cost of assignment of element *i* to position *j*, which corresponds to the motion of the travelling salesman from city *i* to city *j*; v_{ij} is the decision variable: if element *i* is assigned to position *j*, then $v_{ij} = 1$; otherwise, $v_{ij} = 0$.

For solving this problem, J.Wang [10, 11] proposed a recurrent neural network that is described by the differential equation

$$\frac{\partial u_{ij}(t)}{\partial t} = -\eta\left(\sum_{k=1}^{n} v_{ik}(t) + \sum_{l=1}^{n} v_{lj}(t) - 2\right) - \lambda C_{ij} \exp\left(-\frac{t}{\tau}\right), \tag{23}$$

where $v_{ij} = f(u_{ij}(t))$; $f(u) = 1/\left[1 + \exp(-\beta u)\right]$.

The difference variant of this equation has the form of

$$u_{ij}^{t+1} = u_{ij}^{t} - \Delta t \cdot \left[\eta\left(\sum_{k=1}^{n} v_{ik}(t) + \sum_{l=1}^{n} v_{lj}(t) - 2\right) - \lambda C_{ij} \exp\left(-\frac{t}{\tau}\right)\right], \tag{24}$$

where Δt is the time step. Parameters $\Delta t, \eta, \lambda, \tau$, and β are found experimentally and substantially affect the velocity of solving the problem and the quality of the solution.

The computational complexity of iteration (24) is equal to $O(n^3)$ if, for all n^2 elements of the matrix $u_{ij}, i, j = 1,\dots,n$, we recalculate the sum $\sum_{k=1}^{n} v_{ik}(t) + \sum_{l=1}^{n} v_{lj}(t)$. We can accelerate the solution of the system of equations (23) by the following algorithm [9], using the WTA ("Winner takes all") principle [21]:

Step 1. Matrix $\left\| v_{ij}(0) \right\|$ of random values $v_{ij}(0) \in [0,1]$ is generated. Iterations (24) are performed until the following inequality is satisfied for all $i, j = 1,\dots,n$:

$$\sum_{k=1}^{n} v_{ik}(t) + \sum_{l=1}^{n} v_{lj}(t) - 2 \le \delta ,$$

δ is the specified accuracy of satisfying constraints.

Step 2. Transformation of the resultant decision matrix $\|v_{ij}\|$ is performed:

Substep 2.1. i=1.

Substep 2.2. The maximal element $v_{i,j_{\max}}$ is sought in the i-th row of matrix, $j_{\max}$ is the number of the column with the maximum element.

Substep 2.3. Transformation $v_{i,j_{\max}} = 1$ is performed. All the remaining elements of the ith row and of the column numbered $j_{\max}$ are set to zero. Then, there follows a transition to the row numbered $j_{\max}$. Substeps 2.2 and 2.3 are repeated until the cycle returns to the first row, which means that the cycle construction is finalized.

If the cycle returns to the row 1 earlier than the value 1 is assigned to n elements of the matrix $\|x_{ij}\|$, this means that the length of the constructed cycle is smaller than n. In this case, steps 1 and 2 are repeated.

6.2. The Method of Partial Sums

In [9] it is shown that the recurrent Wang network (21)-(23) gave good results in solving the system of equations (24) by Seidel. It is easy to see that the solution of the problem (21)-(23) is associated with multiple calculation of the same partial sums in the equations:

$$\sum_{i=1}^{n} v_{ij} = 1, \quad j = 1,...,n,$$

$$\sum_{j=1}^{n} v_{ij} = 1, \quad i = 1,...,n.$$

In order to avoid redundant computation, let us calculate the partial sums:

"Vertical" partial sums

$$V_{ij} = \sum_{k=i}^{n} v_{kj}, V_{ij}^{'} = \sum_{k=1}^{i} v_{kj}^{'}, \ i, j = 1,...,n ,$$

"Horizontal" partial sums

$$H_{ij} = \sum_{l=j}^{n} v_{il}, H_{ij}^{'} = \sum_{l=1}^{j} v_{il}^{'}, \ i, j = 1,...,n ,$$

where $v_{ij}^{'}$ is the value v_{ij} updated by Seidel.

Let $s_{ij} = \sum_{k=1}^{n} v_{ik}^{*}(t) + \sum_{l=1}^{n} v_{lj}^{*}(t)$ where the matrix v^{*} includes:

1. elements v_{kl} with $k = i, l = j,...,n$ and $k = i+1,...,n, l = 1,...,n$;
2. elements $v_{kl}^{'}$ with $k = 1,...i-1, l = 1,...,n$ and $k = i, l = 1,..., j-1$ updated by Seidel.

Then in (24) we have $s_{11} = V_{11} + H_{11}$. Using s_{11}, we calculate a new $v_{11}^{'}$ value using formula (24) and take $V_{11}^{'} = H_{11}^{'} = v_{11}^{'}$.

For the rest of the first row of matrix $\|v_{ij}\|$ we perform the following:

1) calculate $s_{1j} = H_{1,j-1}^{'} + V_{1j} + H_{1j}$, $j = 2,...,n$.
2) using s_{1j}, calculate $v_{1j}^{'}$ by (24) and take $V_{1j}^{'} = v_{1j}^{'}$, $H_{1j}^{'} = v_{1j}^{'} + H_{1,j-1}^{'}, j = 2,...,n.$

For the rest of the rows with numbers $i = 2,...,n$ and for $j = 1,...,n$:

1. calculate

$$s_{ij} = V_{i-1,j}^{'} + V_{ij} + H_{ij}, j \in \{1,...,n\},$$
$$s_{ij} = s_{ij} + H_{i,j-1}^{'}, \ j \in \{2,...,n\}.$$

2. using s_{ij}, calculate $v_{ij}^{'}$ and take

$$V_{ij}^{'} = v_{ij}^{'} + V_{i-1,j}^{'},$$
$$H_{ij}^{'} = v_{1j}^{'}, j \in \{1,...,n\}, \ H_{ij}^{'} = H_{ij}^{'} + H_{1,j-1}^{'}, j \in \{2,...,n\}.$$

The method of partial sums allows us to reduce the solution time of (24) in the construction of Hamiltonian cycles in distributed computing systems graphs from $O(n^3)$ to $O(n^2)$.

Table 6. Construction of Hamilton Cycle in a 2D-torus

n	144	256	400	576	784	1024
t_{trad}	0,125	1,06	5,2	15,9	39,8	178,7
t_{part}	0,016	0,063	0,188	0,5	1,156	2,047

Table 6 shows the time (in seconds) for the construction of Hamiltonian cycles in a two-dimensional torus with $n = m \times m$ nodes, $m \in \{12,16,20,24,28,32\}$, t_{trad} is the time for building the cycle without considering the repeatability of sums, t_{part} is the time for building the cycle using the method of partial sums (processor Pentium ® Dual-Core CPU E 52000, 2,5 GHz).

An especially big gain of the partial sums method enables the construction of Hamiltonian cycles in three-dimensional tori with a large number (thousands) of vertices. It uses a partition of the three-dimensional torus to two-dimensional tori.

In general, this problem is solved as follows:

1) partition the system graph to $k \geq 2$ connected subgraphs;
2) construct a Hamiltonian cycle in each subgraph by the above algorithm;
3) combine the Hamiltonian cycles of subgraphs in a Hamiltonian cycle.

The three-dimensional torus can be viewed as an aggregate of two-dimensional tori linked by edges together. Therefore, the Hamiltonian cycle for a three-dimensional torus can be realized by the construction of Hamilton cycles for all two-dimensional tori and combining the cycles by the algorithm proposed in [3].

Table 7. Construction of a 3D-torus with the Splitting Method

m	16	20	24	28	32
$n = m^3$	4096	8000	13284	21952	32768
t_{RNseq}	13,19	65,25	243,7	707,5	3354
t_{RNpart}	2,437	7,656	18,64	41,08	84,47

Table 7 shows the time (in seconds) for constructing optimal Hamiltonian cycles for three-dimensional tori with a large (thousands) number of vertices: t_{RNseq} is the running time without the use of partial sums, and t_{RNpart} is the running time using partial sums.

Thus, the results of the experiments show that, in combination with the method of splitting a three-dimensional torus on two-dimensional tori, the algorithm using the partial sums can significantly speed up the construction of cycles in three-dimensional tori with tens of thousands of nodes.

6.3. Permutation Algorithm for the Uniform Mapping Problem

In [3] we proposed the following approach (MB-algorithm) to the problem of mapping. Let us give the initial embedding of vertices in the program graph onto the vertices of the CS graph. For example, $f_m(x) = x$, i.e., the branche numbers of graph $G_p(V_p, P_p)$ coincide with the numbers of ECs containing these branches. Let $e_p(x)$ is an environment (the set of neighbors) of vertex x in graph G_p, and $e_s(x)$ is its environment on graph G_s. For every vertex $x \in V_p$, we test permutation of vertices i and j satisfying the condition

$$i \in e_p(x) \,\&\, i \notin e_s(x) \,\&\, j \in e_s(x) \,\&\, state(j) = 0 .$$

Condition $state(j) = 0$ means that vertex j is not yet permutated in environment $e_s(x)$, otherwise $state(j) = 1$. If the permutation does not worsen the quality of the embedding, we fix it. This approach is based on the assumption of a high probability of a situation where such a permutation, which increases the number of nodes $i \in e_p(x)$ in environment $e_s(x)$, improves (or at least does not worsen) the value of the quality criterion $|f_m|$. The number of permutations tested using a single traversal of all vertices $x \in V_p$ does not exceed $v_p v_s n$, $n = |V_p|$, where v_p and v_s are the maximal degrees of vertices of graphs G_p and G_s respectively. With $v_p v_s < n$, this approach will reduce the amount of calculations, as compared to the known permutation algorithms [2, 17-19] having iteration complexity $O(n^2)$.

Table 8 compares the time (in seconds) of constructing a Hamiltonian cycle by two algorithms: MB-algorithm, and a neural network using the partial sums. From this table, it follows that these algorithms are comparable in their efficiency. The MB-algorithm is designed to use a processor with a fixed point, while the neural network uses the floating-point processor. This fact must be considered when choosing a particular algorithm depending on the speed of the algorithm.

Table 8. Construction of the Hamilton cycle in a 2d-torus by MB-algorithm (t_{MB}) and a recurrent neural network with partial sums (t_{part})

n	144	256	400	576	784	1024
t_{MB}	0,047	0,14	0,343	0,719	1,328	2,25
t_{part}	0,016	0,063	0,188	0,5	1,156	2,05

Conclusion

The problem of mapping a parallel program with weighted vertices (processes) and edges (inter-processor communications) onto a weighted graph of the distributed computing system is considered. An algorithm for solving this problem based on the use of Hopfield networks is proposed. The algorithm is tested on the particular case of this problem – mapping some graphs of parallel programs (homogeneous set of independent tasks - the empty graph, line, ring, mesh, irregular grids) onto a multi-core computer. Experiments have shown, that for graphs of parallel programs with dozens of nodes, the proposed algorithm provides well-balanced sub-optimal mappings. With the increasing number of vertices of the program graph, the share of its edges, corresponding to inter-core data exchanges, is significantly reduced.

Optimal solutions are found for mapping a “line”-graph onto a two-dimensional torus. To increase the probability of finding an optimal mapping, a method for splitting the mapping procedure is proposed. The method’s essence is a reducing solution matrix to a block-diagonal form. The Wang recurrent neural network is used to exclude incorrect solutions of the problem of mapping the line-graph onto a three-dimensional torus.

The construction of Hamiltonian cycles in a graph of distributed computing system by a recurrent neural network is considered. We propose a method of partial sums, which allows one to reduce the time to solve the system of differential equations, describing the neural network, from $O(n^3)$ to $O(n^2)$, where n is a number of graph nodes. It is shown that the neural network algorithm using the partial sums is not inferior to the known permutation methods in time of the cycle construction.

The permutation algorithms do not require a floating point processor and the choice of parameters, but they work with irregular data structures (list-representation of the graph), which may complicate their parallelization. Neural network algorithms require floating-point processors and a choice of parameters, but they work with regular data structures and, therefore, have a high potential for parallelism. Thus, the choice of algorithm for constructing Hamiltonian cycles in graphs of distributed computer systems is determined by the configuration of the hardware processors on which they are executed. Comparison of parallel versions of the considered algorithms is the aim of a further research.

References

[1] Padua, D., (2011). *Encyclopedia of Parallel Computing*, Springer.

[2] Bokhari, S.H.,(1981). On The Mapping Problem, *IEEE Trans. Comp.*, C-30, 3, 207-214.

[3] Tarkov, M.S., (2003). Mapping Parallel Program Structures onto Structures of Distributed Computer Systems, *Optoelectronics, Instrumentation and Data Processing*. 39, 3, 72-83.

[4] Karypis, G., Kumar, V., (2008). Multilevel k-way Partitioning Scheme for Irregular Graphs, *Journal of Parallel and Distributed Computing*, 48, 96–129.

[5] Lakshmivarahan, S., Dhall, S.K., (1999). Ring, torus and hypercube architectures/algorithms for parallel computing. *Parallel Computing*. 25, 1877-1906.

[6] Yu, H., Chung, I-Hsin, Moreira, J., (2006). Topology Mapping for Blue Gene/L Supercomputer. *Proc. of the ACM/IEEE SC2006 Conf. on High Performance Networking and Computing*. ACM Press, 52–64.

[7] Haykin, S., (1999). *Neural Networks. A Comprehensive Foundation*, Prentice Hall Inc.

[8] Smith, K.A., (1999). Neural Networks for Combinatorial Optimization: A Review of More Than a Decade of Research, *INFORMS Journal on Computing*, 11, 1, 15-34.

[9] Tarkov, M.S., (2010). The Construction of Hamiltonian Cycles in Graphs of Distributed Computer Systems by Recurrent Neural Networks, *Numerical Analysis and Applications*, 3, 4, 381-388.

[10] Wang, J., (1993). Analysis and Design of a Recurrent Neural Network for Linear Programming, *IEEE Trans. On Circuits and Systems-I: Fundamental Theory and Applications*, 40, 9, 613-618.

[11] Hung, D.L., Wang, J., (2003). Digital Hardware Realization of A Recurrent Neural Network for Solving The Assignment Problem, *Neurocomputing*, 51, 447-461.

[12] Dijkstra, E.W., (1974). Self-stabilizing systems in spite of distributed control, *Commun. ACM,* 17, 11, 643-644.

[13] Feng, G., Douligeris, C., (2001). The Convergence and Parameter Relationship for Discrete-Time Continuous-State Hopfield Networks, *Proc. of Intern. Joint Conference on Neural Networks*, 376-381.

[14] Li, Y., Peng, S., Chu, W., (2000). Fault-tolerant cycle embedding in dual-cube with node faults, *Int. J. High Performance Computing and Networking*, 3, 1, 45–53.

[15] Akl, S.G., (1997). *Parallel Computation: Models and Methods*, Prentice Hall Inc.

[16] Tsai, P.-Y., Fu, J.-S., Chen, G.-H., (2009). Embedding Hamiltonian cycles in alternating group graphs under conditional fault model, *Information Sciences*, 179, 851–857.

[17] Lee, S.-Y., Aggarval, J.K., (1981). A Mapping Strategy for Parallel Processing, *IEEE Trans. Comput*, C-36, 4, 433–442.

[18] Bollinger S.W., Midkiff, S.F., (1991). Heuristic Technique for Processor and Link Assignment in Multicomputers, *IEEE Transactions on Computers*, 40, 3, 325–333.

[19] Hoefler, T., Snir, M., (2011). Generic Topology Mapping Strategies for Large-scale Parallel Architectures, *Proc. International conference on Supercomputing* (*ICS*'11), 75–84.

[20] Hopfield, J.J., Tank D.W., (1985). «Neural» computation of decisions in optimization problems, *Biological Cybernetics*, 52, 3, 141–152.

[21] Siqueira, P.H., Steiner, M.T.A., Scheer, S., (2007). A new approach to solve the travelling salesman problem, *Neurocomputing*, 70, 1013–1021.

In: Parallel Programming
Editor: Mikhail S. Tarkov ISBN: 978-1-63321-957-1

Chapter 3

LARGE-SCALE AND FINE-GRAIN PARALLELISM IN PLASMA SIMULATION

*A. Snytnikov**
Institute of Computational Mathematics and Mathematical Geophysics, The Siberian Branch of the RAS, Novosibirsk, Russia

Abstract

A 3D kinetic study of the relaxation processes caused by the propagation of an electron beam in high-temperature plasma was carried out. This problem has two different spatial scales: the plasma Debye length and the beam-plasma interaction wavelength, that is some 10 or 100 times larger, thus one needs high-performance computing to observe the two lengths at once. A mathematical model is built on the basis of the Particle-in-Cell (PIC) method. In order to achieve the highest possible computation performance, both large-scale and fine-grain parallel techniques are employed.

The large-scale part is presented by the domain decomposition and is performed by cluster supercomputers. The parallelisation efficiency is presented as well as the performance of the program achieved with different clusters. The performance tests show that it is necessary to provide a good memory bandwidth for the cluster if one wants to achieve good performance on real physical problems.

The fine-grain part is presented by pushing each particle with a separate thread of a GPU (Graphics Processing Unit). Hybrid (GPU-equipped) supercomputers have reached very high performance level recently.

Unfortunately, the solution of real physical problems with such supercomputers is restricted by complexity of the GPU programming. In order to simplify the development of high-performance plasma physics codes for hybrid supercomputers a template implementation of the PIC method was created. The template parameters are the problem-specific implementations of "particles" and "cells" (as C++ classes). Thus, it is possible to develop a PIC code for a new plasma physics problem without studying the GPU programming by a plasma physicist. Instead the new physical features are just included into the existing code as new implementations of "particle" and "cell" classes.

Keywords: Plasma simulation, PIC method, GPU, C++ templates

* E-mail address: snytav@gmail.com

1. Introduction

This work has been inspired by the effect of anomalous heat conductivity observed at the GOL-3 facility in Budker Institute of Nuclear Physics [1]. The GOL-3 facility is a long open trap where the dense plasma is heated up in a strong magnetic field during the injection of the powerful relativistic electron beam of microsecond duration. The effect is the decrease of the plasma electron heat conductivity by 100 or 1000 times compared to the classical value for the plasma with the temperature and density observed in the experiment. Anomalous heat conductivity arises because of the turbulence that is caused by the relaxation of the relativistic electron beam in the high-temperature Maxwellian plasma.

The physical problem is to define the origin and mechanism of the heat conductivity decrease. This is of great importance for the fusion devices because the effect of anomalous heat conductivity helps to heat the plasma and also to confine it. The problem of heat transport in fusion devices has been widely discussed (e.g., [2]).

This problem needs high-performance computing because of the necessity to have a large enough grid to simulate the resonance interaction of the relativistic electron beam with plasma. The beam interacts with the plasma through the electric field (similar to Landau damping), thus it is necessary to observe two different scales simultaneously. The first is the plasma Debye length and the second is the beam-plasma interaction wavelength, which is 10 or 100 times larger than the Debye length. At least 8 grid cells must be defined on the Debye length.

It is also necessary to provide a large number of particles for each cell of the grid for the simulation of turbulence. The level of non-physical statistical fluctuations is inversely proportional to the number of particles per cell. So if there are too few particles, all the physical plasma waves and oscillations will be suppressed by non-physical noise.

2. Large-Scale Parallelism in Plasma Simulation

2.1. Cluster Efficiency Problem

This work also aims at more efficient use of cluster supercomputers. In order to achieve this goal it is necessary to evaluate their performance with some programs solving real physical problems. It would be incorrect to limit performance testing to the general purpose tests like the LinPack package since there is a dramatic difference between the performance of the cluster declared in Top500 list (either peak or LinPack performance) and the performance achieved by a particular user with his particular program. For example, if one employs one fourth of a cluster with peak performance of 5.4 TeraFlOp/S (1 TeraFlOp/S is 10^{12} floating point operations per second), the peak performance should be about 1 TeraFlOp/S. In fact, 0.18 TeraFlOp/S was obtained with the program simulating the beam relaxation in plasma.

The difference between the declared performance (1 TeraFlOp/S) and achieved performance (0.18 TeraFlOp/S) can be explained by the fact that cluster systems are not appropriate for such kind of problem.

2.2. Model Description

The mathematical model employed for the solution of the problem of beam relaxation in plasma consists of the Vlasov equations for ion and electron components of the plasma and also of the Maxwell equation system. The equations have the following form in the usual notation:

$$\frac{\partial f_{i,e}}{\partial t}+\mathbf{v}\frac{\partial f_{i,e}}{\partial \mathbf{r}}+\mathbf{F}_{i,e}\frac{\partial f_{i,e}}{\partial \mathbf{p}}=0,\quad \mathbf{F}_{i,e}=q_{i,e}\left(\mathbf{E}+\frac{1}{c}[\mathbf{v},\mathbf{B}]\right),$$

$$\mathbf{rot\ B}=\frac{4\pi}{c}\mathbf{j}+\frac{1}{c}\frac{\partial \mathbf{E}}{\partial t},$$

$$\mathbf{rot\ E}=-\frac{1}{c}\frac{\partial \mathbf{B}}{\partial t},$$

$$\mathbf{div\ E}=4\pi\rho,$$

$$\mathbf{div\ B}=0.$$

In the present work these equations are solved by the method described in [3]. All the equations will be further given in the non-dimensional form. The following basic quantities are used for the transition to the non-dimensional form:

- characteristic velocity is the velocity of light $v_{ch} = c = 3\times 10^{10}$ cm/sec
- characteristic plasma density $n = 10^{14}$ cm^{-3}
- characteristic time t_{ch} is the plasma period (a value inverse to the electron plasma frequency) $t_{ch} = \omega_{pe}^{-1} = (4\pi n_0 e^2/m_e)^{-0.5} = 5.3\times 10^{-12}$

The Vlasov equations are solved by the PIC method. This method implies the solution of the equation of movement for model particles. The movement equations of the particles are the equations of characteristics of the Vlasov equation.

The scheme proposed by Langdon and Lasinski is used to obtain the values of electric and magnetic fields. The scheme employs the finite-difference form of the Faraday and Ampere laws:

$$\frac{\mathbf{B}^{m+1/2}-\mathbf{B}^{m-1/2}}{\tau}=-rot_h\mathbf{E}^m,$$

$$\frac{\mathbf{E}^{m+1}-\mathbf{E}^{m}}{\tau}=-4\pi\mathbf{j}^{m+1/2}+rot_h\mathbf{B}^{m+1/2}.$$

A detailed description of the scheme can be found in [3]. The scheme gives the second order of approximation with respect to space and time.

2.3. Problem Statement

Let us consider the following problem statement. The 3D computational domain has the shape of a cube with the following dimensions:

$$0 \leq x \leq L_x, 0 \leq y \leq L_y, 0 \leq z \leq L_z,$$

Within this domain there is the model plasma. The model plasma particles are distributed uniformly within the domain. The density of plasma and the temperature of electrons are set by the physicist as well as the electron temperature. The temperature of ions is considered to be zero. Beam electrons are also uniformly distributed within the domain.

Thus, it is believed that the beam is already present in the plasma. The effects that occur when the beam is entering the plasma, are beyond the scope of the study.

The particles simulating beam electrons differ from those simulating plasma electrons by the value of their energy. Initially beam electrons have the energy of about 1 MeV, and the plasma electrons have the energy of about 1 keV.

Moreover, beam electrons have one direction of movement strictly along the X axis, and plasma electrons have the Maxwellian velocity distribution for all the three dimensions.

The main physical parameters of the problem under study are the following: the density and the temperature of the plasma electrons, the ratio of beam density to the plasma density and the energy of the beam.

2.4. Parallel Implementation

The program was parallelised by the domain decomposition method. The computational domain is divided into parts along the direction orthogonal to the direction of the beam (along the Y axis, the beam moving along the X axis). The computational grid in the whole domain is divided into equal parts (subdomains) along the Y axis. Each subdomain is assigned to a group of processors (in the case of a multicore system a single core would be called a processor, since no hybrid parallelization like MPI+OpenMP is employed, just mere MPI).

Furthermore, the particles of each subdomain are distributed uniformly between processors of the group with no regard to their position, as it is shown in Figure 1.

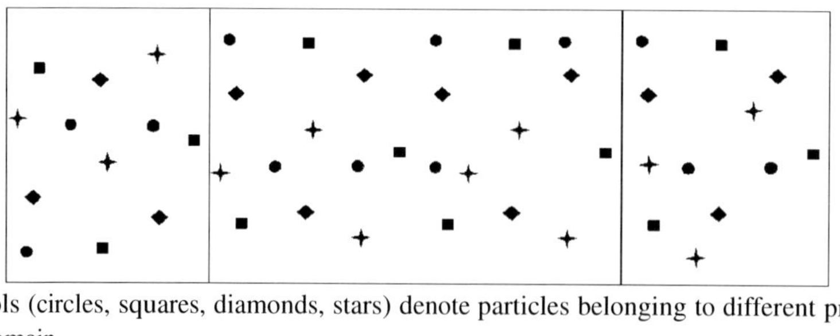

Different symbols (circles, squares, diamonds, stars) denote particles belonging to different processors in the same subdomain.

Figure 1. The scheme of domain decomposition. The computational domain is divided into 4 subdomains. The particles of each subdomain are distributed between four processors uniformly with no regard to their position.

Every processor in the group solves the Maxwell equations in the whole subdomain, and exchanges boundary values of the fields with processors assigned to adjacent subdomains. Then the movement equations for the particles are solved, and the 3D matrix of the current density and the charge density are evaluated by each processor.

But since the processor has only a part of the total number of particles located inside the subdomain, it is necessary to sum the matrices through all the processors of the group to obtain the whole current density matrix in the subdomain. Interprocessor data exchange is performed by the MPI subroutines.

2.5. Parallelization Efficiency

The parallel program has been developed primarily for the simulation of beam interaction with plasma on large computational grids which have large numbers of particles. That is why parallelisation efficiency *k* was computed in the following way:

$$k = T_2/T_1 \times N_1/N_2 \times S_2/S_1 \times 100\ \%$$

Here T_1 - is the computation time with N_1 processors, T_2 is the computation time with N_2 processors, S is the characteristic size of the problem in each case. Here the characteristic size is the grid size along the X axis. In this section the characteristic size *S* is proportional to the number of processors *N*.

It means that the workload of a single processor is constant. The purpose of such a definition of efficiency is to find out what the communication overhead is when the number of processors is increased with the constant workload for each processor.

In the ideal case the computation time must remain the same (the ideal k=100 %). In the computations devoted to efficiency evaluation the X axis grid size only increased, all the other parameters remained constant, the results are shown in Figure 2.

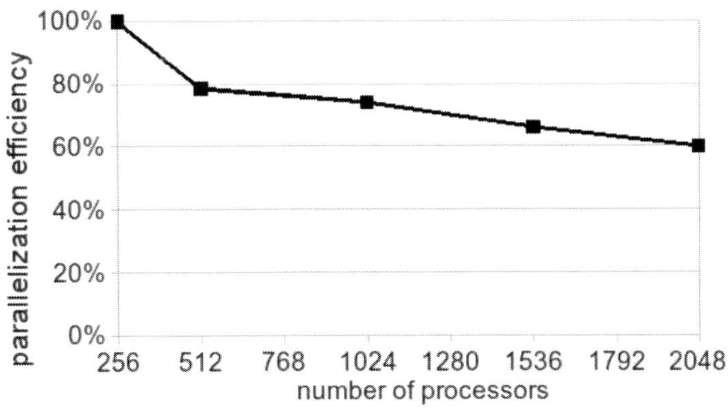

Figure 2. Parallelization efficiency measured with the cluster named MVS-100K, Joint Supercomputer Centre of the RAS (Russian Academy of Sciences). The grid size along Y and Z is 64 nodes, the grid size along X is equal to the number of processors (150 particles per cell for all the cases).

2.6. Cluster Performance Comparison

Every time step consists of the following procedures:

- Computation of electric and magnetic fields
- Computation of the movement of particles
- Evaluation of the new values of current and charge density

In addition, during selected time steps (usually one time step of a hundred) the physical data are filed for future analysis. The most important part of the data is the Fourier Transform of main physical quantities (current and charge densities, absolute values of electric and magnetic fields). The worktime of the above listed procedures was measured with the GnuProf (gprof) profiler. In each case the worktime of a single procedure call is given.

The program was tested with four cluster supercomputers. The first one is installed in Tomsk State University. It has 564 Xeon 5150 processors and is called SKIF Cyberia. The second one is the MVS-100K. It is installed in the Joint Supercomputer Center, Moscow and is equipped with different Xeon Processors. Most of them are Xeon E5450 and the total number of cores is 7920. The third one is called the SKIF MSU. It is installed in the Research Computing Center of Moscow State University. It has 1250 processors (mostly Xeon E5472. The forth cluster is installed in Novosibirsk State University, so it will be called here the NSU cluster. It is equipped with Xeon 5355 processors with the total number of cores 512. A more detailed description for these clusters can be found at http://supercomputers.ru (the list of most powerful supercomputers in Russia. All the clusters are equipped with similar processors, but with different networks, and this results in a dramatic performance difference.

In order to evaluate the new values of position and impulse of a particle it is necessary to know the values of electric and magnetic fields at the present position of the particle. Each of the three components of the field is stored in a separate 3D array. In such a way six 3D arrays are accessed at each time step for each particle. Since the particles are situated randomly in the subdomain, the access to the arrays is also unordered. It means that the use of the cache memory can not reduce the computation time. If a part of the field array were fetched to the cache in the process of computation of the particle movement, it would be impossible to use this part of the field array for the computation with the next particle, because it is (most likely) situated in a completely different part of the subdomain.

Since the cache memory can not store all the six arrays for fields, one has to access the RAM (Random Access Memory) for computation of the particle movement. And since the performance of the processor is usually limited by the memory bandwidth, it is the memory bandwidth that determines the speed of the computation with particles and the performance of the program as a whole (particles take over 60 % of the total time). Figure 3 shows the time of computation with particles during one timestep.

The conclusion of the major influence of the memory bandwidth on the particle computation time is confirmed by the comparison of the times obtained with the MVS-100K and the SKIF MSU clusters. Both clusters are equipped with similar processors, thus the resulting time difference (almost twofold) can only be explained by the difference of the memory bandwidth. Figure 3 also shows that there are opportunities for performance optimization. One of the possible ways is to sort particles along their position to enable the efficient use of cache memory.

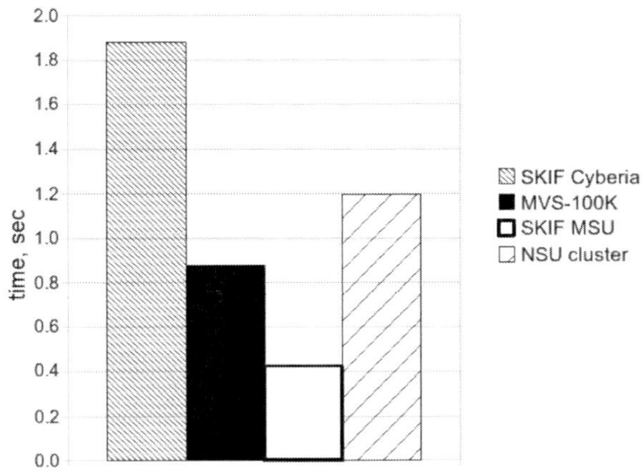

Figure 3. The worktime for the procedure of particle movement computation. The test computations were conducted with the SKIF Cyberia, MVS-100K, the SKIF MSU and the NSU cluster.

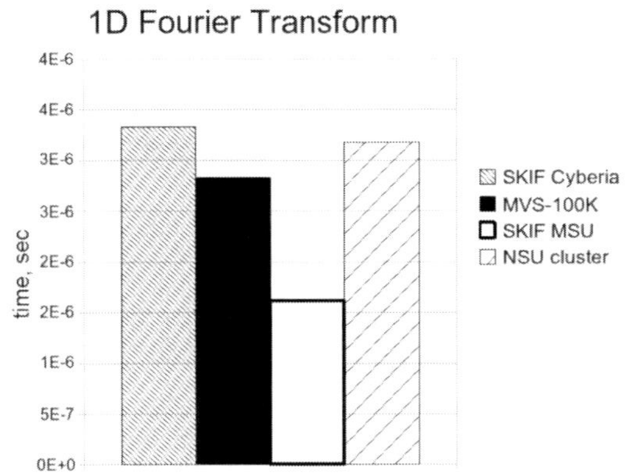

Figure 4. The worktime for the procedure implementing 1D Fast Fourier Transform. The test computations were conducted with the SKIF Cyberia, the MVS-100K, the SKIF MSU and the NSU cluster.

The computation with particles takes the most time (from 92 % with the SKIF Cyberia up to 64 % with the SKIF MSU). This is the part of the program that is parallelized with the highest efficiency. So the optimization of this procedure might spoil the parallelization efficiency, but the decrease of the total time appears to be more important.

In order to separate the computation time from the memory access time in the Figure 4 Fast Fourier Transform procedure is considered. This procedure takes 1D complex array with the size of either 512 as the input and performs the Fast Fourier Transform.

All the local variables of this procedure fit well in the cache memory. In such a way, through the example of this procedure one can see that it is possible to measure the speed of the "fast" computation, with no access to the RAM, using only cache memory.

The speed of interprocessor communication was measured by way of example of the procedure implementing the transfer of particles between processors. This procedure involves the search for particles that have flown out of the subdomain and that are now situated in the additional buffer layer.

These particles are then excluded from the particle array and put into the transfer buffer. Next, the buffers are transmitted to the processors assigned to adjacent subdomains. If the rank of the current subdomain is even, the particles are first transmitted "to the left", that is, to the subdomain with the Y coordinates less than those in the current subdomain, and then "to the right". If the number of the current subdomain is odd, exactly the opposite happens - first the particles are transmitted to the right, and then to the left.

Consequently the time shown in Figure 5 includes the search through the list of particles and four transmitting operations MPI_SendRecv.

The number of particles being transmitted cannot be large due to physical considerations. In plasma physics no large differences in density may occur within the Debye length, 10 % being a large difference in this case. The Debye length, as pointed above, must be not less than 8 grid cells for the correct simulation of wave dynamics.

With the grid size of 512×64×64 nodes, and the domain being divided into 32 subdomains, the width of a subdomain along the Y axis is just 2 cells.

Thus the densities in adjacent subdomains should not differ by more than 10 %. If particle flux from one processor to another one is large, the computation is physically incorrect. In such a way it is possible to set the size of the transfer buffer to 5 % of the size of the particle array, the number of particles sent being usually much less.

Figure 5 shows that the loss of transfer time is minimal with the SKIF Cyberia and the SKIF MSU. This is possibly because is the ServNet technology installed on the SKIF machines. The maximal time is wasted for transfer with the MVS-100K. This is probably because of the large size and heterogenous nature of this supercomputer.

3. Fine-Grain Parallelism in Plasma Simulation

The fine-grain level of parallelism is represented here by assigning separate particles in the PIC method to the processes or threads in the computational system. Assigning each particle to a single core or processor is impractical since the number of cores is usually much less than the number of particles (usually thousands and millions, respectively).

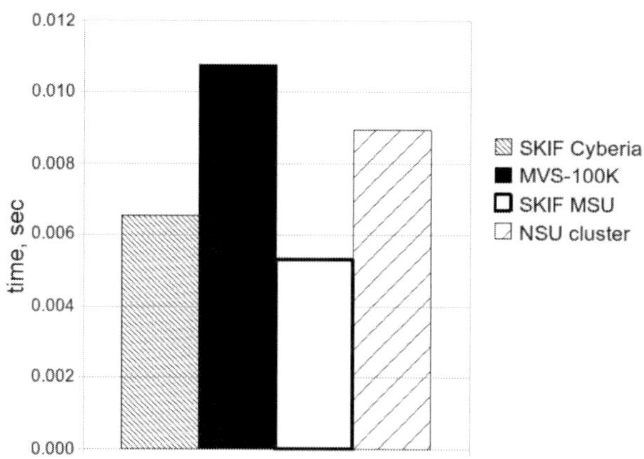

Figure 5. The worktime for the procedure of particle transfer. The test computations were conducted with the SKIF Cyberia, the MVS-100K, the SKIF MSU and the NSU cluster.

But with a GPU-equipped cluster the things are different. First, the number of computational cores is greater than in CPU cluster. Second, the concurrent processing of a large number of particles is performed much more effectively. With the GPU computations the same computational model and numerical methods are used, as those described above.

3.1. GPU Implementation

The implementation of the above PIC algorithm for the GPUs is quite standard. The field evaluation method is ported to the GPU almost without any change. The computation speed is high enough even without optimization. The field arrays are stored in the GPU global memory. The bottleneck of PIC codes is the particle push. With the CPUs it takes up to 90 % of runtime. The first step is the distribution of particles among cells. This step only reduces the push time twice with the CPUs. With the GPUs it is even more important than with the GPUs since it enables the use of texture memory (texture memory is limited and the whole particle array will never fit). The second step is keeping the field values related to the cell (and also to the adjacent cells) in the cell itself. This is important since each particle needs 6 field values and writes 12 current values to the grid nodes.

Now it all is done within a small amount of memory (the cell) without addressing the global field or current arrays that contain the whole domain. Then the evaluated currents from all cells are added to the global current array.

Figure 6 shows the ratio of the computation time with a GPU (Nvidia Tesla 2070 or the latest Nvidia Kepler) to the computation time with 4 cores of Intel Xeon CPU. It is seen from the Figure 6 that particle push is accelerated better than field evaluation. Particle push is the most important for the PIC method. This speedup means that it might be possible to perform the plasma simulation of the necessary scale (grid of 1000×1000×1000 nodes with 10000 particles each) with a cluster equipped with Kepler GPUs.

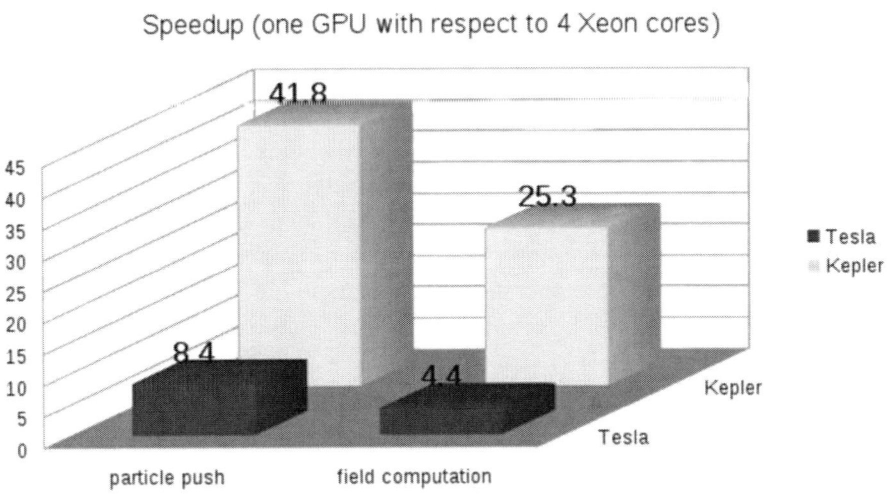

Figure 6. The ratio of computation time with a GPU (Nvidia Tesla 2070 or the latest Nvidia Kepler) to the computation time with 4 core of Intel Xeon CPU.

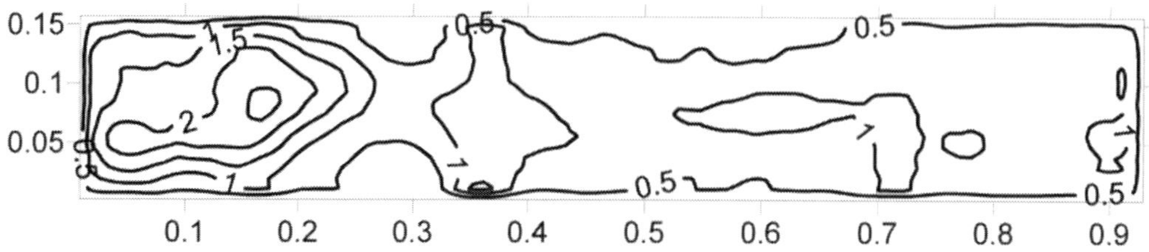

Figure 7. Electron density contours in the XY plane, $z=L_z/2$, moment of time t=91.7 (in terms of the plasma period). The density is given in terms of the initial values of density.

3.2. The Template Implementation of the PIC Method

In order to provide the tool for fast development of the new problem-oriented PIC codes for GPUs it is necessary

- to develop an optimized GPU implementation of the PIC method for a particular problem
- to create a set of diagnostic tools to facilitate the analysis of results by a physicist
- to provide an option to replace the problem-specific parts of the computational algorithm

In order to achieve the third point the C++ templates are used. It means that the "computation domain" class is implemented that contains "cell" class objects. "Cell" class contains "particle" class objects. Here "computation domain" class is a template class with "cell" class as a parameter. "Cell" is a template itself, "particle" being its parameter.

For a wide variety of PIC method implementations most of the operations of a cell with its particles are absolutely the same (adding/removing a particle, particle push, the evaluation of the particle's contribution to the current).

Only the gridless particles method of gyrokinetic codes might be an exception. And even they fit into the proposed scheme since they just don't need some of the operations, they don't introduce anything new. This fact brings hope that these operations once implemented as a template will be efficient for a number of problems solved with the PIC method.

The operations of the computation domain with cells are absolutely the same for all implementations of the PIC method. The things that differ are the initial distribution and boundary conditions. Thus these operations must be implemented as virtual functions.

Since particle attributes and the operations with particle are similar in most cases, it is possible to create a basic implementation of the "particle" class containing particle position, momentum, charge and mass.

If for some new physical problem the "particle" needs new attributes, then a derived class is implemented. And this new class "derived particle" is used as the parameter to "cell" template class.

At present there are object-oriented implementations of the PIC method (e.g., OOPIC library). There are also the template libraries for PIC method [4] but only for the CPU-based supercomputers, not for the hybrid ones.

4. Electron Heat Conductivity in Computational Experiments

This section displays a sketch of the anomalous heat conductivity effect. The exact physics needs much greater numbers of particles and grid sizes. In order to simulate the interaction of the electron beam with plasma the following values of the main physical parameters were set:

- electron temperature of 1 KeV
- the mass of ion 1836 electron masses (hydrogen ions)
- plasma density of 10^{14} cm^{-3}
- the ratio of beam density to plasma density of 10^{-3}
- beam energy of 1 MeV
- the size of the domain of $L_x = 0.065$ cm and Ly = Lz = 0.008 cm.
- grid size of 512×64×64 nodes, 150 particles per cell

The modulation of electron density was observed in the computational experiments. The amplitude of the modulation is 220 % of the initial value of density. Modulation in this case means the emergence of regions with very high or very low density in the previously uniform-density plasma as it is shown in Figure 7. It is seen from Figure 7 that the density becomes non-uniform not only along the direction of the beam (the X axis), but also along the Y axis. Thus, the density is modulated not along X, that seems quite natural, but also along Y and Z. It corresponds to the physics of the process well, because it is known that the waves propagating in plasma due to beam relaxation have all the three components of wave-vector as non-zeros.

Conclusion

The parallel implementation of the PIC-based plasma model has been developed for both the CPU and the GPU-based supercomputers. The resulting code is able to simulate plasma with high resolution needed to study the turbulent transport in plasma.

Through the example of beam-plasma interaction problem the large-scale and fine-grain aspects or parallel programming have been shown. The main conclusion is that the parallelisation can not be limited to large-scale for the PIC method. In order to obtain best performance the fine-grain (e.g., GPU-based) parallelisation is also necessary.

The research work was supported by the RFBR grants 14-07-00241 and 14-01-31088.

References

[1] Astrelin, V. T., Burdakov, A. V., Postupaev, V. V., (1998). Generation of Ion-Acoustic Waves and Suppresion of Heat Transport during Plasma Heating by an Electron Beam. *Plasma Physics Reports*. 24, 5. 414-425.

[2] Cohen, B. I., Barnes, D. C., Dawson, J. M., Hammett, G. W., Lee, W. W., Kerbel, G. D., Leboeuf, J.-N., Liewer, P. C., Tajima, T., Waltz, R. E., (1995). The numerical

tokamak project: simulation of turbulent transport. *Computer Physics Communications*, 87, 1-2, 1-15.

[3] Grigoriev, Yu., Vshivkov, V., Fedoruk, M., (2002). Numerical «particle-in-cell» methods: theory and applications. *De Gruyter*, 249 p.

[4] Decyk, V. K., (1995). Skeleton PIC codes for parallel computers, *Computer Physics Communications,* 87.

In: Parallel Programming
Editor: Mikhail S. Tarkov

ISBN: 978-1-63321-957-1

Chapter 4

NUMERICAL MODELLING OF ASTROPHYSICAL FLOW ON HYBRID ARCHITECTURE SUPERCOMPUTERS

***I. Kulikov*[1,2,3], *I. Chernykh*[1,2], *A. Snytnikov*[1,2], *V. Protasov*[3], *A. Tutukov*[4], *and B. Glinsky*[1,2,*]**

[1]Institute of Computational Mathematics and Mathematical Geophysics, Siberian Branch RAS, Novosibirsk, Russia
[2]Novosibirsk State University, Novosibirsk, Russia
[3]Novosibirsk State Technical University, Novosibirsk, Russia
[4]Institute of Astronomy of the Russian Academy of Sciences, Moscow, Russia

Abstract

This chapter describes a comprehensive computer technology of numerical modeling of astrophysical flows on hybrid supercomputer equipped with computations accelerators (NVIDIA and/or Intel accelerators). The design of parallel computing algorithms for modeling the gas-dynamic, magnetic gas dynamic, collisionless component of astrophysical objects with consideration of chemical processes is presented. There are three software packages described in this chapter: GPUPEGAS code designed for simulation of astrophysics objects on hybrid supercomputers; AstroPhi code which is used for the dynamics of stars and molecular clouds simulation on hybrid supercomputers equipped with Intel Xeon Phi accelerators; PADME code for simulation of planetary systems formation on hybrid supercomputers.

Keywords: Co-design of parallel algorithms, parallel programming, computational astrophysics, hybrid architecture of computational systems, GPU-accelerators NVIDIA, Intel Xeon Phi accelerators

[*] Corresponding author: B. Glinsky. E-mail: kulikov@ssd.sscc.ru.

$$R\frac{\partial u}{\partial t} + RL\Lambda R\frac{\partial u}{\partial x} = 0,$$

And making the substitution $w = Ru$, we arrive to independent equations:

$$\frac{\partial w}{\partial t} + \Lambda\frac{\partial w}{\partial x} = 0.$$

This system of equations has the exact solution at each of the cell boundaries, depending on the sign of the eigenvalues. Let us make the inverse substitution in $u = Lw$ and being the exact solution of Riemann problem at the Eulerian stage. For the approximation of flux in the gas dynamics equations at Euler stage the velocity and pressure computed by the formulas:

$$V = \frac{v_L + v_R}{2} + \frac{p_L - p_R}{2}\sqrt{\frac{\rho_L + \rho_R}{\rho_L \rho_R \gamma (p_L + p_R)}}$$

$$P = \frac{p_L + p_R}{2} + \frac{v_L - v_R}{2}\sqrt{\frac{\rho_L \rho_R \gamma (p_L + p_R)}{\rho_L + \rho_R}}.$$

Material flow, which will remain in the cell after a time τ, can be calculated using the following simple formula:

$$M_{i,j}^{n+1} = M_{i,j}^{n} + \frac{\tau}{h_x}\left(x\_flow\_in_{i,j} - x\_flow\_out_{i,j}\right) + \frac{\tau}{h_y}\left(y\_flow\_in_{i,j} - y\_flow\_out_{i,j}\right)$$

To determine flows across borders a modification of the classical method of calculation is used which takes into account possible slant of the boundary (Figure 1) due to the different speeds in knots [30].

Incoming flow by axis x calculated as

$$x\_flow\_in_{i,j} = \frac{1}{2}\left(v_{x\,i-\frac{1}{2},j-\frac{1}{2}} \cdot \begin{cases} M_{i-1,j}, & v_{x\,i-\frac{1}{2},j-\frac{1}{2}} > 0 \\ M_{i,j}, & v_{x\,i-\frac{1}{2},j-\frac{1}{2}} \le 0 \end{cases} + v_{x\,i-\frac{1}{2},j+\frac{1}{2}} \cdot \begin{cases} M_{i-1,j}, & v_{x\,i-\frac{1}{2},j+\frac{1}{2}} > 0 \\ M_{i,j}, & v_{x\,i-\frac{1}{2},j+\frac{1}{2}} \le 0 \end{cases} \right).$$

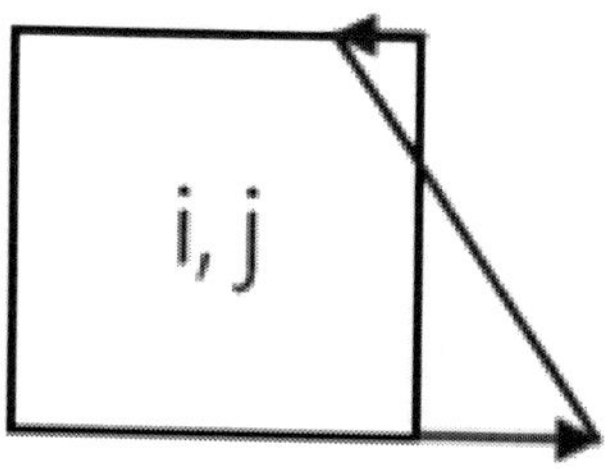

Figure 1. Bevel border cells for two-dimensional case.

Condition for the stability of the method is formulated as:

$$CFL = \frac{\tau\left(\sqrt{\gamma\frac{p}{\rho}} + \boldsymbol{max}\{|v_x|, |v_y|\}\right)}{\boldsymbol{min}\{h_x, h_y\}}$$

The primary particle dynamics simulation algorithmic complexity is to determine the force acting on each particle from other particles. Besides it is necessary to take into account the interaction of the gravitational field of gas and particles. In this chapter the Particle-Mesh method [22] used.

This method allows to reduce the computational cost of this step of the simulation. The Particle-Mesh method is based on the fact that we divide the computational domain into a finite set of cells (in our implementation exactly coinciding with the computational grid for the gas components) and in each of them calculating the particle density.

Then to obtain the density distribution, the Poisson equation is solved for the gravitational potential. Knowing the potential can easily calculate the gravity force:

$$F = -grad\Phi$$

where Φ determines from:

$$\nabla\Phi = 4\pi\left(\rho_{gas} + \rho_{particles}\right)$$

This method has a significant drawback - accuracy. Using the classical approach the calculation accuracy of the attractive force depends only on the accuracy of summation. By the same method, there are several sources of error:

1 Calculation particle density in the cell. As the Harlow method is not avoid fluctuations of the particle density in the transition from cell to cell, which leads to fluctuations in unphysical solutions.
2 Calculation of gravitational force. The gravitational potential is bound to the center of the cell.

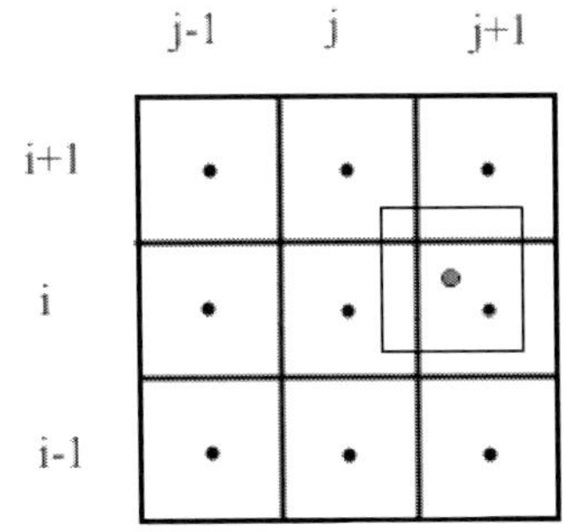

Figure 2. Dencity of the particle is distributed between cells *(i, j), (i+1, j), (i, j+1), (i+1, j+1)*.

To reduce the influence of these factors the cell density of the particles and the force acting on it are determined according to the method Clouds-In-Cells (CIC) (Birdsall 1997).

With this approach the coordinates of the particles are the coordinates of the center of mass of the "cloud" of finite size. The density of such clouds is distributed between the cells in which it fell (Figure 2). Thus, the particle density in a cell and the force acting on a particle is calculated as:

$$\rho_{i,j} = \sum_{clouds} W_{i,j}(x,y)\rho_c(x,y)$$

$$F_c = -\sum_{i,j} W_{i,j}(x,y)\, grad\Phi_{i,j}$$

where

$$W_{i,j}(x,y) = \begin{cases} \left(1-\frac{|x-x_i|}{h_x}\right)\left(1-\frac{|y-y_j|}{h_y}\right), & |x-x_i| \le h_x \;\&\; |y-y_j| \le h_y \\ 0, & other \end{cases}$$

This approach does not solve the problem completely but it can significantly reduce the error of calculations that considered in detail [7].

Are traditionally, collisionless component is described using N-body models. Nevertheless, this model has disadvantages as a spurious generation of entropy, increased communication overhead and poor load balancing [36]. Therefore, in co-design algorithms to describe collisionless components in the context of modeling the galaxies collision was selected "Collisionless Stellar Hydrodynamics" approach. This approach is based on the equations for the first moments of the collisionless Boltzmann equation. The first moments of the collisionless Boltzmann moment equations are:

$$\frac{\partial n}{\partial t} + div(n\vec{u}) = 0,$$

$$\frac{\partial n\vec{u}}{\partial t} + div(\vec{u}n\vec{u}) = -grad(n\sigma^2) - \rho grad(\Phi_{gas} + \Phi_{\star}),$$

$$\frac{\partial nE_{ij}}{\partial t} + div(nE_{ij}\vec{u}) = -div(2n\sigma_{ij}^2\vec{u}) - 2(n\vec{u}, grad(\Phi_{gas} + \Phi_{\star})),$$

$$nE_{ij} = n\sigma_{ij}^2 + \rho u_i u_j,$$

$$\Delta(\Phi_{gas} + \Phi_{\star}) = 4\pi(\rho + n),$$

where n is density, $\vec{u}$ is the velocity vector, σ^2 is the velocity dispersion tensor, nE_{ij} is the density of total energy, Φ_{gas} is the gravitational potential of the gas itself, $\Phi_{\square}$ is the contribution of the dark matter and stars to the gravitational potential. The solver for the system of collisionless Boltzmann equation is based on the combination of Fluids-in-Cells and Godunov method.

On Euler stage numerical method must drop the advective terms in the equations of continuity, motion and velocity dispersion tensor. As a result the equation in one-dimensional case should be written as:

$$\frac{\partial n}{\partial t}+\left[u_x\frac{\partial n}{\partial x}\right]+n\frac{\partial u_x}{\partial x}=0,$$

$$\frac{\partial u_i}{\partial t}+\left[u_x\frac{\partial u_i}{\partial x}\right]+\frac{1}{n}\frac{\partial \sigma^2{}_{xi}}{\partial x}=0,$$

$$\frac{\partial \sigma^2{}_{ij}}{\partial t}+\left[u_x\frac{\partial \sigma^2{}_{ij}}{\partial x}\right]+\sigma^2{}_{ij}\frac{\partial u_x}{\partial x}+\sigma^2{}_{xj}\frac{\partial u_i}{\partial x}+\sigma^2{}_{xi}\frac{\partial u_j}{\partial x}=0.$$

Discard the advective terms (we take them into account at the transfer stage) and rewrite the system in the quasi-linear form.

$$\frac{\partial}{\partial t}\begin{pmatrix} n \\ u_x \\ u_y \\ u_z \\ \sigma^2{}_{xx} \\ \sigma^2{}_{xy} \\ \sigma^2{}_{xz} \\ \sigma^2{}_{yy} \\ \sigma^2{}_{yz} \\ \sigma^2{}_{zz} \end{pmatrix}+\begin{pmatrix} 0 & n & 0 & 0 & 0 & 0 & 0 & 0 & 0 & 0 \\ 0 & 0 & 0 & 0 & n^{-1} & 0 & 0 & 0 & 0 & 0 \\ 0 & 0 & 0 & 0 & 0 & n^{-1} & 0 & 0 & 0 & 0 \\ 0 & 0 & 0 & 0 & 0 & 0 & n^{-1} & 0 & 0 & 0 \\ 0 & 3\sigma^2{}_{xx} & 0 & 0 & 0 & 0 & 0 & 0 & 0 & 0 \\ 0 & 2\sigma^2{}_{xy} & \sigma^2{}_{xx} & 0 & 0 & 0 & 0 & 0 & 0 & 0 \\ 0 & 2\sigma^2{}_{xz} & 0 & \sigma^2{}_{xx} & 0 & 0 & 0 & 0 & 0 & 0 \\ 0 & \sigma^2{}_{yy} & 2\sigma^2{}_{xy} & 0 & 0 & 0 & 0 & 0 & 0 & 0 \\ 0 & \sigma^2{}_{yz} & \sigma^2{}_{xz} & \sigma^2{}_{xy} & 0 & 0 & 0 & 0 & 0 & 0 \\ 0 & \sigma^2{}_{zz} & 0 & 2\sigma^2{}_{xz} & 0 & 0 & 0 & 0 & 0 & 0 \end{pmatrix}\frac{\partial}{\partial x}\begin{pmatrix} n \\ u_x \\ u_y \\ u_z \\ \sigma^2{}_{xx} \\ \sigma^2{}_{xy} \\ \sigma^2{}_{xz} \\ \sigma^2{}_{yy} \\ \sigma^2{}_{yz} \\ \sigma^2{}_{zz} \end{pmatrix}=0$$

As one can see, the first and last three columns are zero columns. This means that the corresponding eigen values are equal to zero and the corresponding macro parameters as in the case with classical gas density in the dynamic equations will be included in the scheme as the arithmetic mean.

Thus, we consider the system of equations of the sixth order of the form:

$$\frac{\partial}{\partial t}\begin{pmatrix} u_x \\ u_y \\ u_z \\ \sigma^2_{xx} \\ \sigma^2_{xy} \\ \sigma^2_{xz} \end{pmatrix} + \begin{pmatrix} 0 & 0 & 0 & n^{-1} & 0 & 0 \\ 0 & 0 & 0 & 0 & n^{-1} & 0 \\ 0 & 0 & 0 & 0 & 0 & n^{-1} \\ 3\sigma^2_{xx} & 0 & 0 & 0 & 0 & 0 \\ 2\sigma^2_{xy} & \sigma^2_{xx} & 0 & 0 & 0 & 0 \\ 2\sigma^2_{xz} & 0 & \sigma^2_{xx} & 0 & 0 & 0 \end{pmatrix} \frac{\partial}{\partial x}\begin{pmatrix} u_x \\ u_y \\ u_z \\ \sigma^2_{xx} \\ \sigma^2_{xy} \\ \sigma^2_{xz} \end{pmatrix} = 0$$

Solution of the system has the form:

$$U_x = \frac{u_x^L + u_x^R}{2} + \frac{\left[\sigma^2\right]_{xx}^L - \left[\sigma^2\right]_{xx}^R}{2}\sqrt{\frac{n^L + n^R}{3n^L n^R\left(\left[\sigma^2\right]_{xx}^L + \left[\sigma^2\right]_{xx}^R\right)}},$$

$$U_{y,z} = \frac{u_{y,z}^L + u_{y,z}^R}{2} + \frac{\left[\sigma^2\right]_{xy,xz}^L - \left[\sigma^2\right]_{xy,xz}^R}{2}\sqrt{\frac{n^L + n^R}{n^L n^R\left(\left[\sigma^2\right]_{xx}^L + \left[\sigma^2\right]_{xx}^R\right)}} +$$

$$\frac{\left[\sigma^2\right]_{xx}^L - \left[\sigma^2\right]_{xx}^R}{2}\sqrt{\frac{n^L + n^R}{3n^L n^R\left(\left[\sigma^2\right]_{xx}^L + \left[\sigma^2\right]_{xx}^R\right)}}\frac{\left(\left[\sigma^2\right]_{xy,xz}^L + \left[\sigma^2\right]_{xy,xz}^R\right)(1-\sqrt{3})}{\left[\sigma^2\right]_{xx}^L + \left[\sigma^2\right]_{xx}^R},$$

$$\left[\sigma^2\right]_{xx} = \frac{\left[\sigma^2\right]_{xx}^L + \left[\sigma^2\right]_{xx}^R}{2} + \frac{u_x^L - u_x^R}{2}\sqrt{\frac{3n^L n^R\left(\left[\sigma^2\right]_{xx}^L + \left[\sigma^2\right]_{xx}^R\right)}{n^L + n^R}},$$

$$\left[\sigma^2\right]_{xy,xz} = \frac{\left[\sigma^2\right]_{xy,xz}^L + \left[\sigma^2\right]_{xy,xz}^R}{2} + \frac{u_y^L - u_y^R}{2}\sqrt{\frac{n^L n^R\left(\left[\sigma^2\right]_{xx}^L + \left[\sigma^2\right]_{xx}^R\right)}{n^L + n^R}} +$$

$$\frac{u_x^L - u_x^R}{2}\sqrt{\frac{n^L + n^R}{n^L n^R\left[\sigma^2\right]_{xx}^L + \left[\sigma^2\right]_{xx}^R}}\frac{n^L n^R\left(\left[\sigma^2\right]_{xy,xz}^L + \left[\sigma^2\right]_{xy,xz}^R\right)(\sqrt{3}-1)}{n^L + n^R}.$$

The MHD equations in 3D case are:

$$\frac{\partial \rho}{\partial t} + \frac{\partial\left(\rho v_x\right)}{\partial x} + \frac{\partial\left(\rho v_y\right)}{\partial y} + \frac{\partial\left(\rho v_z\right)}{\partial z} = 0,$$

$$\frac{\partial p}{\partial t}+\left[v_x\frac{\partial p}{\partial x}\right]=-\gamma p\frac{\partial v_x}{\partial x},$$

$$\frac{\partial B_y}{\partial t}+\left[v_x\frac{\partial B_y}{\partial x}\right]+B_y\frac{\partial v_x}{\partial x}-\frac{\partial\left(B_x v_y\right)}{\partial x}=0,$$

$$\frac{\partial B_z}{\partial t}+\left[v_x\frac{\partial B_z}{\partial x}\right]+B_z\frac{\partial v_x}{\partial x}-\frac{\partial\left(B_x v_z\right)}{\partial x}=0.$$

Discard the advective terms (we will take them into account at the transfer stage) and rewrite the system in the quasi-linear form.

$$\frac{\partial}{\partial t}\begin{pmatrix}\rho\\ v_x\\ v_y\\ v_z\\ p\\ B_y\\ B_z\end{pmatrix}+\begin{pmatrix}0&\rho&0&0&0&0&0\\ 0&0&0&0&\frac{1}{\rho}&\frac{B_y}{\rho}&\frac{B_z}{\rho}\\ 0&0&0&0&0&-\frac{B_x}{\rho}&0\\ 0&0&0&0&0&0&-\frac{B_x}{\rho}\\ 0&\gamma p&0&0&0&0&0\\ 0&B_y&-B_x&0&0&0&0\\ 0&B_z&0&-B_x&0&0&0\end{pmatrix}\frac{\partial}{\partial x}\begin{pmatrix}\rho\\ v_x\\ v_y\\ v_z\\ p\\ B_y\\ B_z\end{pmatrix}=0.$$

As can be seen the system is degenerate by the first column and it is obvious that one of the eigenvalues is zero, which effectively means no mass transfer at Euler stage. Therefore, we will consider a system of quasi-linear equations $\frac{\partial u}{\partial t}+B\frac{\partial u}{\partial x}=0$ of the sixths order:

$$\frac{\partial}{\partial t}\begin{pmatrix}v_x\\ v_y\\ v_z\\ B_y\\ B_z\\ p\end{pmatrix}+\begin{pmatrix}0&0&0&\frac{B_y}{\rho}&\frac{B_z}{\rho}&\frac{1}{\rho}\\ 0&0&0&-\frac{B_x}{\rho}&0&0\\ 0&0&0&0&-\frac{B_x}{\rho}&0\\ B_y&-B_x&0&0&0&0\\ B_z&0&-B_x&0&0&0\\ \gamma p&0&0&0&0&0\end{pmatrix}\frac{\partial}{\partial x}\begin{pmatrix}v_x\\ v_y\\ v_z\\ B_y\\ B_z\\ p\end{pmatrix}=0.$$

We will use the average values of magnetic dynamic parameters for constructing the scheme.

$$\left(b_x, b_y, b_z\right) = \frac{1}{\sqrt{\rho}}\left(B_x, B_y, B_z\right),$$

$$b^2 = b_x^2 + b_y^2 + b_z^2.$$

The speed of sound c, Alfven speed c_a, fast c_f and slow c_s magnetic speed are:

$$c = \sqrt{\frac{\gamma p}{\rho}},$$

$$c_a = \left|b_x\right| = \left|\frac{B_x}{\sqrt{\rho}}\right|,$$

$$c_{f,s} = \sqrt{\frac{\left(c^2 + b^2\right) \pm \sqrt{\left(c^2 + b^2\right)^2 - 4c^2 c_a^2}}{2}}.$$

It is worth noting that the eigenvectors can have singularities as the degeneracy of eigenvalues. To avoid this situation we introduce a special notation [46, 9, 42]:

$$\left(\beta_y, \beta_z\right) = \begin{cases} \dfrac{\left(B_y, B_z\right)}{\sqrt{B_y^2 + B_z^2}}, & B_y^2 + B_z^2 \neq 0 \\ \left(\dfrac{1}{\sqrt{2}}, \dfrac{1}{\sqrt{2}}\right), & B_y^2 + B_z^2 = 0 \end{cases}$$

$$\left(\alpha_f, \alpha_s\right) = \begin{cases} \dfrac{\left(\sqrt{c^2 - c_s^2}, \sqrt{c_f^2 - c^2}\right)}{\sqrt{c_f^2 - c_s^2}}, & B_y^2 + B_z^2 \neq 0 \vee \gamma p \neq B_x^2 \\ \left(\dfrac{1}{\sqrt{2}}, \dfrac{1}{\sqrt{2}}\right), & B_y^2 + B_z^2 = 0 \,\&\, \gamma p = B_x^2 \end{cases}$$

As a result we obtain the following formula to determine the unknowns on the boundary of two cells:

$$V_x = \frac{v_x^L + v_x^R}{2} + \frac{B_y^L - B_y^R}{2}\left[\frac{\beta_y \alpha_s \alpha_f (c_f - c_s)}{c\sqrt{\rho}}\right] + \frac{B_z^L - B_z^R}{2}\left[\frac{\beta_z \alpha_s \alpha_f (c_f - c_s)}{c\sqrt{\rho}}\right] + \frac{p^L - p^R}{2}\left[\frac{\alpha_f^2 c_f + \alpha_s^2 c_s}{\rho c^2}\right]$$

$$V_y = \frac{v_y^L + v_y^R}{2} + \frac{B_y^L - B_y^R}{2}\left[sign(B_x)\frac{\beta_y^2 - 1}{\sqrt{\rho}} - sign(B_x)\frac{\beta_y^2 (c_f \alpha_f^2 + c_s \alpha_s^2)}{c\sqrt{\rho}}\right] +$$
$$\frac{B_z^L - B_z^R}{2}\left[\frac{\beta_y \beta_z sign(B_x)}{\sqrt{\rho}} - \frac{\beta_y \beta_z sign(B_x)(c_f \alpha_f^2 + c_s \alpha_s^2)}{c\sqrt{\rho}}\right] + \frac{p^L - p^R}{2}\left[\frac{\alpha_f \alpha_s \beta_y sign(B_x)(c_f - c_s)}{c^2 \rho}\right]$$

$$V_z = \frac{v_z^L + v_z^R}{2} + \frac{B_y^L - B_y^R}{2}\left[\frac{\beta_y \beta_z sign(B_x)}{\sqrt{\rho}} - \frac{\beta_y \beta_z sign(B_x)(c_s \alpha_s^2 + c_f \alpha_f^2)}{c\sqrt{\rho}}\right] +$$
$$\frac{B_z^L - B_z^R}{2}\left[sign(B_x)\frac{\beta_z^2 - 1}{\sqrt{\rho}} - sign(B_x)\frac{\beta_z^2 (c_s \alpha_s^2 + c_f \alpha_f^2)}{c\sqrt{\rho}}\right] + \frac{p^L - p^R}{2}\left[\frac{\alpha_f \alpha_s \beta_z sign(B_x)(c_f - c_s)}{c^2 \rho}\right]$$

$$B_y = \frac{B_y^L + B_y^R}{2} + \frac{v_x^L - v_x^R}{2}\left[\frac{\alpha_f \alpha_s \sqrt{\rho}\beta_y (c_f - c_s)}{c}\right] +$$
$$\frac{v_y^L - v_y^R}{2}\left[sign(B_x)\sqrt{\rho}(\beta_y^2 - 1) - \frac{\sqrt{\rho}\beta_y^2 sign(B_x)}{c}(c_s \alpha_s^2 + c_f \alpha_f^2)\right] +$$
$$\frac{v_z^L - v_z^R}{2}\left[\sqrt{\rho}\beta_y \beta_z sign(B_x)\left(1 - \frac{c_s \alpha_s^2 + c_f \alpha_f^2}{c}\right)\right]$$

$$B_z = \frac{B_z^L + B_z^R}{2} + \frac{v_x^L - v_x^R}{2}\left[\frac{\alpha_f \alpha_s \sqrt{\rho}\beta_z (c_f - c_s)}{c}\right] +$$
$$\frac{v_y^L - v_y^R}{2}\left[\sqrt{\rho}\beta_y \beta_z sign(B_x)\left(1 - \frac{c_s \alpha_s^2 + c_f \alpha_f^2}{c}\right)\right] +$$
$$\frac{v_z^L - v_z^R}{2}\left[sign(B_x)\sqrt{\rho}(\beta_z^2 - 1) - \frac{\sqrt{\rho}\beta_z^2 sign(B_x)}{c}(c_s \alpha_s^2 + c_f \alpha_f^2)\right]$$

$$P = \frac{p^L + p^R}{2} + \frac{v_x^L - v_x^R}{2}\left[\rho\left(c_f - \alpha_s^2 (c_f - c_s)\right)\right] +$$
$$\frac{v_y^L - v_y^R}{2}\left[sign(B_x)\rho \alpha_s \alpha_f \beta_y (c_f - c_s)\right] + \frac{v_z^L - v_z^R}{2}\left[sign(B_x)\rho \alpha_s \alpha_f \beta_z (c_f - c_s)\right]$$

These formulas will be used for Euler stage of the numerical method. To ensure zero divergence of the magnetic field will use the additional equation:

$$\frac{\partial \mathbf{B}}{\partial t} = rot(\vec{v} \times \mathbf{B})\,.$$

To solve the Poisson equation using an approach based on the fast Fourier transform. This combination of mathematical approaches and numerical methods can be used as unified computing technology to solve the gas dynamics equations, magnetic gas dynamics and the equations for the first moments of the collisionless Boltzmann equation.

3. Verifcation of Implementation

Simulation often is the only way to validate new theories in astrophysics. Thus researchers especially need to employ reliable and trustworthy programs. Ahead of the presentation of simulation results a number of various tests must be conducted for validation and verification of the program being used. Validation and verification are the main stages of the development of any technology, either a simulation package or an observational tool. The goal of such a testing stage is estimate of the correctness and precision of the simulation.

A great work of validation and verification is done in computational fluid dynamics. During the development of the program package the numerical algorithm was verified by the test problem with the solutions from the special data bank (see the table 1). One of the problems is the shock wave simulation. It is known that different methods simulate the shock wave region in a different way: either with oscillations or with dissipation. In the case of the gravitational gas dynamics the oscillations are less tolerant since any density wave will attract the neighboring gas resulting in non-physical fluctuations of the gas values.

Also there is a problem of simulation of the essential rarefaction region. It is known that a lot of methods give the non-physical growth of the inner energy is this region. Moreover the great initial drop of pressure (5 decimal orders) is the standard robustness test for the method. This test must show the capability of the method to simulate the intense perturbations with quickly spreading shock waves robustly.

The results of simulation are given in figures 3 – 5.

The MHD shock tube are [42]:

$$\left[\rho, p, v_x, v_y, v_z, \sqrt{4\pi}B_y, \sqrt{4\pi}B_z\right] = \begin{cases} [0.18405, 0.3541, 3.8964, 0.5361, 2.4866, 2.394, 1.197], & x < 0.5 \\ [0.1, 0.1, -5.5, 0, 0, 2, 1], & x \geq 0.5 \end{cases}$$

where $\sqrt{4\pi}B_x \equiv 4$. The results of simulation on time $t = 0.15$ are given in figure 6.

The collisionless Boltzmann equation shock tube are [30]:

$$\left[n, \sigma^2_{xx}, \sigma^2_{xy}, \sigma^2_{xz}, \sigma^2_{yy}, \sigma^2_{yz}, \sigma^2_{zz}, v_x, v_y, v_z\right] = \begin{cases} [2,2,1,1,1,1,1,0,0,0], x < 0.5 \\ [1,1,1,1,1,1,1,0,0,0], x \geq 0.5 \end{cases}$$

Table 1. The initial state of the shock tube

№	ρ_L	p_L	v_L	ρ_R	p_R	v_R	x_0	t
1	1	1	1	0.125	0.1	0	0.3	0.2
2	1	0.4	-2	1	0.4	2	0.5	0.15
3	1	1000	0	1	0.01	0	0.5	0.012

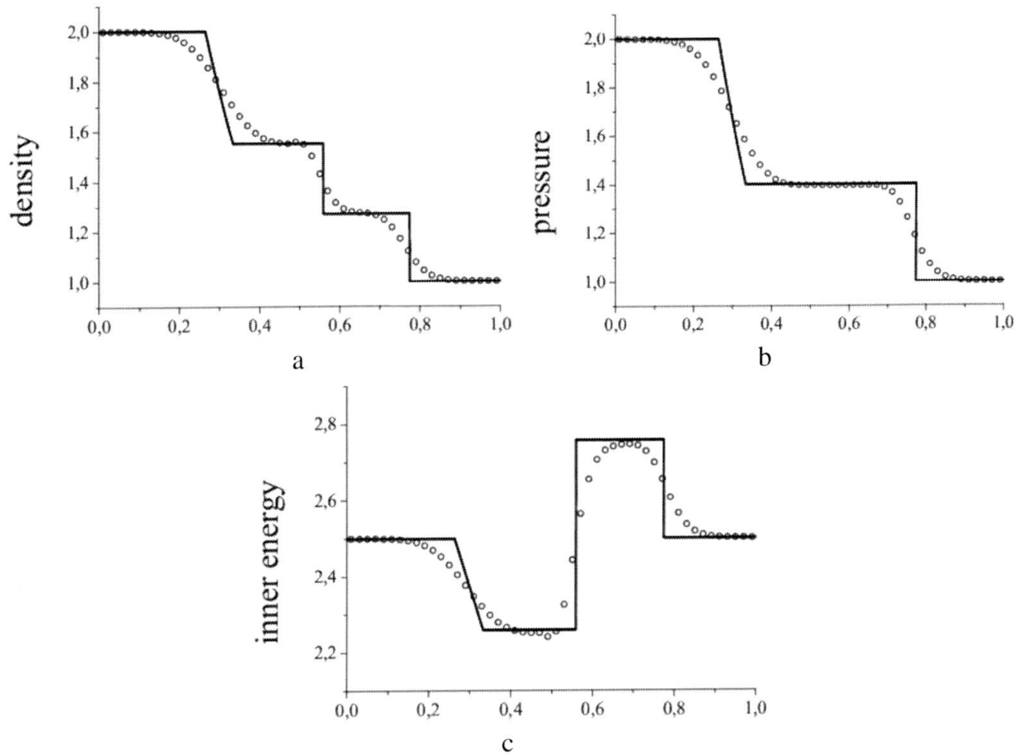

Figure 3. The simulation of the first test.

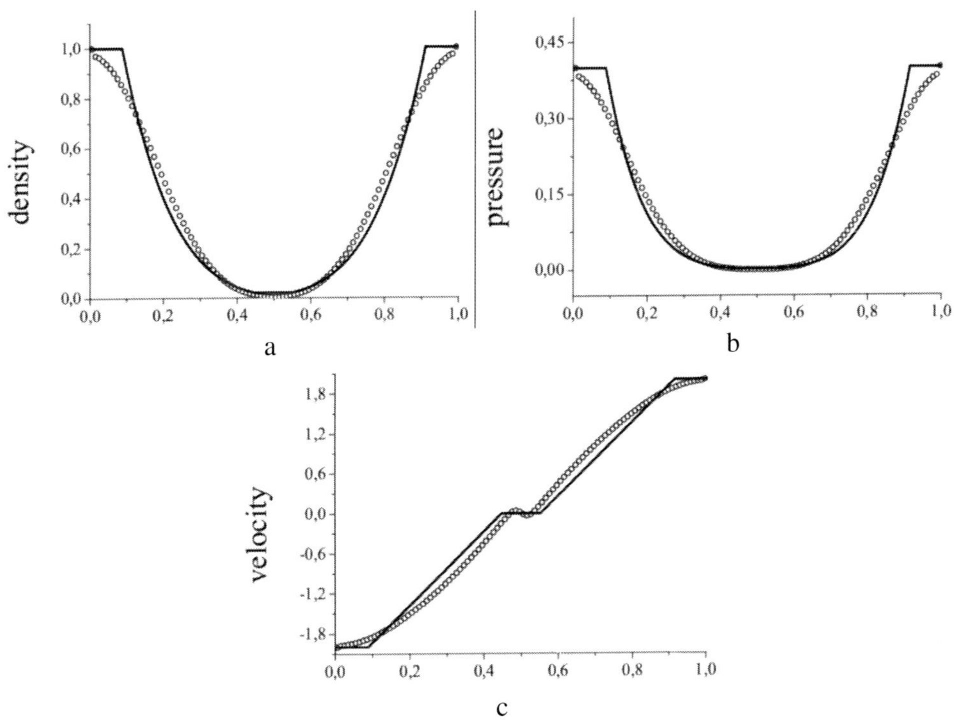

Figure 4. The simulation of the second test.

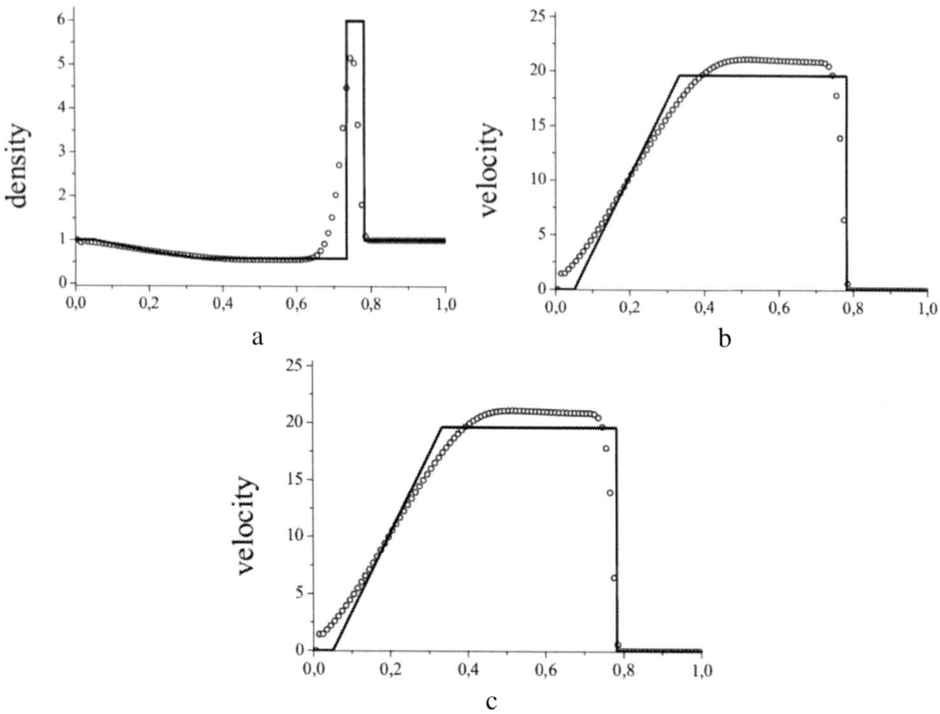

Figure 5. The simulation of the third test.

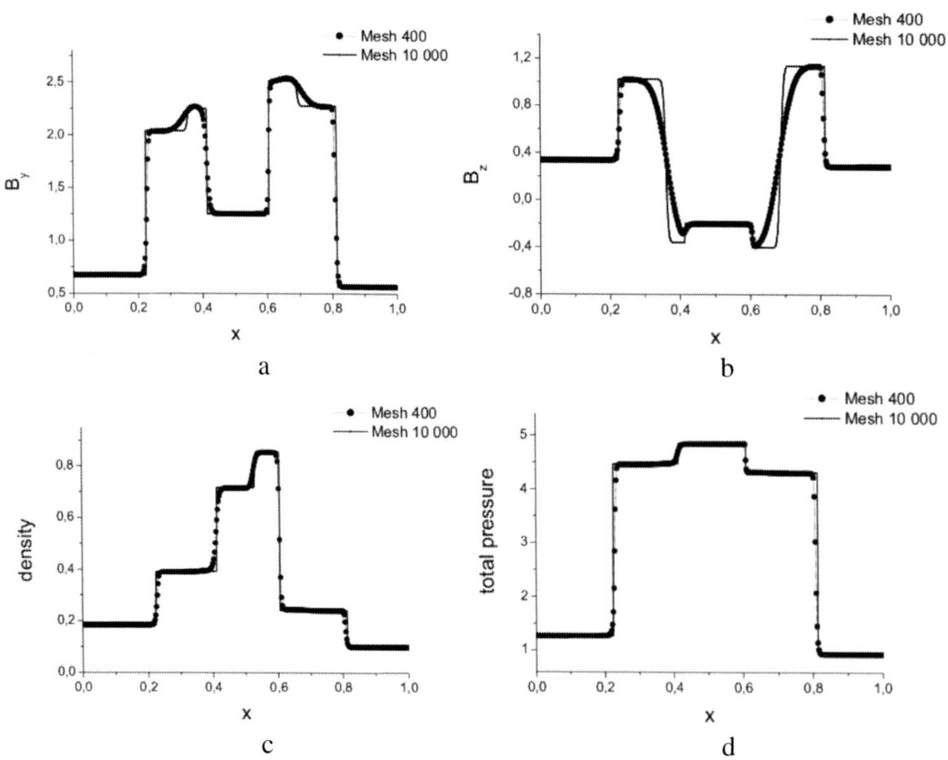

Figure 6. Continued on next page.

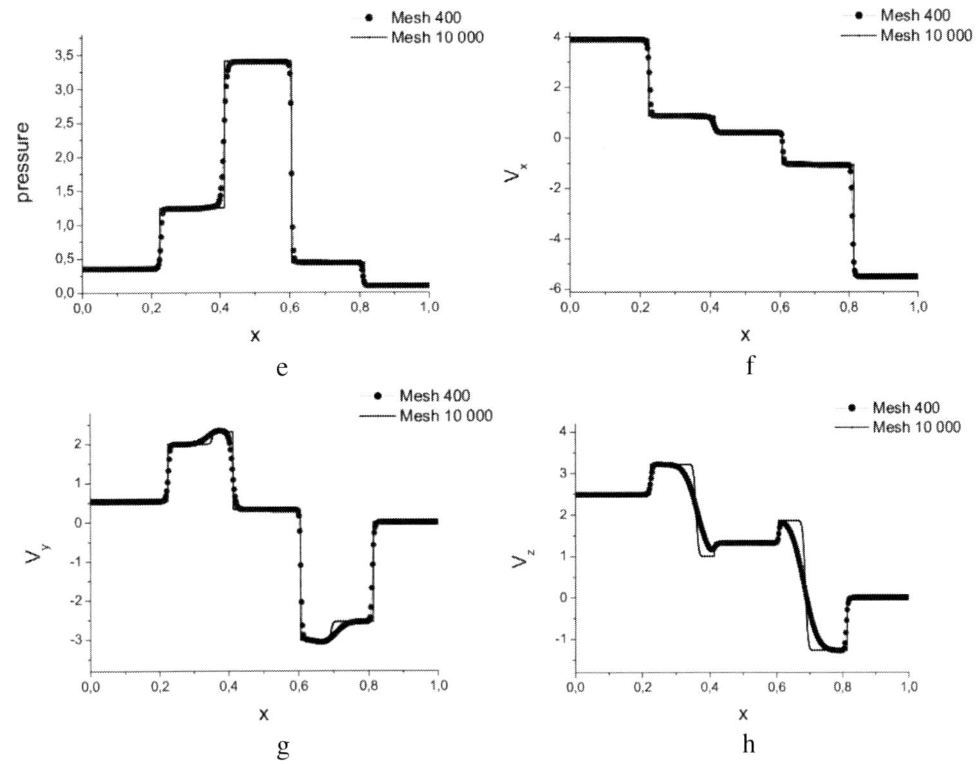

Figure 6. The simulation of MHD shock tube.

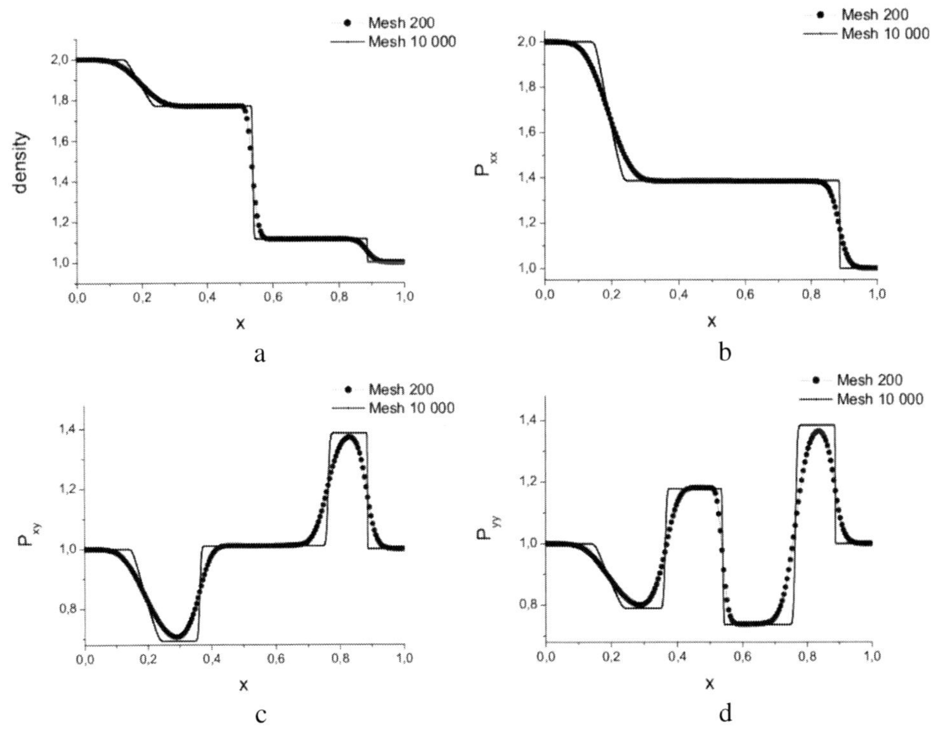

Figure 7. Continued on next page.

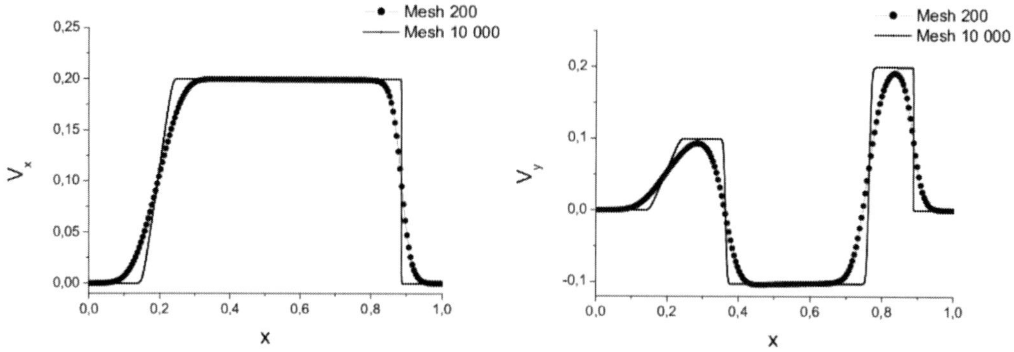

e f

Figure 7. The collisionless Boltzmann equation shock tube.

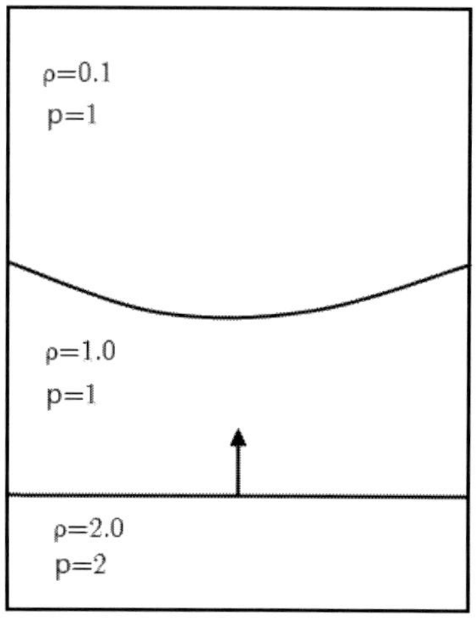

Figure 8. The Richtmyer–Meshkov instability.

The Richtmyer-Meshkov instability occurs at the boundary between two media, while passing through her shock. Consider the configuration shown in Figure 8. In the given two different densities of the gas layer and the shock wave.

The results of simulation are given in figure 9.

The initial data for the interacting shock wave and rarefied gas: $[-1,\ 1]\times[-0.5,\ 0.5]$ – the domain, density and pressure are $p=\rho=1$. In domain $[0.375,\ 0.625]\times[-0.125,\ 0.125]$ density and pressure are $\rho=1/29$, $p=1$. In domain $x>0.75$ density and pressure are $p=\frac{3}{2}$, $\rho=\frac{4}{3}$. The results of simulation are given in figure 10.

The initial data for the Rayleigh–Taylor and the Kelvin–Helmholtz instabilities: $[-0.5,\ 0.5]\times[-0.5,\ 0.5]$ – the domain,

$$\rho=\begin{cases}1,\ y\le 0\\ 2, y>0\end{cases},$$

$$v_y = A(y)\cdot\left[1+\cos(2\pi x)\right]\left[1+\cos(2\pi y)\right],\quad A(y)=\begin{cases}10^{-2}, & |y|\le 0.01\\ 0, & |y|>0.01\end{cases}$$

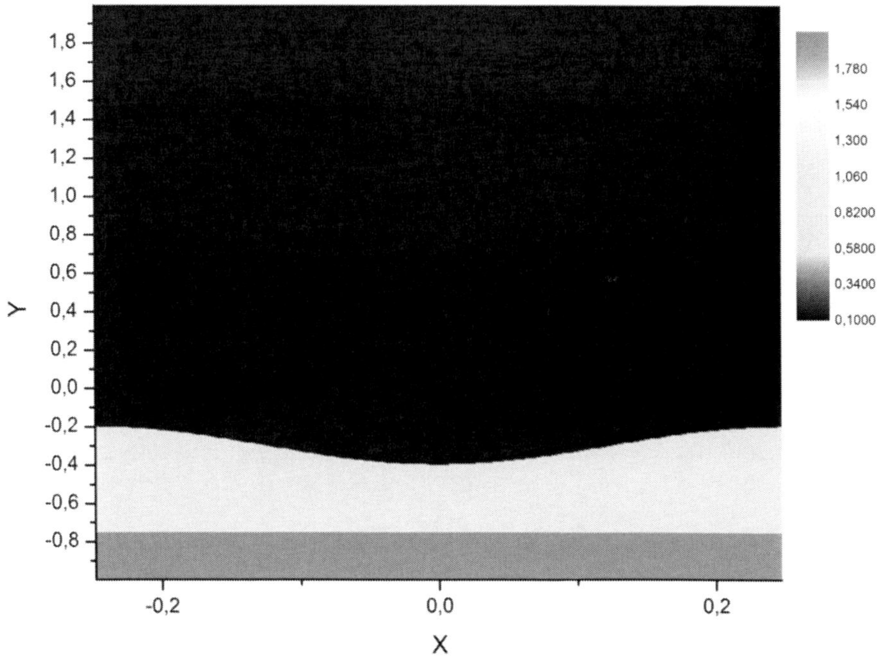

a

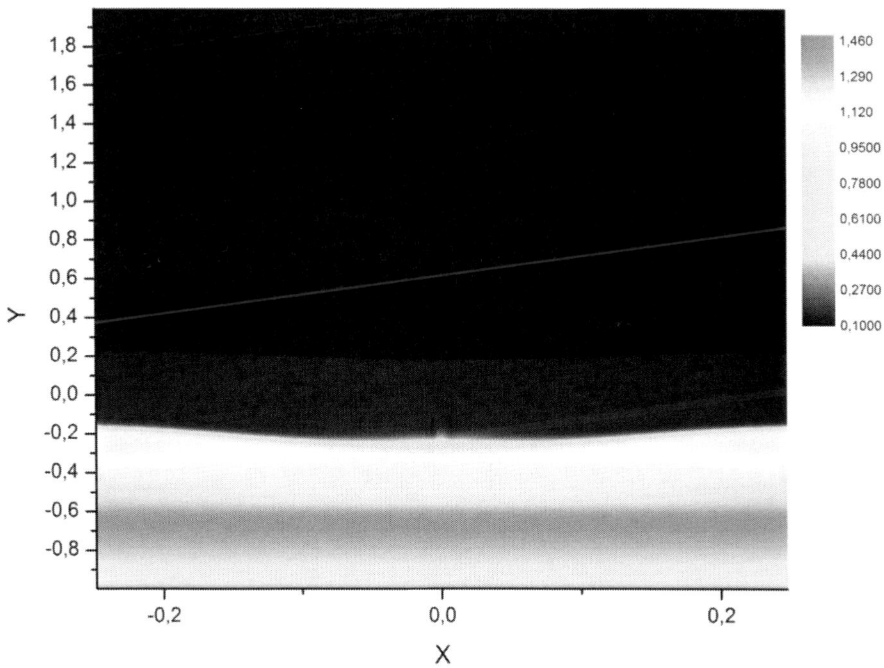

b

Figure 9. Continued on next page.

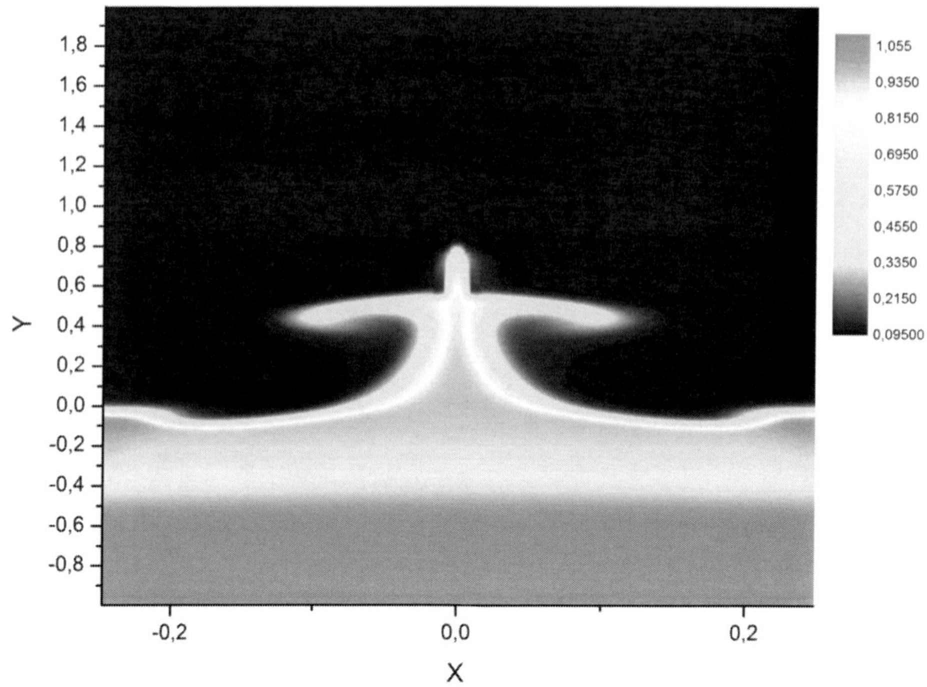

c

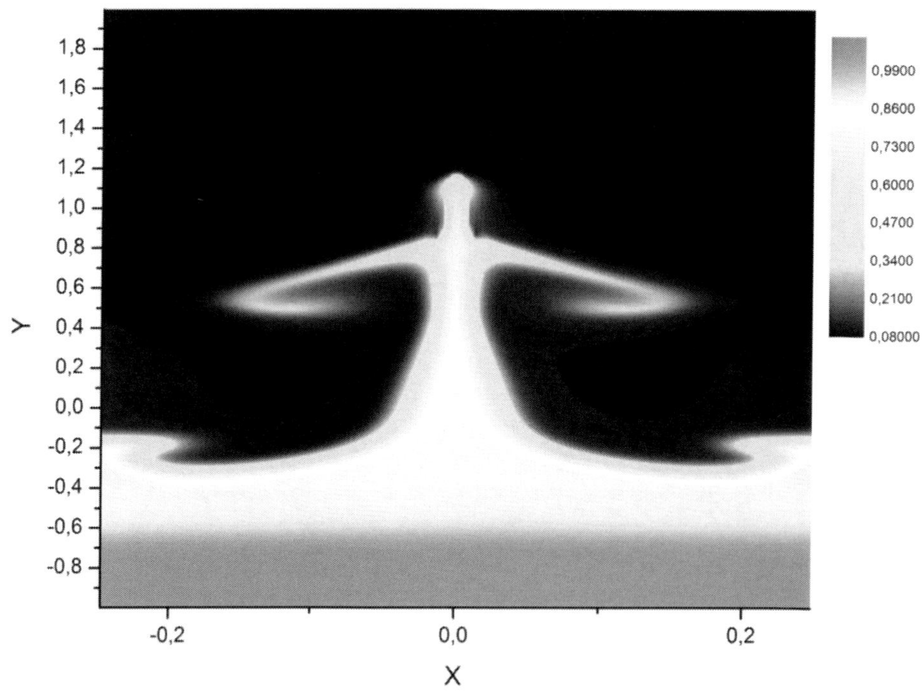

d

Figure 9. The simulation of the Richtmyer–Meshkov instability.

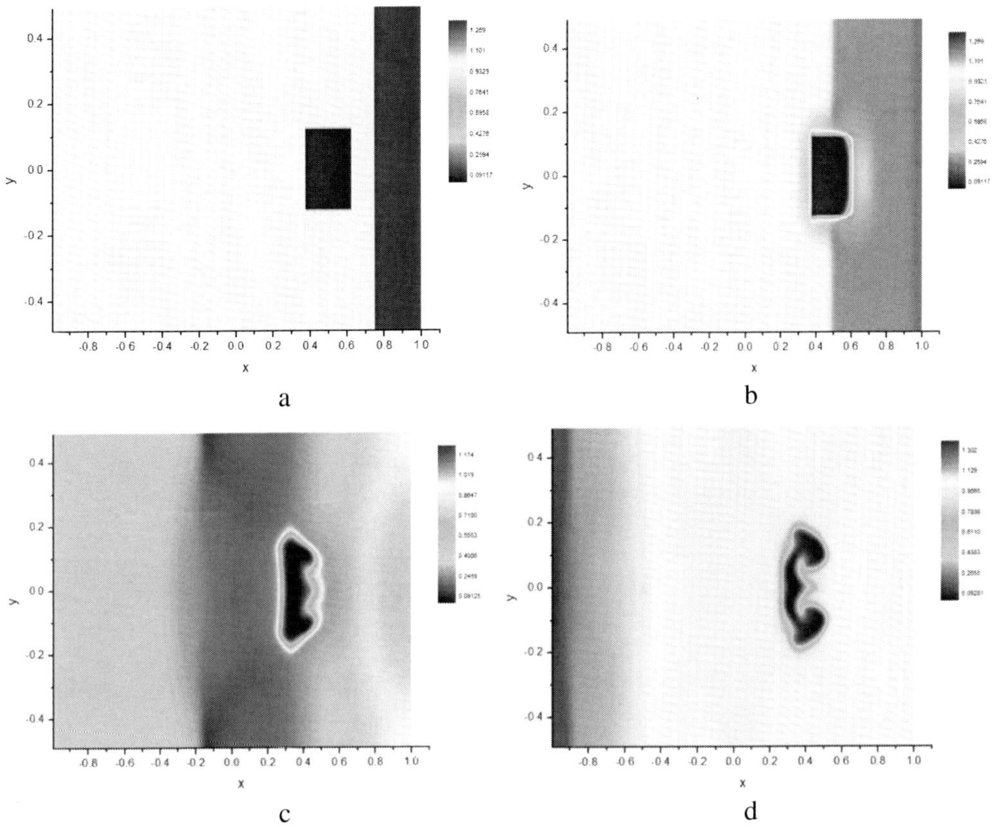

Figure 10. The interacting shock wave and rarefied gas.

For the Kelvin–Helmholtz instability are:

$$\rho = \begin{cases} 2, & |y| \le 0.25 \\ 1, & |y| > 0.25 \end{cases},$$

the pressure $p = 2.5$, the velocity is

$$v_x = \begin{cases} 0.5, & |y| \le 0.25 \\ -0.5, & |y| > 0.25 \end{cases},$$

$$v_y = \begin{cases} 0.01\left[1+\cos(8\pi x)\right]\left[1+\cos(8\pi y)\right], & |y-0.25| \le 0.1 \\ -0.01\left[1+\cos(8\pi x)\right]\left[1+\cos(8\pi y)\right], & |y+0.25| \le 0.1 \end{cases}$$

The results of simulation are given in figure 11 (the Rayleigh–Taylor instability on left and the Kelvin–Helmholtz instability on right).

The solution of Poisson equation was investigated by decreasing the mesh step with the known gravitational potential and density:

$$\Phi(r)=\begin{cases}\frac{4}{15}\pi r^5-\frac{3\pi}{5}r^4+\frac{2\pi}{3}r^2-\frac{3\pi}{5}, & r\le 1\\ -\frac{4\pi}{15r}, & r>1\end{cases}$$

$$\rho(r)=\begin{cases}2r^3-2r^2+1, & r\le 1\\ 0, & r>1\end{cases}$$

Table 2 gives the values of the relative residual with the decreasing grid step. It is seen from the table that the second order of convergence is reached.

Consider a configuration of three particles (Figure 12).

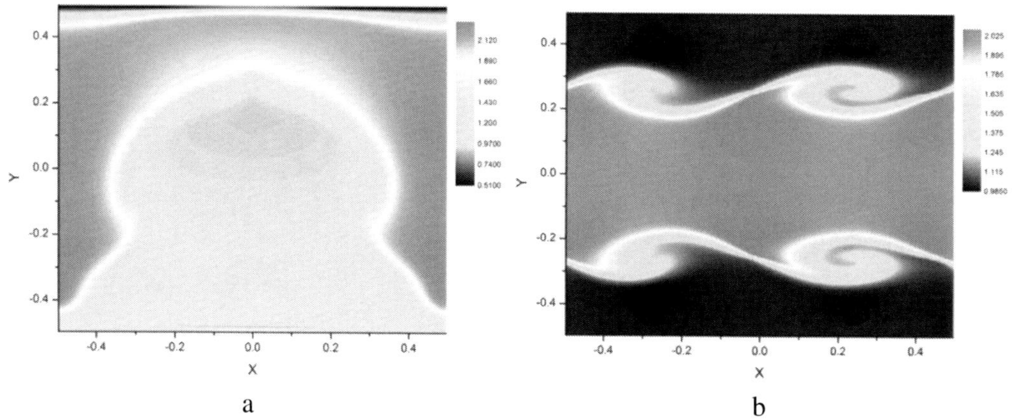

Figure 11. The Rayleigh–Taylor instability on left and the Kelvin–Helmholtz instability on right.

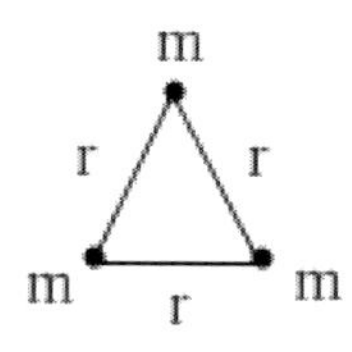

Figure 12. The configuration ensemble of three particles.

Table 2. The Euclidean norm of the deviation of the solution with the decreasing grid step

The mesh	The relative residual
16^3	6.425461E-003
32^3	1.593152E-003
64^3	4.012327E-004
128^3	1.040856E-004
256^3	2.462044E-005

Three particles of equal mass located at the vertices of an equilateral triangle. If the particles are rotated at the same speed, the distance between them should be stored. The results of simulation are given in table 3.

More tests can be found in [31].

4. Parallel Implementation

The main problem within the astrophysical code development is the efficient solution of gas dynamics equations and the Boltzmann moment equations since it takes up to 94% of computation time (Figure 13).

The uniform mesh in Cartesian coordinates is used for the solution of gas dynamics equations. Thus it is possible to use the arbitrary Cartesian topology for domain decomposition. Such a combination of mesh and topology enables potentially infinite scalability. The GPUPEGAS code is an MPI decomposition along the coordinate, while the other two coordinates the CUDA technology is used. The AstroPhi code uses 1D domain decomposition. Along one of the directions the decomposition is performed by the MPI tools, and further deomposition is perfomed by OpenMP tools within each subdomain. The parallel implementation is related to the topology and architecture of a hybrid supercomputer NKS-G6 of the Siberian Supercomputer Center ICMandMG SB RAS. The co-design of the numerical method for solving the hydrodynamic equations is implemented at every stage irrespective computation of the fluxes through each cell. In this case, the one-layer overlapping of the boundary points of the neighboring subdomains is needed. In order to increase the scalability of the numerical method the next step will be to abandon the solution of Poisson equation and to evaluate the field from the equivalent evolution equation of the Cauchy-Kowalewskaya type for the gradient of potential.

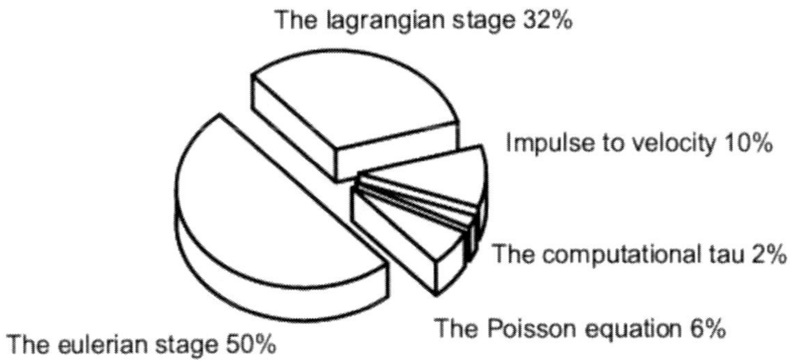

Figure 13. Computational workload in percent for each stage of the algorithm.

Table 3. Distance between the particles after the 1/3 turnover

τ	R
0,1	0, 42641
0,01	0, 44064
0,001	0, 44333

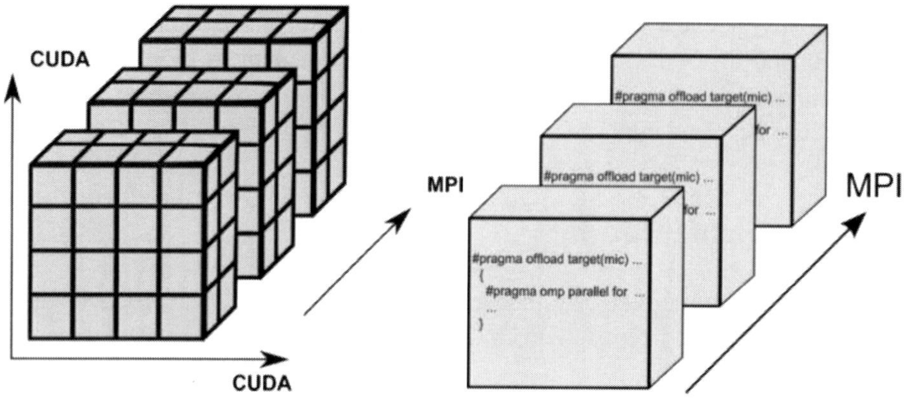

Figure 14. Domain decomposition for the solution of hydrodynamic equations.

It will be then possible to compute gravitational field in the same way as the gas flows are now computed, on Intel Xeon Phi and GPU accelerators. The method based on Cauchy-Kowalewskaya type equation has been already tested for the problem of the self-gravitating gas cloud expansion. It will be included into AstroPhi and GPUPEGAS codes after the publication of the present paper.

3D FFT which is used for Poisson equation solution is taken from the FFTW library. The distribution of field arrays among processors is set by FFTWand this FFTW-given distribution defines how are the gas values distributed. FFTW requires no overlapping. The block diagram of codes is shown by the figure 15.

For all the procedures executed by GPU accelerators within GPUPEGAS code or by Intel Xeon Phi accelarators within AstroPhi code the same programming pattern is used:

```
for(i=0; i<NX; i++)
  for(k=0; k<NY; k++)
   for(l=0; l<NZ; l++)
    {
     a[i*NZ*NY+k*NZ+l];
    }
```

For computation of hydrodynamic parameters on GPU was used following algorithm:

- Transfer arrays from CPU to GPU by means cudaMemcpy function with option cudaMemcpyHostToDevice,
- Run procedure on GPU,
- Transfer arrays from GPU to CPU by means cudaMemcpy function with option cudaMemcpyDeviceToHost.

The details can be found in code listing for GPU:

```
cudaMemcpy(acu, a, NX*NY*NZ*sizeof(real),
               cudaMemcpyHostToDevice);
dim3 threads(BLOCK_SIZE,BLOCK_SIZE,1);
```

```
dim3 blocks(NY/threads.x,NZ/threads.y,1);
function<<<blocks, threads>>>(acu,tau,NX,NY,NZ,h);
cudaMemcpy(anext, acu, NX*NY*NZ*sizeof(real),
            cudaMemcpyDeviceToHost);
...
__device__void gpu_function(real acuelem,
                              real tau, real h)
{
            return acuelem * h/tau;
}
...
__global__void function(real* acu, real tau,
                         int NX, int NY, int NZ, real h)
{
k = blockIdx.y * blockDim.y + threadIdx.y;
l = blockIdx.x * blockDim.x + threadIdx.x;
for(i=0; i<NX; i++)
     acu[i*NZ*NY+k*NZ+l] =
            gpu_function(acu[i*NZ*NY+k*NZ+l],tau,h);
}
```

The details can be found in code listing for Intel Xeon Phi:

```
...
// MIC mode
#ifndef MIC_DEV
#define MIC_DEV 0
#endif
...
// Number of MIC-threads
#define MIC_NUM_THREADS 60
...
#pragma offload_attribute(push,target(mic))
double function(double *a, double x, int number)
{
            return a[number] * x;
}
#pragma offload_attribute(pop)
...
#pragma offload target(mic) in(a: length(NX*NY*NZ)) \
                         out(c: length(NX*NY*NZ))
{
#pragma omp parallel for default(none) shared(a,x,c) \
                         num_threads(MIC_NUM_THREADS)
for(int i=1; i<NX-1; i++)
  for(int k=1; k<NY-1; k++)
    for(int l=1; l<NZ-1; l++)
```

```
        {
          c[i*NZ*NY+k*NZ+l] = function(a,x,i*NZ*NY+k*NZ+l);
        }
    }
    ...
```

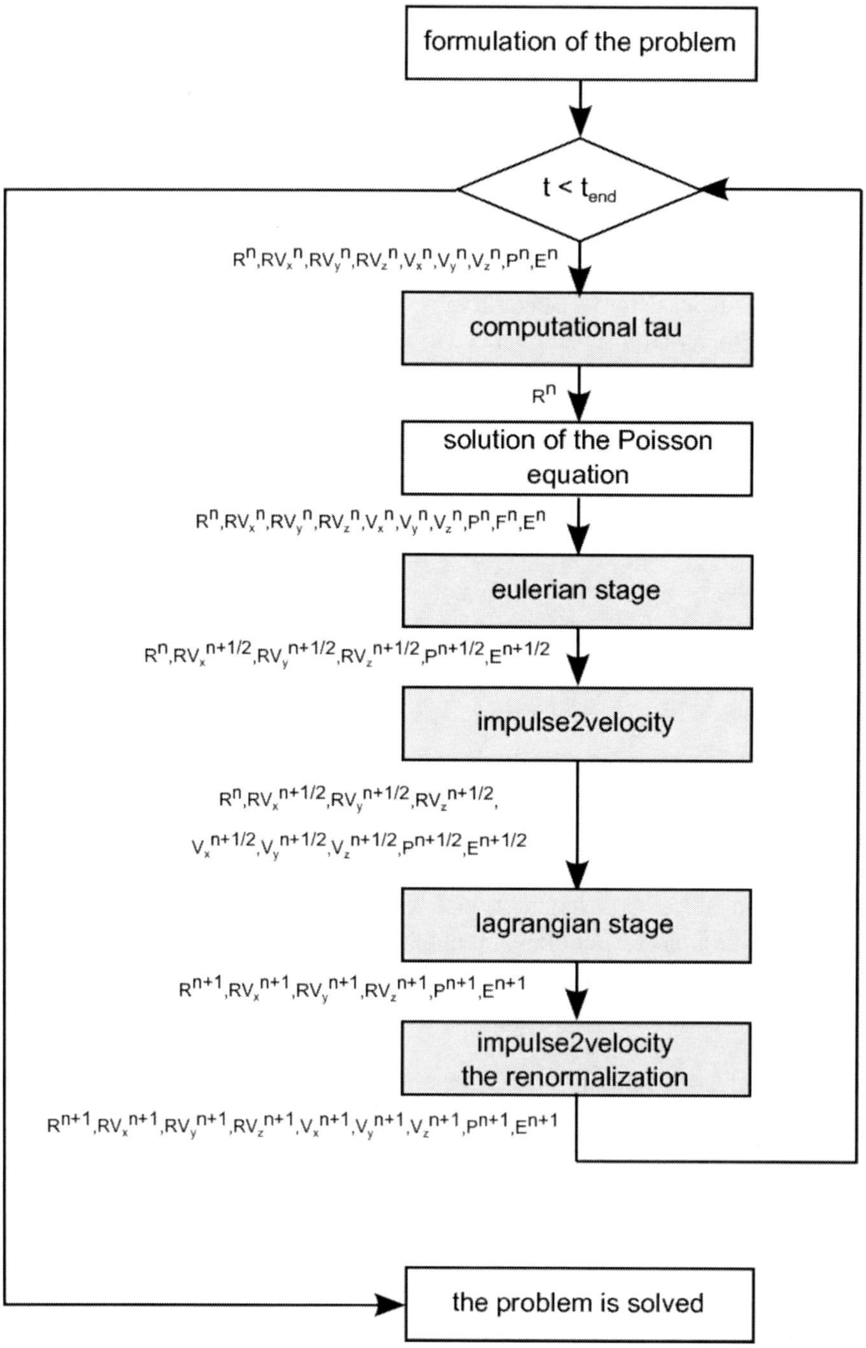

Figure 15. The block diagram of the AstroPhi code and GPUPEGAS code.

There is one remarkable point that should be mentioned here. It is the time-step evaluation procedure. In the case when GPUs were used (GPUPEGAS code), this procedure could be run only on CPU (the same in GAMER code). The reason is the absence of efficient global minimum operation (min) in CUDA. On the contrary, in OpenMP such an efficient operation is present. The computational cost of this operation is about 1%. Thus it doesn't affect the performance of the single-core run. But when the number of GPU cores is raised up to several thousand and the speed-up is about one hundred within one GPU, then time-step evaluation procedure may become the most expensive. This situation may easily become possible in the next couple of years since the speed-up of 55 times was already obtained in GPUPEGAS code with a single Nvidia Tesla and since the number of GPU cores in constantly increasing. It should be noticed that such a problem with very expensive min procedure is not at all possible with Intel Xeon Phi accelerators.

Thus, for the hybrid parallel implementation let us define three different kinds of scalability.

1. SingleDevice scalability (high scalability within one single Intel Xeon Phi or GPU) significant computation time decrease during one timestep as a result of using a large number of Intel Xeon Phi or GPU cores.
2. MultiDevice scalability (low scalability for the case of many Intel Xeon Phi or GPU accelerators). The computation time for one timestep remains constant using a larger number of Intel Xeon Phi or GPU accelerators.
3. FFTW scalability (high scalability for FFTW library). It means the significant decrease of computation time for one timestep using more CPUs or CPU cores.

The mesh of the size 256^3 was used for speed-up evaluation within a single Intel Xeon Phi or GPU. In this case each of the Intel Xeon Phi accelerators contained a portion of the whole mesh, the size of the portion being equal to 256^3. Let us remind that accelerators were not used for Poisson equation solution. The speed-up is given in figure 16 for GPUPEGAS code and figure 17 for AstroPhi code.

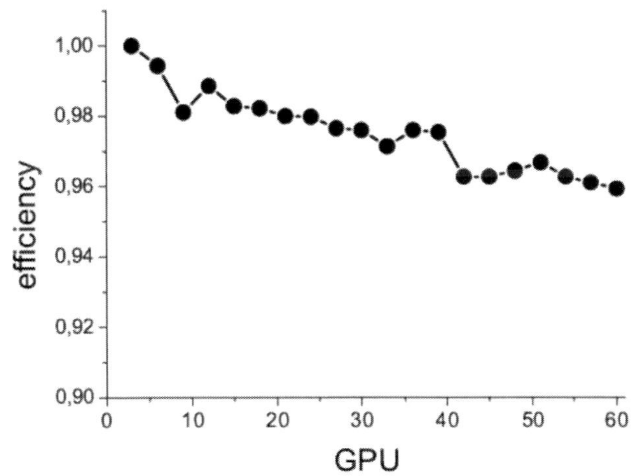

a

Figure 16. Continued on next page.

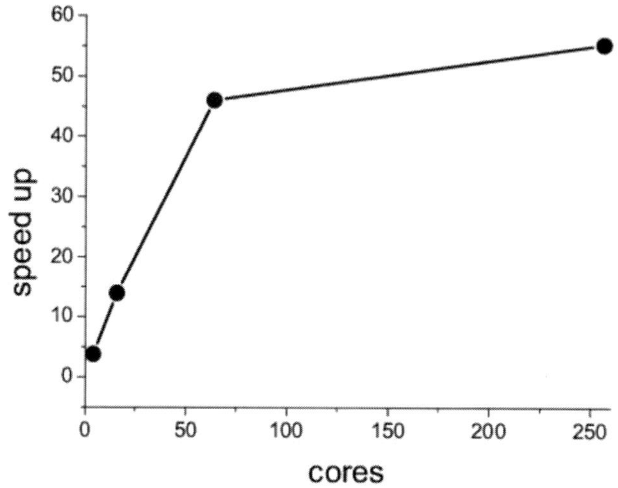

b

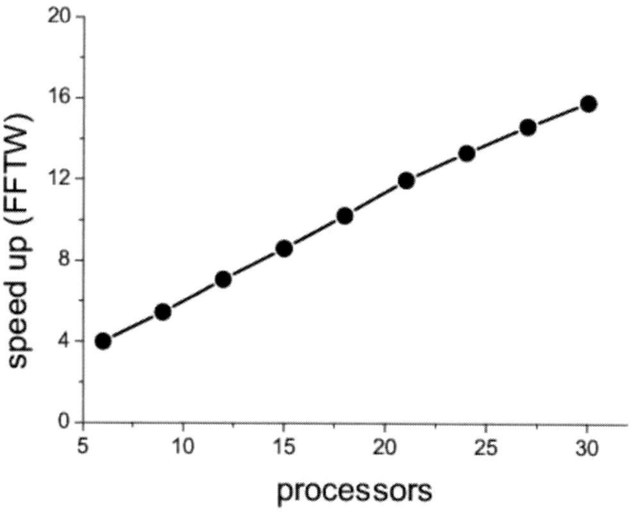

c

Figure 16. GPUPEGAS code performance.

In order to compare the computation time with a number of CPU/GPU accelerators and the single core CPU/GPU computation time let us perform the following test. Let us trace the computation time separetly for each part of the numerical method: for Eulerian (*Euler*) and Lagrangian (*Lagrange*) stages, for Poisson (*Poisson*) equation solution, for velocity computation (*imp2vel*) and renorming and also for time-step (*tau*) evaluation. Let us use the mesh with the size 256^3 and 4 nodes of NKS-30T cluster at SSCC, Novosibirsk (www2.sscc. ru).

Time measurement was performed in three different configurations of the program:

1 Configuration 1 – computation time for one time-step with one core of Intel Xeon X5670 and one core of NVidia Tesla M2090.
2 Configuration 2 – computation time for one time-step with for 4 nodes of cluster, each node using one core of Intel Xeon X5670 and one core of NVidia Tesla M2090.

3 Configuration 3 – computation time for one time-step with for 4 nodes of cluster, each node using one core of Intel Xeon X5670 and 256 cores of NVidia Tesla M2090.

The results of time measurement are presented in table 4.

Small number of cores in the experiment allowed to get superlinear speedup (because more efficient use of the cache memory). We do not were compared performance of the solution of hydrodynamic equations on single core of GPU and a single core of CPU.

Because of comparable performance of a single core graphics accelerator and the CPU core on acoustical problems. Situation becomes complicated by the fact that time of computation of hydrodynamic equations in this case is approximately 20% of the full time, and almost coincides with time of computational τ and three times slower, than solving the Poisson equation.

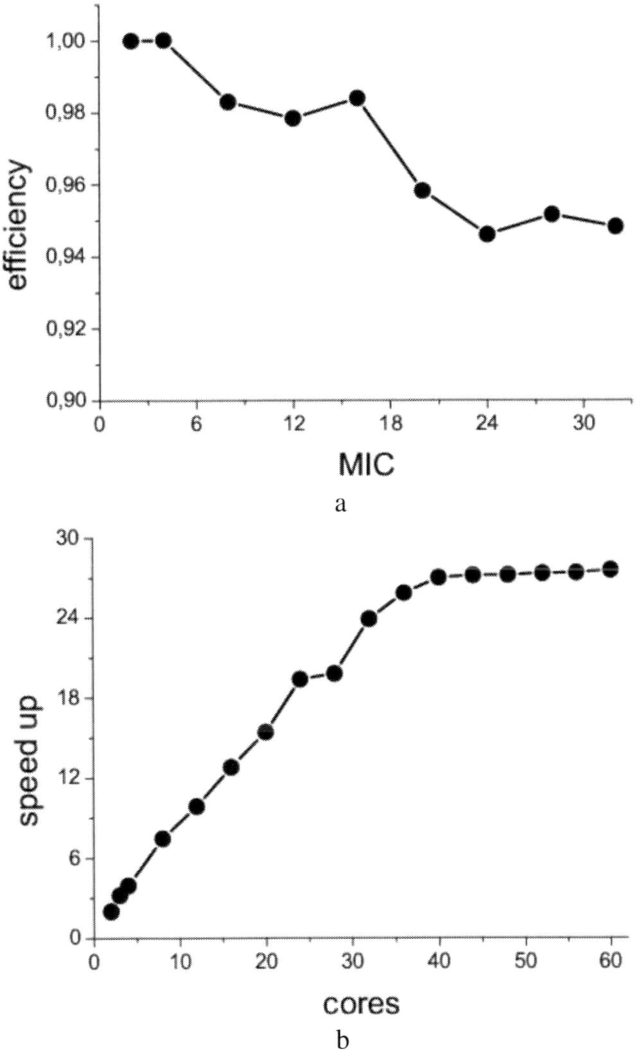

Figure 17. Continued on next page.

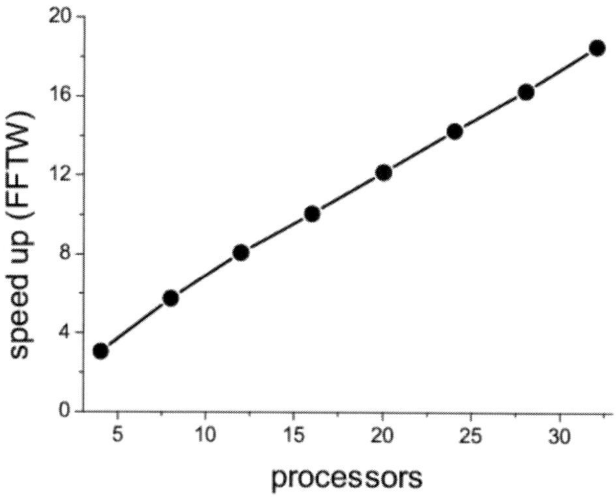

c

Figure 17. AstroPhi code performance.

Table 4. GPUPEGAS code performance

№	Euler	Lagrange	Imp2Vel	Poisson	Tau	Total
1	34,72	22,87	8,43	4,02	1,22	71,26
2	8,62	5,51	2,11	1,03	0,31	17,58
3	0,17	0,095	0,035	1,03	0,31	1,64

In the following papers is planned to addition of multicomponent medium, non-equilibrium chemodynamics, and improving order accuracy of the numerical method, which will increase the time for solve of hydrodynamic equations.

But requires a qualitative improvements parallel algorithm for solving the Poisson equation and create an efficient GPU-reducing operations to compute τ.

In order to compare the computation time with a number of Intel Xeon Phi accelerators and the single core CPU computation time let us perform the following test. Let us trace the computation time separetely for each part of the numerical method: for Eulerian and Lagrangian stages, for Poisson equation solution, for velocity computation and renorming and also for time-step evaluation.

Let us use the mesh with the size This test was peformed with four nodes of the MVS-10P cluster at JSCC, Moscow (www.jscc.ru). At each node one Intel Xeon E5-2690 processor was use in a single-thread mode and also one Intel Xeon Phi 7110 acelerator. The program was compiled in the following way:

```
mpicc -o astrophi -O2 -openmp \
    -I /home1/kulikov/fftw-2.1.5/include \
    -L /home1/kulikov/fftw-2.1.5/lib astrophi.cpp \
    -lrfftw_mpi -lfftw_mpi -lrfftw -lfftw -lm
```

Time measurement was performed in four different configurations of the program:

1 Configuration 1 – computation time for one time-step with one core of the Intel Xeon E5-2690 processor.
2 Configuration 2 – computation time for one time-step with for nodes of the cluster, each node using one core of the Intel Xeon E5-2690 processor.
3 Configuration 3 – computation time for one time-step with for nodes of the cluster, each node using one core of the Intel Xeon E5-2690 processor for Poisson equation solution and also one core of the Intel Xeon Phi 7110 accelerator for hydrodynamics equation solution.
4 Configuration 4 – computation time for one time-step with for nodes of the cluster, each node using one core of the Intel Xeon E5-2690 processor for Poisson equation solution and 60 cores of the Intel Xeon Phi 7110 accelerator for hydrodynamics equation solution.

The results of time measurement are presented in table 5.

As it is seen from the table 5, using 4 CPUs in a single-thread mode results in almost linear speed-up (in this case, everything is computed by the CPU). But when gas dynamics equations are solved by Intel Xeon Phi accelerator in the single-thread mode then the gas dynamics solver works slower approximatrly 8 times. It is explained by the relatively low performance of a single core of Intel Xeon phi accelerator.

It seems that single core of Intel Xeon Phi accelerator is comparable with top PentiumII or early PentimuIII processors. Using all the cores of one Intel Xeon Phi accelerator results in a speed-up of 3 times compared to four CPUs in a single-thread mode (60 Intel Xeon Phi cores compared to 4 Intel Xeon cores), or in speed-up of 10 times compared to mere sequential program (60 Intel Xeon Phi cores compared to 1 Intel Xeon core).

5. The Computational Experiments

The initial data for the simulation of protoplanetary system: $[-2.5,\ 2.5]\times[-2.5,\ 2.5]$ is domain. The density, pressure and angular velocity are:

$$\rho(R)=\begin{cases}3, & R<0.25\\ 2, & R<2\end{cases},\quad p(R)=\begin{cases}2, & R<0.25\\ 1, & R<2\end{cases},\quad \omega(R)=2(2-R)^2$$

Table 5. AstroPhi code performance

№	Euler	Lagrange	Other	Poisson	Total
1	6,032	42,230	5,453	5,965	59,680
2	1,523	10,664	1,387	1,950	15,524
3	11,672	81,708	10,552	1,950	105,882
4	0,456	2,960	0,440	1,950	5,806

Also in domain $R \in [0.5, 2.0]$ are uniformly distributed 50 000 particles with mass $m_i = 5 \cdot 10^{-5}$ and angular velocities $\omega_i = 2 \cdot (2 - R_i)^2 + \varepsilon_i$, where ε_i – dispersion of velocity for particle. The results of simulation are given in figure 18.

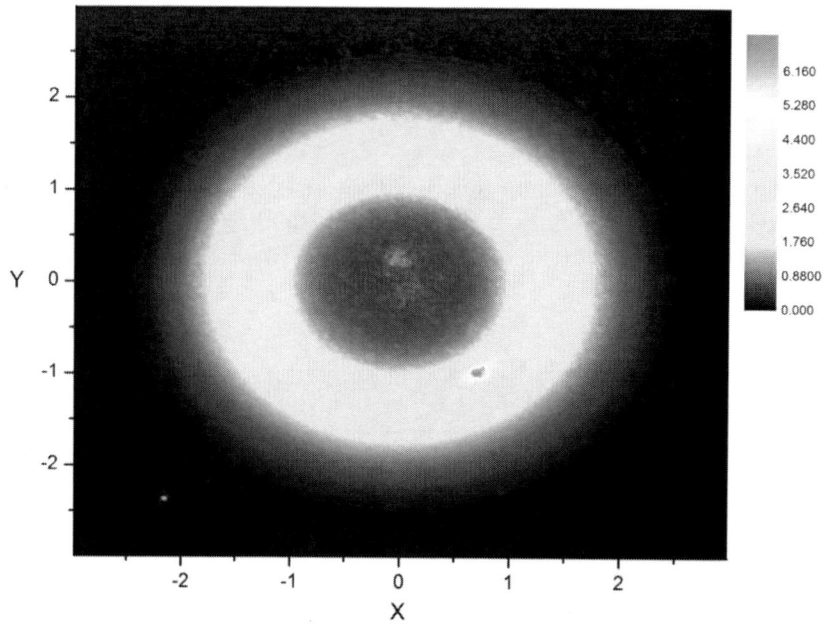

a

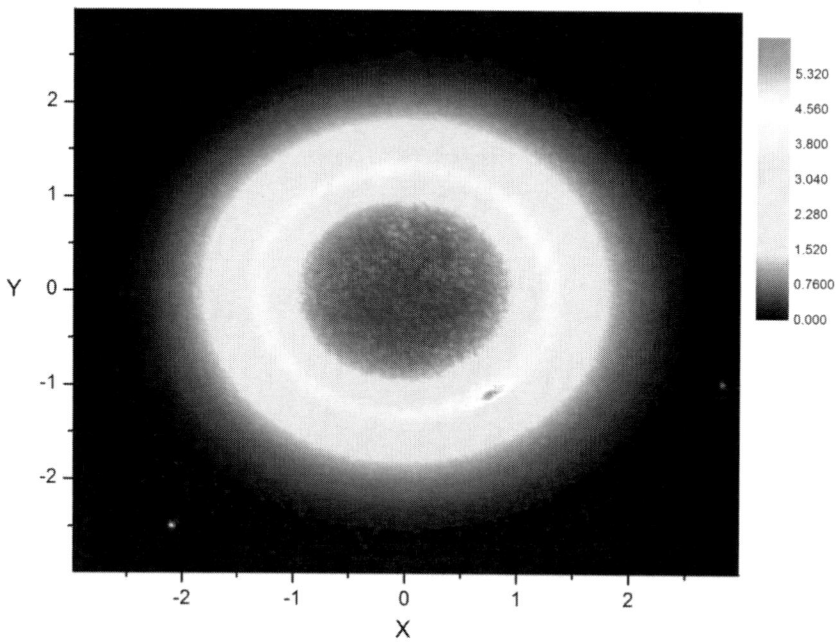

b

Figure 18. Continued on next page.

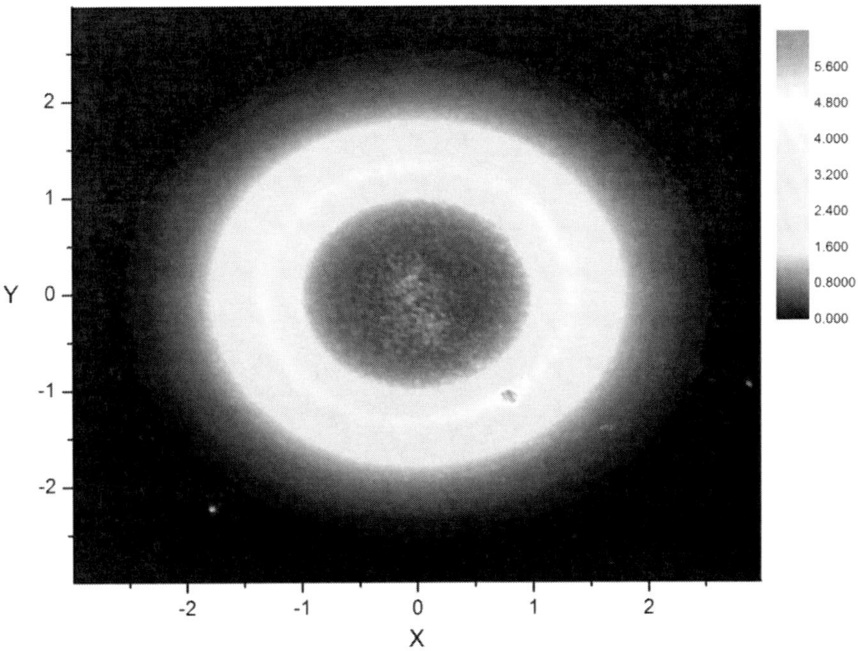

c

Figure 18. The simulation of protoplanetary system.

Figure 18 shows the formation of a ring of gas and dust, in which the soliton is formed consisting primarily of particles.

The problems of gravitational collapse of astrophysical objects are widely studied due to significant growth of observational astronomic data. Gravitational collapse takes place on initial stage of star evolution and also at the final stage (supernova explosion with collapsing core). In this section the capabilities of AstroPhi code will be shown with the exapmle of several collapse problems: the collapse of a rapidly rotating cloud [4], Evrard collapse [53], the collapse of rotating molecular cloud [41].

In order to simulate the collapse of a rotating proto-stellar cloud let us set the gas cloud inside a sphere with the radius $R_0 = 3.81 \cdot 10^{14}$ m, the mass $M_g = 3.457 \cdot 10^{30}$ kg, with uniform distribution of density $\rho = 1.492 \cdot 10^{-14}$ kg/m^3 and pressure $p = 0.1548 \cdot 10^{-10}$ H/m^2. The cloud rotates with the angular velocity $\omega = 2.008 \cdot 10^{-12}$ rad/sec. Adiabatic exponent corresponds to hydrogen $\gamma = 5/3$.

The mass of the central body is $M_{\odot} = 1.998 \cdot 10^{30}$ kg. The main parameters used for transition to non-dimensional form are the following: $L_0 = 3.81 \cdot 10^{14}$ m, $\rho_0 = 1.492 \cdot 10^{-14}$ kg/m^3, $p = 0.1548 \cdot 10^{-7}$ H/m^2, $v_0 = 1010$ m/sec, $t = 3.7 \cdot 10^{11}$ sec, $\omega_0 = 0.27 \cdot 10^{-11}$ rad/sec. Then in non-dimensional values the problem is set as follows: $\rho = 1.0$ is the density of the gas cloud, $p = 10^{-3}$ is the pressure inside the gas cloud, $\omega = 0.744$ is the angular velocity, $m_{\odot} = 2.42$ is the mass of the central body, $\gamma = 5/3$ is adiabatic index, $[0;6.4]^3$ is the computation domain.

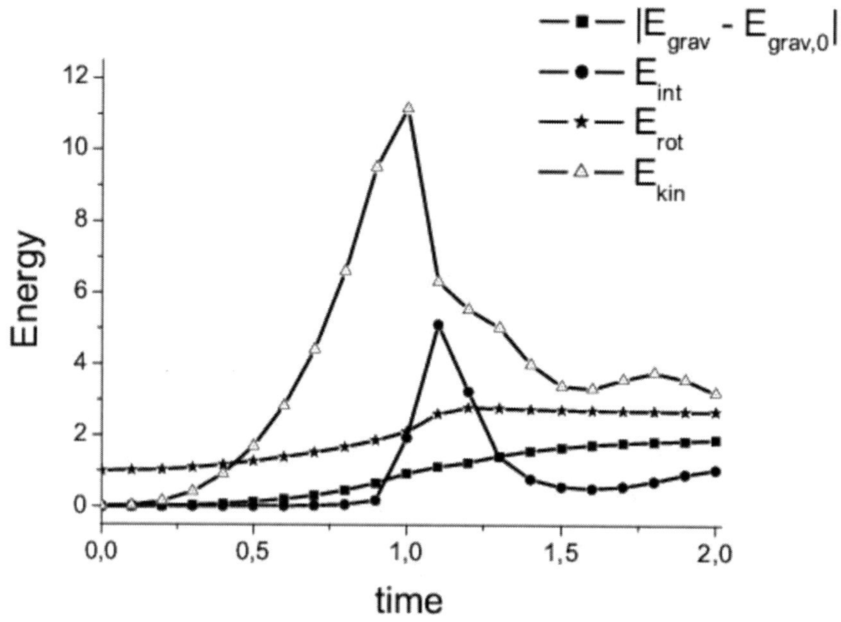

Figure 19. The behaviour of different types of energy in AstroPhi code in the simulation of rapidly rotating cloud.

There is a number of papers considering the collapse of proto-stellar clouds. In these papers there is a question what is the density distribution in the equatorial plane of the cloud after collapse. There is still no straight answer. The main result in this problem is the energy behaviour (Figure 19) and toroidal density distribution in the equatorial plane. The origin of such a distribution is the result of the momentum transport. This origin is illustrated by the behaviour of rotational and kinetic energy, and also by the potential energy after collapse 6. The potential energy is much better than the result obtained by S. G. Moiseenko et al. with the code specially designed for such kind of problems. Nevertheless there is a reasonable quantitative accordance in the behaviour of rotational and kinetic energy at the initial stage of cloud evolution. It is remarkable that the behaviour of inner energy exactly corresponds the results of S. G. Moiseenko et al. Moreover the behavior of all types of energy qualitatively, and before collapse there is even quantitative agreement with the results of other authors. It should be notice that the problem of the collapse of a rapidly rotating cloud can not be solved with AstroPhi, or any other code based on SPH, AMR or ALE approach. Here the close quantitative or qualitative accordance to the results of this Lagrangian code speaks about the capability of AstroPhi code to simulate the rapidly forming high gradients.

So, having considered the differences shown in Figure 19, it is possible to state that AstroPhi code successfully simulated the collapse of a rapidly rotating cloud.

Evrard collapse is often used to test SPH methods. The problem is interesting because of the sequence of processes in the initial stage. First, there is a short term collapse of hte central part, then fast heating of the central part, and its further expasnsion resulting in a shock wave. In order to simulate Evrard collapse let us set a a non-rotating cloud with non-dimensional radius $R_0 = 1$, with the density distribution $\rho(r) = 1/(2\pi r)$, adiabatic index $\gamma = 5/3$ and total inner energy $u = 0.05$.

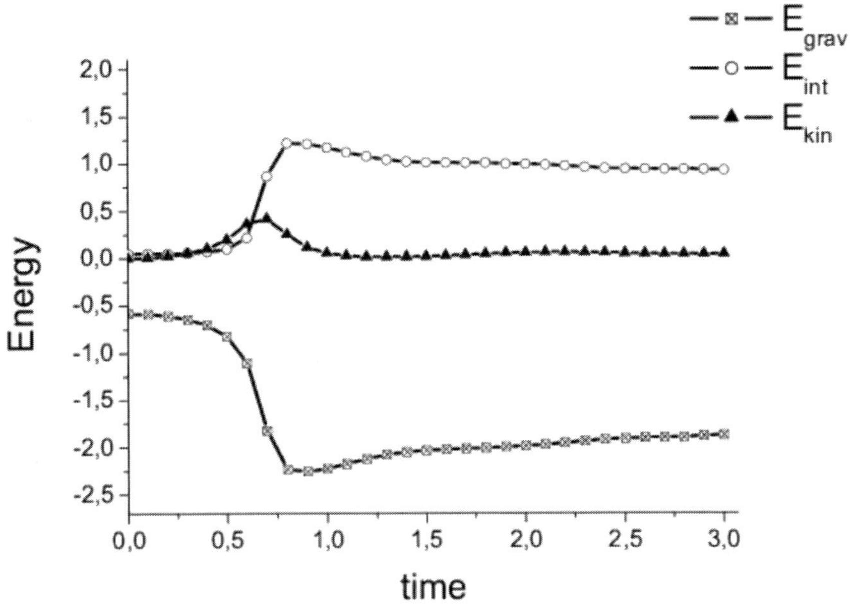

Figure 20. The behaviour of different types of energy in AstroPhi code on Evrard collapse test.

The results of AstroPhi simulation the behaviour of energy is in a quantitative agreement with the result of [53] (Figure 20) before the moment of collapse. After the moment of collapse there is qualitative agreement. It should be noticed that the collapse takes place atexactly the same moment of time. The qualitative difference in the behaviour of inner and potential energy as stipulated by the fundamental restrictions of the AREPO code in simulating high density gradients.

It is necessary to take into account that AREPO code shows decrease of potential energy and increase of inner energy with the increase of mesh size. AstroPhi code shows lower values of potential energy and higher values of inner energy, the behaviour of kinetic energy being the same for all the stages of collapse. It is not clear why do the potential energy and the inner energy differ in AstroPhi ang AREPO.

It would be interesting to test energy behaviour for a number of different codes (in particular, mesh-based codes) with different mesh sizes. It could be than possible to make the "standard" self-gravitating gas sphere collapse test.

In order to simulate the collapse of rotating molecular cloud let us set the gas cloud inside a sphere with the radius $R_0 = 100$ pc, the mass $M_g = 10^7 M_\odot$ and density distribution $\rho(r) \sim 1/r$, temperature $T \approx 2000$ K, rotation velocity $\omega = 21$ km/sec. The adiabatic index corresponds to hydrogen $\gamma = 5/3$. The Sound velocity $c \approx 3.8$ km/sec. The main parameters used for transition to non-dimensional form are the following: $L_0 = 100$ pc, $\rho_0 = 1.2 \times 10^{-18}$ kg/m^3, $v_0 = 21$ km/sec. Then in non-dimensional values the problem is set as follows: $\rho = 1.0$ is the density in the centre of the gas cloud, $p = 2 \times 10^{-2}$ is the pressure in the centre of the gas cloud, $\omega = 1$ – angular velocity, $\gamma = 5/3$ – adiabatic index, $[0; 6.4]^3$ – computation domain.

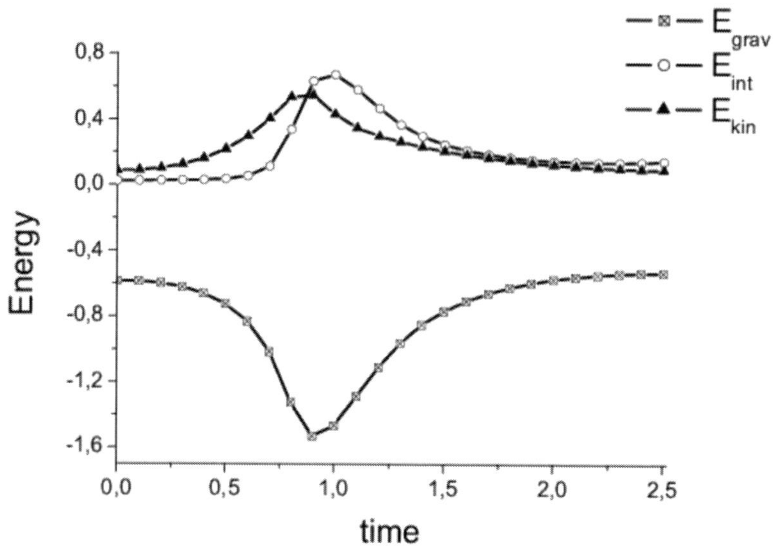

Figure 21. The behaviour of different types of energy in AstroPhi code on Molecular cloud collapse.

The behaviour of energy in this simulation of the rotating molecular cloud is in quantitative agreement with the results of other authors (Figure 21) before the moment of collapse. And after the moment of collapse there is qualitative agreement. It should be noticed that the collapse takes place at exactly the same moment of time. The qualitative difference in the behaviour of inner and potential energy as stipulated by the fundamental restrictions of SPH method in simulating high density gradients.

Special interest is the problem in the presence of a vertical magnetic field. The presence of the forces associated with the magnetic field at the time of compression allow you to get the polar flows, which are often observed in the collapse of astrophysical objects.

Figure 22 shows the distribution of the density of the magnetized gas in the collapse. Formation takes place polar flows.

Conclusion and Future Work

In this paper new software codes AstroPhi and GPUPEGAS is proposed. The codes are designed for simulation of astrophysical objects dynamics on hybrid supercomputers equipped with Intel Xenon Phi and GPU computation accelerators. The details of parallel implementation are described. Also the changes to the computational algorithm are shown that enable the efficient parallel implementation. The speed-up of 27 times was obtained within a single Xeon Phi accelerator. The use of 32 Xeon Phi accelerator resulted in 94% parallel efficiency. The speed-up of 55 times was obtained within a single GPU accelerator. The use of 60 GPU-accelerator resulted in 96% parallel efficiency. This work is part of project "Hydrodynamical Numerical Modelling of Astrophysical Flow at the Peta- and Exascale", developed by the present authors in the Siberian Supercomputer Center, ICMMG SB RAS in collaboration with the Institute of Astronomy RAS.

Further on the AstroPhi code will be developed in different directions. For example, the technique used for flow computation at Lagrangian stage.

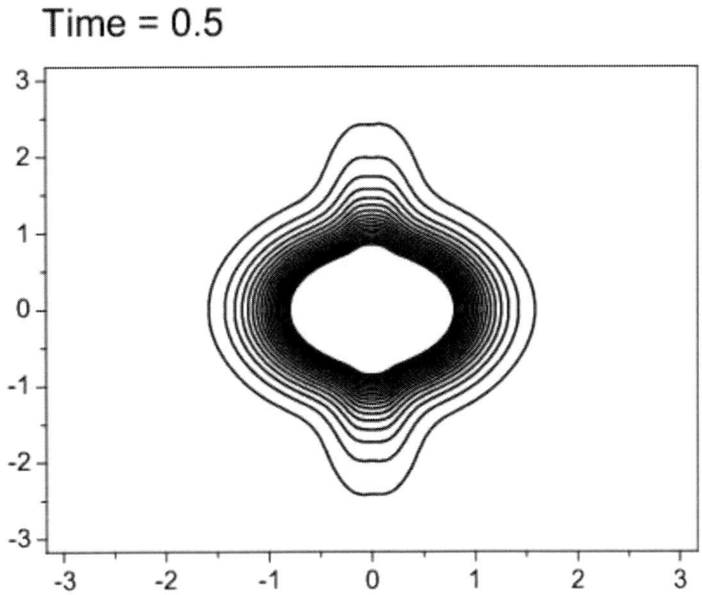

Figure 22. The MHD collapse.

At present this technique provides, the necessary level of Galilean invariance, but in future will be improved with full 3D cell deformation. The chemical processes are of great interest. In order to increase the scalability of the numerical method the next step will be to abandon the solution of Poisson equation and to evaluate the field from the equivalent evolution equation of the Cauchy-Kowalewskaya type for the gradient of potential. It will be then possible to compute gravitational field in the same way as the gas flows are now computed, on Intel Xeon Phi accelerators. The method based on Cauchy-Kowalewskaya type equation has been already tested for the problem of the self-gravitating gas cloud expansion. It will be included into AstroPhi code after the publication of the present paper.

The authors are grateful to the Nikolay V. Kuchin, Chief Engineer of the Siberian Supercomputer Centre. The authors are grateful to Eduard Vorobyov and Nigel Mitchell for for useful discussions about model of collisionless components.

The research work was supported by the Grant of the President of Russian Federation for the support of young scientists number MK – 4183.2013.9, RFBR grants 13-07-00589 and 14-01-31199, by the Grant of the Russian Scientific Foundation.

References

[1] Agertz, O., 2007. Fundamental differences between SPH and grid methods. *Monthly Notices of the Royal Astronomical Society*. 380, 963-978.

[2] Ardeljan, N., Bisnovatyi-Kogan, G., Moiseenko, S., 1996. An implicit Lagrangian code for the treatment of nonstationary problems in rotating astrophysical bodies. *Astronomy and Astrophysics*. 115, 573-594.

[3] Almgren, A., et al., 2010. CASTRO: A New Compressible Astrophysical Solver. I. Hydrodynamics and Self-gravity. *The Astrophysical Journal*. 715, 1221-1238.

[4] Ardeljan, N., Bisnovatyi-Kogan, G., Moiseenko, S., 1996. An implicit Lagrangian code for the treatment of nonstationary problems in rotating astrophysical bodies. *Astronomy and Astrophysics*. 115, 573-594.

[5] Attwood, R., Goodwin, S., Whitworth, A., 2007. Adaptive smoothing length in SPH. *Astronomy and Astrophysics*. 464, 447-450.

[6] Batten, P., Clarke, N., Lambert, C., Causon, D. M., 1997. On the Choice of Wavespeeds for the HLLC Riemann Solver. *Society for Industrial and Applied Mathematics Journal on Computing*. 18, 6, 1553-1570.

[7] Birdsall, C., 1997. Clouds-in-Cells Physics for Many-Body Plasma Simulation. *Journal of Computational Physics*. 135, 141-148.

[8] Brandenburg, A., Dobler, W., 2002. Hydromagnetic turbulence in computer simulations. *Computer Physics Communications*. 147, 471-475.

[9] Brio, M., Wu, C., 1988. An Upwind Differencing Scheme for the Equations of Ideal Magnetohydrodynamics. *Journal of Computational Physics*. 75, 400-422.

[10] Collela, P., Woodward, P. R., 1984. The Piecewise Parabolic Method (PPM) Gas-Dynamical simulations. *Journal of Computational Physics*. 54, 174-201.

[11] Courant, R., Isaacson, E., Rees, M., 1952. On the solution of nonlinear hyperbolic differential equations by finite differences. *Communications on Pure and Applied Mathematics*. 5, 243-255.

[12] Dolag, K., Vazza, F., Brunetti, G., Tormen, G., 2005. Turbulent gas motions in galaxy cluster simulations: the role of smoothed particle hydrodynamics viscosity. *Monthly Notices of the Royal Astronomical Society*. 364, 753-772.

[13] Einfeld, B., 1988. On Godunov-type methods for gas dynamics. *Society for Industrial and Applied Mathematics Journal on Numerical Analysis*. 25, 2, 294-318.

[14] Engquist, B., Osher, S. J., 1981. One-sided difference approximations for nonlinear conservation laws. *Mathematics of Computation*. 36, 321-351.

[15] Ferrari, A., Dumbser, M., Toro, E., Armanini, A. 2009. A New Parallel SPH Method for 3D Free Surface Flows. *High Performance Computing on Vector Systems 2009*. 179-188.

[16] Fletcher, A., Beck, R., Shukurov, A., Berkhuijsen, E., Horellou, C. 2011. Magnetic fields and spiral arms in the galaxy M51. *Monthly Notices of the Royal Astronomical Society*. 412, 4, 2396-2416.

[17] Gingold, R. A., Monaghan, J. J., 1977. Smoothed particle hydrodynamics – Theory and application to non-spherical stars. *Monthly Notices of the Royal Astronomical Society*. 181, 375-389.

[18] Godunov, S. K., Manuzina, Yu. D., Nazareva, M. A., 2011. Experimental analysis of convergence of the numerical solution to a generalized solution in fluid dynamics. *Computational Mathematics and Mathematical Physics*, 51, 88-95.

[19] Godunov, S., Kulikov, I., 2014. The computational of hydrodynamics equation discontinuous solutions with a guarantee of non-decreasing entropy. *Computational Mathematics and Mathematical Physics*. (in print).

[20] Goloviznin, V., Karabasov, S., Kondakov, V., 2013. Generalization of CABARET scheme for two-dimensional orthogonal computational grid. *Mathematical Modelling*. 25, 7, 103-136 (in russian).

[21] Gonzalez, M., Audit, E., Huynh, P., 2007. HERACLES: a three-dimensional radiation hydrodynamics code. *Astronomy and Astrophysics*. 464, 429-435.

[22] Grigoriev, Yu., Vshivkov, V., Fedoruk, M., 2002. Numerical «particle-in-cell» methods: theory and applications. *De Gruyter*, 249 p.

[23] Haghighipour, N., 2010. Planets in Binary Star Systems. *Series: Astrophysics and Space Science Library*. 366, 332 p.

[24] Harten, A., Lax, P. D., Van Leer, B., 1983. On upstream differencing and Godunov-type schemes for hyperbolic conservation laws. *Society for Industrial and Applied Mathematics Review*. 25, 35-61.

[25] Hayes, J., et al., 2006. Simulating Radiating and Magnetized Flows in Multiple Dimensions with ZEUS-MP. *The Astrophysical Journal Supplement Series*. 165, 188-228.

[26] Jin, S., Xin, Z., 1995. The Relaxation Schemes for Systems of Conservation Laws in Arbitrary Space Dimensions. *Communications on Pure and Applied Mathematics*. 48, 3, 235-276.

[27] Khoperskov, S., Vasiliev, E., Sobolev, A., Khoperskov, A., 2013. The simulation of molecular clouds formation in the Milky Way. *Monthly Notices of the Royal Astronomical Society*. 428, 2311-2320.

[28] Kravtsov, A., Klypin, A., Hoffman, Y., 2002. Constrained Simulations of the Real Universe. II. Observational Signatures of Intergalactic Gas in the Local Supercluster Region. *The Astrophysical Journal*. 571, 563-575.

[29] Krumholz, M. R., Klein, R. I., McKee, C. F., Bolstad, J., 2007. Equations and Algorithms for Mixed-frame Flux-limited Diffusion Radiation Hydrodynamics. *The Astrophysical Journal*. 667, 626-643.

[30] Kulikov, I., 2013. PEGAS: Hydrodynamical code for numerical simulation of the gas components of interacting galaxies. *Book Series of the Argentine Astronomical Society*. 4, 91-95.

[31] Kulikov, I., Chernykh, I., Glinsky, B., 2013. AstroPhi: a hydrodynamical code for complex modelling of astrophysical objects dynamics by means of hybrid architecture supercomputers on Intel Xenon Phi base. *Bulletin of South Ural State University. Series: Computational mathematics and software engineering*. 2, 57-79 (in russian).

[32] Lucy, L. B., 1977. A numerical approach to the testing of the fission hypothesis. *The Astrophysical Journal*. 82, 1013-1024.

[33] Matthias, S., 1996. GRAPESPH: cosmological smoothed particle hydrodynamics simulations with the special-purpose hardware GRAPE. *Monthly Notices of the Royal Astronomical Society*. 278, 1005-1017.

[34] Mignone, A., Plewa, T., Bodo, G., 2005. The Piecewise Parabolic Method for Multidimensional Relativistic Fluid Dynamics. *The Astrophysical Journal*. 160, 199-219.

[35] Mignone, A., et al., 2007. PLUTO: a Numerical Code for Computational Astrophysics. *The Astrophysical Journal Supplement Series*. 170, 228-242.

[36] Mitchell, N., Vorobyov, E., Hensler, G., 2013. Collisionless Stellar Hydrodynamics as an Efficient Alternative to N-body Methods. *Monthly Notices of the Royal Astronomical Society*. 428, 2674-2687.

[37] Mocz, P., Vogelsberger, M., Sijacki, D., Pakmor, R., Hernquist, L. 2014. A discontinuous Galerkin method for solving the fluid and magnetohydrodynamic equations in astrophysical simulations. *Monthly Notices of the Royal Astronomical Society*. 437, 397-414.

Nevertheless, using parallel high performance computers it is possible reduce the computational cost and get results of simulation in a reasonable time. A question is how to develop efficient parallel algorithms and implement them on modern parallel computers.

In this chapter, we present an effective technology of the distributed stochastic simulation. Also, we describe the software library PARMONC intended for the distributed stochastic simulation. The PARMONC launches the stochastic simulation on supercomputers with different architectures: massive-parallel and hybrid ones. In the PARMONC, a special parallel random generation technique is used which, in particular, enables one to get correlated results of different Monte Carlo computations. We also study a scalability of the distributed stochastic simulation based on the use of the PARMONC, namely, study estimation of its scalability up to future exaflop supercomputers.

As an example of application of the PARMONC to real-life problems, we consider solving an actual problem arising in the physics of plasma, namely, simulation of electron avalanches in gases. We present a probabilistic model which is detailed enough and enables one to get adequate description of the electron avalanche evolution. We consider a scenario in which the number of transitions in the avalanche tree and the total number of electrons is rather great (up to several billions). To make the stochastic simulation of the avalanche evolution we used a supercomputer with massive parallel architecture. To enhance the efficiency of computations, we also used Intel Xeon Phi coprocessors. To this goal, we modified the parallel Monte Carlo algorithm defining new levels of parallelism. This technique enables one to load both the CPU and co-processor with computational burden in a balanced manner.

The structure of the chapter is as follows. In Section 2 we describe main ideas of the distributed stochastic simulation including the question of the parallel random numbers generation. In Section 3 we present the software library PARMONC. In Section 4 we describe the Monte Carlo algorithm for the electron avalanche simulation and discuss ways of its parallel implementation on supercomputers with different architectures.

2. Parallelization of Stochastic Simulation

2.1. Distributed Stochastic Simulation

The stochastic simulation is numerical realization of probabilistic representation of a certain object in order to estimate its desired integral features by the law of large numbers [1], [5]. We assume that a functional of interest $\varphi \in R$ is represented as an expectation of some random variable ζ:

$$\varphi \approx \mathrm{E}\zeta,$$

provided that its variance $\mathrm{Var}\zeta$ is finite. In this case, one can evaluate the value of $\mathrm{E}\zeta$ using a sample mean:

$$\mathrm{E}\zeta \approx \bar{\zeta} = L^{-1} \sum_{i=1}^{L} \zeta_i \tag{1}$$

where ζ_i are statistically independent realizations of the random variable ζ. The value of $\bar{\zeta}$ is called a *stochastic estimator for* φ.

One also needs to evaluate a second moment $\mathrm{E}\zeta^2$ of the random variable

$$\mathrm{E}\zeta^2 \approx \bar{\xi} = L^{-1}\sum_{i=1}^{L}\zeta_i^2$$

in order to estimate the variance and standard deviation of the random variable ζ:

$$\mathrm{Var}\zeta \approx \bar{\sigma}^2 = \bar{\xi} - \bar{\zeta}^2, \ (\mathrm{Var}\zeta)^{0.5} \approx \bar{\sigma}.$$

In the Monte Carlo method, a complex random variable is represented as a function

$$\zeta = \zeta(\alpha_1, \alpha_2, \dots, \alpha_k), \tag{2}$$

where $\alpha_1, \alpha_2, \dots, \alpha_k$ are independent random variables which have uniform distribution on the interval $(0, 1)$ [1], [5]. These variables are called *base random numbers*. A sequence of the base random numbers $\{\alpha_k\}$ is usually generated with the help of some deterministic numerical algorithm called a *random number generator (RNG)*. Usually, iterative formulas are used:

$$\alpha_{k+1} = f(\alpha_k), k = 0, 1, 2, \dots$$

where α_0 is some fixed quantity.

Thus, while calculating the realizations $\zeta_i, i = 1, 2, \dots, L$ the base random numbers are in turn produced by the RNG. To calculate the sample mean, we need a finite set of independent random numbers $R = \{\alpha_1, \alpha_2, \dots, \alpha_S\}$. We call a *stochastic experiment* a process of calculating the sample mean $\bar{\zeta}$ using a particular set of base random numbers R. Usually, R is a subsequence of general sequence $\{\alpha_k\}$ of base random numbers. Using some different set $R' = \{\alpha'_1, \alpha'_2, \dots, \alpha'_{S'}\}$ (or a different subsequence) of the base random numbers that are independent of the base random numbers from R, we finally obtain an independent value of the sample mean. In other words, we make the stochastic experiment which is independent of the first one.

A λ confidence interval for the expectation $\mathrm{E}\zeta$ is defined by the formula

$$\lambda = \mathrm{P}(|\bar{\zeta} - \mathrm{E}\zeta| \le \gamma(\lambda)(\mathrm{Var}\zeta)^{0.5}L^{-0.5}) \approx \mathrm{P}(|\bar{\zeta} - \mathrm{E}\zeta| \le \gamma(\lambda)\bar{\sigma}L^{-0.5}). \tag{3}$$

According to tables of a standard normal distribution, $\gamma(\lambda) = 3$ for $\lambda = 99.7\%$. A value of an *absolute (stochastic) error* $\bar{\varepsilon}$ of the stochastic estimator $\bar{\zeta}$ is given by the formula

$$\bar{\varepsilon} = 3(\mathrm{Var}\zeta)^{0.5}L^{-0.5} \approx 3\bar{\sigma}L^{-0.5}$$

and the value of a *relative (stochastic) error* is given by the formula

$$\bar{\rho} = \bar{\varepsilon}/\bar{\zeta} \cdot 100\%.$$

Let us consider a matrix representation of the realization ζ_i which is useful when the software library PARMONC is used (see Section 3). Assume the simulation gives different independent values simultaneously. It is convenient to represent them as the matrix $[\zeta_{ij}], 1 \le i \le n_1, 1 \le j \le n_2$. We will also call it a realization (a realization of a random object). After averaging, the following matrices are calculated:

- $[\bar{\zeta}_{ij}]$ – the matrix of the sample means,
- $[\bar{\varepsilon}_{ij}]$ – the corresponding matrix of the absolute errors,
- $[\bar{\rho}_{ij}]$ – the corresponding matrix of the relative errors,
- $[\bar{\sigma}^2_{ij}]$ – the corresponding matrix of the sample variances.

A *computational cost* of the estimator is proportional to the value

$$C(\zeta) = \tau_\zeta \text{Var}\zeta,$$

where τ_ζ is a average computer time to simulate a single realization of ζ. The value of $C(\zeta)$ corresponds to computational expenses to obtain a desired level of the absolute or relative error. It is clear from the formula (3) that the sample volume L which is necessary to achieve a desired level of accuracy is proportional to the variance Varζ.

To decrease the computational cost, the simulation of the statistically independent realizations may be distributed among M processors (numbered from 0 to $M - 1$). At some moment all the processors send subtotal sample means to a dedicated processor (e.g., to the processor with 0-th number), and the parallel modification of the estimator is given by the formula

$$\bar{\zeta}_M = (\sum_{m=0}^{M-1} l_m)^{-1} \sum_{m=0}^{M-1} l_m \bar{\zeta}^{(m)}, \tag{4}$$

where l_m is the sample volume corresponding to the m-th processor, $\bar{\zeta}^{(m)}$ is the corresponding sample mean.

According to this parallelization technique, the stochastic simulation of the realizations on different processors is performed in an asynchronous mode. It is clear that it is possible to neglect the time expenses for quite rare data exchanges between the 0-th processor and the other ones. In this case, the variance Varζ remains the same but the value of τ_ζ is decreased. As a result, the value of τ_ζ (and, respectively, the value of $C(\zeta)$) is decreased by M times thus giving the nearly optimal parallelization [6].

Obviously, it is possible to exchange data at the end of simulation. However, it is not advisable for several reasons. First of all, it is desirable to control the absolute and relative stochastic errors during the simulation. On the other hand, it is useful to create periodic "save-points" of the simulation. For this reason, we modify the parallelization technique in the following way.

Let the m-th processor ($m = 0, 1, \ldots, M-1$) periodically sends entries of the matrices $[\bar{\zeta}^{(m)}_{ij}]$ and $[\bar{\xi}^{(m)}_{ij}]$ and the corresponding sample volume l_m (calculated by the moment of sending data) to the 0-th processor. In turn, the 0-th processor periodically receives all the sums $\{\bar{\zeta}^{(m)}_{ij}\}$, $\{\bar{\xi}^{(m)}_{ij}\}$ and the sample volumes $\{l_m\}$, $m = 0, 1, \ldots, M-1$, that were sent to it. Then the 0-th processor averages the sample moments:

$$\bar{\zeta}_{ij} = l^{-1} \sum_{m=0}^{M-1} l_m \bar{\zeta}^{(m)}_{ij}, \; \bar{\xi}_{ij} = l^{-1} \sum_{m=0}^{M-1} l_m \bar{\xi}^{(m)}_{ij}, \tag{5}$$

where $l = \sum_{m=0}^{M-1} l_m$, calculates the sample variances $\bar{\sigma}_{ij}^2$, the absolute $\bar{\varepsilon}_{ij}$ and the relative $\bar{\rho}_{ij}$ errors of the estimators $\bar{\zeta}_{ij}$. Then the 0-th processor saves the matrices $[\bar{\zeta}_{ij}]$, $[\bar{\varepsilon}_{ij}]$, $[\bar{\rho}_{ij}]$ and $[\bar{\sigma}_{ij}^2]$ to a disk. Note that the sample volumes l_m, $m = 0, 1, \ldots, M-1$ may be different at the moment of passing data. A reason for this fact may consist in different performances of processors or in the diversity of time expenses for the computation of different realizations.

If the frequency of the data exchange with the 0-th processor is not very high, we can neglect time expenses for the periodical data exchange and averaging. Therefore, the modified parallelization technique enables us to reduce the computational cost of the stochastic simulation nearly by M times. There is also no need to use any load balancing techniques because all the processors work independently and make data exchange in asynchronous mode. This conclusion is proved by an example presented in Subsection 3.3.

2.2. Parallel Random Numbers Generation

For massively parallel stochastic simulation, necessary quantity of base random numbers is quite large, and choice of a parallel random number generator (RNG) must be made with care. An important requirement for a parallel RNG is that sequences of base random numbers $\{\alpha_k\}$ which are generated on different processors must be statistically independent of each other and have good statistical properties [6]. For a properly chosen parallel RNG the parallel modification of the estimator (4) goes to $\mathrm{E}\zeta$ while the number of processors M and total sample volume $\sum_{m=0}^{M-1} l_m$ increases.

There is a series of publications devoted to parallel random numbers generation, e.g., [7] - [13]. Some of these approaches were implemented for high-performance many-core coprocessors such as graphics processing units (GPUs). Note that the RNG [8] is widely used in massive-parallel computations. Despite such variety of RNGs, we exploit our own approach which was carefully tested theoretically and also with the help of statistical tests. The generator was practically justified for more than decade in large-scale computations by the Monte Carlo method.

The following linear congruential generator [5] is used to produce a *general sequence of base random numbers* $\{\alpha_k\}$:

$$u_0 = 1,\ u_{k+1} \equiv u_k A \pmod{2^r},\ \alpha_k = u_k 2^{-r}, \qquad k = 0, 1, 2, \ldots. \tag{6}$$

A period of the generator is

$$L_P = 2^{r-2}. \tag{7}$$

We use the following parameters for the generator [14]:

$$r = 128,\ A \equiv 5^{100109} \pmod{2^{128}}.$$

Therefore, the period of this generator is $2^{126} \approx 10^{38}$.

In order to obtain independent streams of the base random numbers the general sequence $\{\alpha_k\}$ is divided into subsequences of length n that start with the initial numbers $\tilde{\alpha}_m = \alpha_{nm}$, $m = 0, 1, \ldots$. We may say that "leaps" of length n are made within th general sequence of base random values. *Initial numbers of the subsequences* $\{\tilde{\alpha}_m\}$ are calculated by the formula

$$\tilde{u}_0 = 1,\ \tilde{u}_{m+1} = \tilde{u}_m A(n)\ (\mathrm{mod}\ 2^r),\ \tilde{\alpha}_m = \tilde{u}_m\ 2^{-r}, \qquad m = 0, 1, 2, \ldots \qquad (8)$$

The multiplier $A(n)$ of this auxiliary generator is calculated as follows:

$$A(n) \equiv A^n (\mathrm{mod}\ 2^r).$$

This parallel generator enables convergence of the parallel modification of the estimator (4) to $\mathrm{E}\zeta$. Now it is implemented as a well tested, fast and reliable routine on supercomputers with different architectures[15] – [17].

In some special cases, it is useful to exploit an additional RNG together with the basic generator (6). This is the case when one wants to get correlated results of several computations but some elements of the realization of random object undergo appreciable changes according to some parameters of probabilistic model. To this goal we recommend to use the congruential generator (6) with the following parameters: $r = 40,\ A \equiv 5^{17}\ (\mathrm{mod}\ 2^{40})$. Also, it is useful to randomize it with the help of the RNG (6):

$$v_0 = \tilde{v},\ v_n \equiv v_{n-1} A\ (\mathrm{mod}\ 2^{40}), \qquad \beta_n = v_n 2^{-40}, \qquad n = 1, 2, \ldots \qquad (9)$$

In this formula, to define the initial value $\tilde{v}$ the major 40 bits of u_n from the RNG (6) are used. For example, for electron avalanche simulation we used the additional RNG to simulate a free path length Δl for different values of Δt (see Section 4). As a result, we got high correlation between estimators for different values of Δt. The use of the additional RNG also enables a speed-up of the simulation.

For effective correlation of results of different Monte Carlo simulations on parallel high performance clusters, it is desirable to define a hierarchy of embedded subsequences of the general sequence $\{\alpha_k\}$. To this goal subsequences of base random numbers may be assigned to: a) different stochastic experiments, b) different processors and c) different realizations:

- within the general sequence $\{\alpha_k\}$, the "leaps" of length n_e are made using (8) in order to define the initial numbers of subsequences that will be used to perform stochastic experiments (when doing it, *"experiments" subsequences* are produced),
- within each "experiment" subsequence, the "leaps" of length $n_p < n_e$ are made using (8) to define the initial numbers of embedded subsequences that will be used on different processors (when doing it, *"processors" subsequences* are produced),
- within each "processor" subsequence, the "leaps" of length $n_r < n_p$ are made using (8) to define the initial numbers of embedded subsequences that will be used to simulate independent realizations (when doing it *"realizations" subsequences* are produced).

Thus, the hierarchy of the embedded subsequences is as follows:

general sequence ⊃ "experiments" subsequences

"experiments" subsequence ⊃ "processors" subsequences

"processors" subsequence ⊃ "realizations" subsequences

For example, in the PARMONC (see Section 3) an initialization of the parallel RNG is made as follows: the "experiment" subsequence number is defined by the user; the "processor" subsequence number is automatically defined by the PARMONC with a number of parallel branch provided by MPI or OpenMP runtime environment; the "realizations" subsequence number is automatically defined by the PARMONC before starting the simulation of a realization.

In the PARMONC, the default lengths of "leaps" are as follows:

- $n_e = 2^{115} \approx 10^{34}$ - for "experiments" subsequences,
- $n_p = 2^{98} \approx 10^{29}$ - for "processors" subsequences,
- $n_r = 2^{43} \approx 10^{13}$ - for "realizations" subsequences.

One can therefore perform approximately $2^{125} \cdot 2^{-115} = 2^{10} \approx 10^3$ stochastic experiments; within a single experiment one can use $2^{115} \cdot 2^{-98} = 2^{17} \approx 10^5$ processors at most and on a processor one can simulate at most $2^{98} \cdot 2^{-43} = 2^{55} \approx 10^{16}$ independent realizations.

In the PARMONC, the corresponding generator multipliers $A(n_e)$, $A(n_p)$ and $A(n_r)$ are defined to use by default. Nevertheless, one can redefine the default values of $A(n_e)$, $A(n_p)$ and $A(n_r)$ with the use of special command.

3. Software Library PARMONC for Implementation of Distributed Stochastic Simulation

Let us introduce a software library PARMONC (an acronym for PARallel MONte Carlo) – a library of easy-to-use programs that was implemented on high-performance clusters of the Siberian Supercomputer Center and can also be used in other supercomputer centers [18]. A description of the PARMONC can be found on the web site of the Siberian Supercomputer Center [19]; full description is provided in , [20].

The main objectives of the PARMONC development are as follows:

- creation of a software tool suitable for the massively parallel stochastic simulation for a wide range of applications,
- creation of an easy-to-use software framework to parallelize stochastic simulation to be applied without knowledge of MPI language.

A number of publications are devoted to the development of software packages for parallel computations with the Monte Carlo method (see, e.g., [21] – [23]). Different hardware and software platforms are reported in these publications. In our opinion, the following features distinguish the PARMONC from other software tools and make it an easy-to-use instrument for specialists in the field of stochastic simulation:

- The only thing the user has to do in order to parallelize stochastic simulation is to write in C, C++ or in FORTRAN a sequential subroutine to simulate a single realization of a random object of interest and to pass its name to the PARMONC routines.

- In his/her sequential code, he/she uses a PARMONC function, which implements a parallel RNG, in a usual and convenient way.
- In the course of simulation, the PARMONC periodically calculates and saves in files the subtotal results of simulation and the corresponding computation errors.
- The PARMONC provides an easy-to-use technique to resume stochastic simulation after its termination with automatic averaging of the results of the previous simulation.

3.1. Transformation of the Sequential Code to Parallel One for the PARMONC

For simplicity let us consider a problem of evaluation of the expectation $E\zeta$ of a scalar random variable ζ using the sample mean (1). A typical sequential code (written in C) consists of the following operations:

```
int i, L;
double s, t=0.0;
for(i=0;i<L;i++){
   realization(s);
   t=t+s;
}
t=t/(double)L;
```

Here the argument L is the number of independent realizations; *realization* is the name of a sequential routine, which computes a single realization of the random variable ζ and returns its value to the argument s. Finally, the variable t gives the value of the sample mean. In the routine *realization* the user calls a function which implements a RNG. The usual use of this function (named *rng()*, e.g.) is as follows:

```
a = rng();
```

Here a is the base random number which has the uniform distribution on the interval $(0, 1)$. These numbers are used to simulate necessary complex distributions by formula (2). Given statistically independent outputs from the function *rng()*, all the return values s from the subroutine *realization* are statistically independent.

Thereby, a routine, which computes a single realization of a random object, takes the return values from a function that implements a RNG and returns a single realization of a random object. This routine and the specifications for the random object realization are provided by the user. The routine that implements a RNG is considered to be an external routine. In Figure 1 we explain the relationship between main program and data elements in the stochastic simulation.

To implement the above-mentioned parallelization technique, the most convenient way is to use a user-defined routine that computes a single realization of a random object as the major piece of the code to be launched on different processors (see Figure 1). Like in a sequential code, each copy of the routine takes return values from a function that implements the parallel RNG and returns a single realization of a random object. The outputs from all

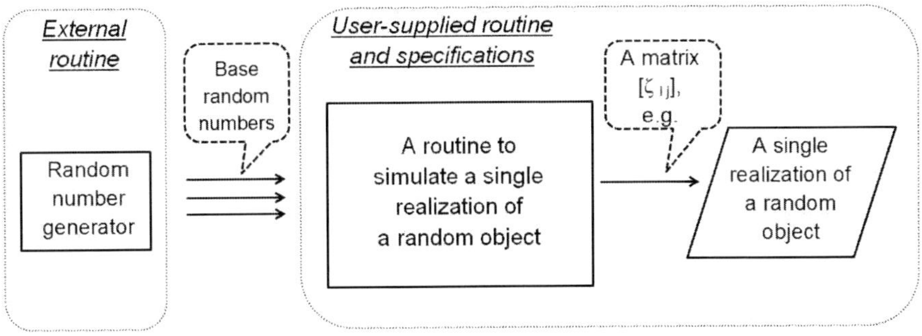

Figure 1. Relationship between the main program and data elements in stochastic simulation.

```
int i, L;
double s, t=0.0;
for(i=0;i<L;i++){
   realization(s);
   t=t+s;
}
t=t/(double)L;
```

→

```
int L;
double s;
parmoncc( realization, L, s );
```

Figure 2. Transformation of the sequential code to parallel one for the PARMONC.

the copies of the user-defined routine (realizations) are taken into account in the course of averaging with the use of formulas (5). This approach is very convenient for specialists in the stochastic simulation because it takes them minimal efforts to adapt their sequential programs for using the PARMONC.

To implement the above-mentioned parallelization technique, the most convenient way is to use a user-defined routine that computes a single realization of a random object as the major piece of the code to be launched on different processors (see Figure 1). Like in a sequential code, each copy of the routine takes return values from a function that implements the parallel RNG and returns a single realization of a random object. The outputs from all the copies of the user-defined routine (realizations) are taken into account in the course of averaging with the use of formulas (5). In Figure 2 we present the idea of transformation of the sequential code to parallel one for the PARMONC. This approach is very convenient for specialists in the stochastic simulation because it takes them minimal efforts to adapt their sequential programs for using the PARMONC.

3.2. Contents of the Library

Contents of the PARMONC is as follows:

- *rnd128* - a function to producc a single base random number,
- *parmoncf* - the main subroutine to perform parallel stochastic simulation (for programs written in FORTRAN),

- *parmoncc* - the main subroutine to perform parallel stochastic simulation (for programs written in C),

- *manaver* - a program to average subtotal sample moments calculated on processors (in a manual mode),

- *genparam* - a program to calculate multipliers of the parallel RNG (in a manual mode).

Here *rnd128, parmoncf and parmoncc* are library routines to use in FORTRAN or C/C++ user-supplied programs, *genparam* and *manaver* are executable files to run from a command line. Object files for the library routines are archived to a static library *libparmonc.a*.

The PARMONC software realization does not use any unique features of a specific FORTRAN compiler or a specific MPI implementation. Therefore, it can be compiled and built with any FORTRAN compiler and MPI library and ported to different high-performance clusters or powerful personal computers with multi-core processors.

The subroutine *parmoncf/parmoncc* initializes the parallel RNG, distributes the simulation of independent realizations among processors, makes all operations to pass, to collect and to average data and to save the simulation results in files. The simulation results are stored in several files in a special subdirectory of the user's working directory.

These subroutines take a name of a user-defined routine which computes a single realization of a random object as argument. The main user-supplied program where a call to *parmoncf/parmoncc* is located is considered as a MPI program despite the fact that it does not contain any MPI instructions (see an example in Section 3.3). This means that it must be compiled, linked and launched according to specific rules determined by a particular MPI realization on the computer.

The argument *res* is a resumption flag. It defines whether the present simulation resumes the previous one or not:

- *res* = 0 in case of a new simulation. In this case the *parmonc* creates brand new files with results.

- *res* = 1 in case of resuming the previous simulation. In this case the *parmonc* automatically takes into account results of the previous simulation (from the corresponding files) and averages it by formulas (5).

The argument *seqnum* is the "experiments" subsequence number (it is equal to 0,1,2, ...). In case of resuming the previous simulation, this argument must be different from the same argument of the previous use of *parmoncf/parmoncc*.

Also, there are parameters *perpass, peraver* defining the periods of data passing and averaging, respectively, as the number of minutes.

The double precision function *rnd128* is written using 64-bit integer arithmetic. The function has no arguments. After the initialization of the parallel RNG, *rnd128* starts returning base random numbers from a selected subsequence. Thus, on different processors, parallel streams of base random numbers are generated independently.

The program *manaver* is used to average and to save in files the subtotal sample moments calculated on processors. It is launched after the termination of a job on a cluster.

The application of *manaver* is useful in the case when by the moment of terminating the job, the sample moments stored in the files with results correspond to a smaller sample volume than to the one that was actually obtained on all the processors.

If one wants to define different values of the parallel RNG multipliers $A(n_e), A(n_p)$ and $A(n_r)$ in comparison with the default ones, he runs the program *genparam* from a command line in his working directory in the following way:

```
$ genparam ne np nr
```

where *ne, np* and *nr* are exponents of 2. As a result, a file *parmonc_genparam.dat* is created in the user's working directory. Hereupon, the PARMONC routines use the multipliers' values from this file instead of the default ones.

When the user launches a job on a cluster, a subdirectory */parmonc_data* is automatically created by the PARMONC in his/her working directory. In the directory */parmonc_data/results* one can find the results of computation stored in the files *func.dat*, *func_ci.dat* and *func_log.dat*:

- *func.dat* stores a matrix of the sample means,
- *func_ci.dat* encapsulates a matrix of the sample means together with matrices of absolute and relative errors and variances,
- *func_log.dat* stores information about the stochastic simulation: the total sample volume, the mean computer time per a realization, the upper bounds for absolute and relative errors, etc.

Also, in this directory, one can find a file *parmonc_exp.dat* containing information about each stochastic experiment that was started by the user.

3.3. Performance Test

The following example may be found in the full documentation to the PARMONC [20]. Also, it is available for the users of the the Siberian Supercomputer Center in the directory of the library [19].

We consider a 2-dimensional system of stochastic differential equations (SDEs) over a time interval $[0, 100]$:

$$d\bar{y}(t) = Cdt + Dd\bar{w}(t),$$

where

$$\bar{y}(0) = \begin{pmatrix} 0 \\ 0 \end{pmatrix}, \bar{y}(t) = \begin{pmatrix} y_1(t) \\ y_2(t) \end{pmatrix}, C = \begin{pmatrix} 1.0 \\ 1.0 \end{pmatrix}, D = \begin{pmatrix} 10^{-2} & 0 \\ 0 & 10^{-2} \end{pmatrix},$$

and $\bar{w}(t) = \begin{pmatrix} w_1(t) \\ w_2(t) \end{pmatrix}$ is a 2-dimensional Wiener process. Our objective is to evaluate expectations of its components $\mathrm{E}y_1(t)$, $\mathrm{E}y_2(t)$ at fixed points $t_i = i{\cdot}10^{-1}$, $i = 1, \ldots, 1000$. We simulate trajectories of thc SDE system using a generalized Euler method with a mesh size $h = 10^{-6}$:

$$\bar{y}^{(n+1)} = \bar{y}^{(n)} + hC + \sqrt{h}D\bar{\xi}^{(n)}, n = 0, 1, 2, \ldots, 10^8, \tag{10}$$

where

$$\bar{y}^{(0)} = \begin{pmatrix} 0 \\ 0 \end{pmatrix}, \bar{y}^{(n)} = \begin{pmatrix} y_1^{(n)} \\ y_2^{(n)} \end{pmatrix}, \bar{\xi}^{(n)} = \begin{pmatrix} \xi_1^{(n)} \\ \xi_2^{(n)} \end{pmatrix},$$

all quantities $\{\xi_i^{(n)}\}$ being independent in total and having a standard normal distribution. The simulation yields a matrix $[\zeta_{ij}]$:

$$\zeta_{ij} = y_j^{(n)}, n = i10^5, 1 \leq i \leq 1000, 1 \leq j \leq 2.$$

Thus, each entry of the matrix after averaging gives:

$$\bar{\zeta}_{ij} \approx \mathrm{E}y_j(t_i), t_i = i \cdot 10^{-1},\ i = 1, \ldots, 1000, j = 1, 2.$$

Below, as an example, the main user's program in C containing a call to *parmoncc* is provided.

```
int main()
{
   int nrow = 1000, ncol = 2, res = 1, seqnum = 2, perpass = 10,
       peraver = 20;
   long long int maxsv = pow(10,9);
   parmoncc ( difftraj, &nrow, &ncol, &maxsv, &res, &seqnum,
              &perpass, &peraver );
   return 0;
}
```

Here *difftraj* is the name of the user-supplied subroutine implementing the simulation of a realization of an approximate diffusion trajectory according to (10) and returning a realization of matrix $[\zeta_{ij}]$; *nrow* and *ncol* define dimensions of the matrix; *maxsv* is a maximal sample volume to simulate on processors; *res* is a resumption flag; *seqnum* defines the "experiments" subsequence number; *perpass* and *peraver* define the period of sending and receiving data, respectively (in minutes).

In this example *res* = *1*. This means the case of resuming the previous simulation: the PARMONC automatically takes into account results of the previous simulation (from the corresponding files) and averages it by formulas (5). Also, *seqnum* = *2*. This means that we use the "experiments" subsequence with number 2. Processors send subtotal data to the 0-th processor every 10 minutes. In turn, the 0-th processor receives data every 20 minutes. The argument *maxsv* is chosen to be sufficiently large in order to have an "endless" stochastic simulation that is limited only by the time framework of a job on a cluster (it is defined by the user when starting the job).

In the subroutine *difftraj*, the parallel RNG is called in the following simple way:

```
a = rnd128();
```

This way of calling the RNG seems the most natural for specialists in the stochastic simulation.

The above-mentioned diffusion problem was computed on 1, 8, 16, 32, 64, 128, 256 and 512 processors to compare the speedup of parallelization. All the processors sent data to the 0-th processor after having simulated each realization. In turn, the 0-th processor received

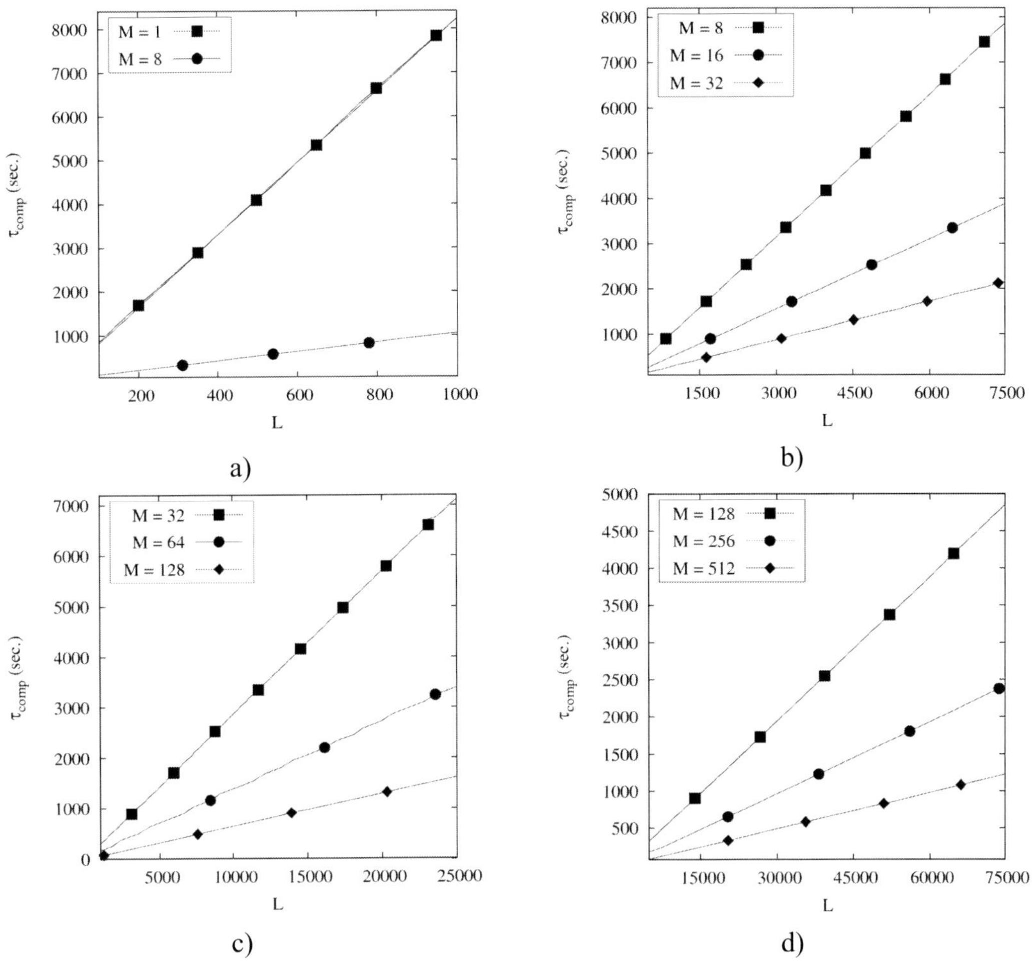

Figure 3. Results of a PARMONC performance test: comparison of the computer time $\tau_{comp} = \tau_{comp}(L)$ for different numbers of processors: a) M = 1 and 8, b) M = 8, 16 and 32, c) M = 32, 64 and 128, d) M = 128, 256 and 512. In each graph X-axis corresponds to the total sample volume L, Y-axis corresponds to τ_{comp} measured in seconds.

data after having simulated each realization. Such conditions are assumed to be strictest in terms of the parallel algorithm performance. A mean computer time τ_ζ to simulate a single realization is approximately 7.7 sec., the bulk of data which is periodically sent by every processor to the 0-th processor is approximately 120 Kbytes.

For different numbers of processors M we compare the computer time it takes to simulate L realizations in total $\tau_{comp} = \tau_{comp}(L)$. A value of τ_{comp} is evaluated after the 0-th processor has received, averaged and saved data in files.

It is seen from the graphs in Figure 3 that for all the values of L the speedup of parallelization is in direct proportion to the number of processors despite "strict" conditions related to data exchange.

3.4. Evaluation of Scalability of Distributed Stochastic Simulation on Supercomputers

The problem of studying the properties of scalability of parallel algorithms and programs when transferring their implementation from current computer to more powerful (up to future exaflop supercomputers) reached the level of technological challenges and requires thorough researches. Computational algorithms are generally more conservative compared with the development of computer technology. Evaluating future behavior of an algorithm developed by a given computational scheme can be done by simulating its execution. Such model can represent usage of thousands or millions of computational cores by a parallel program. By simulation, it is possible to find bottlenecks in algorithms for understanding how to modify them for achieving efficient scaling onto a large number of cores.

In many cases, we need estimating scalability rate of parallel programs only, not exact loading of computer's kernels and memory and/or computation time. For this purpose, we use the agent-based simulation system named AGNES (AGent NEtwork Simulator) [24]. The AGNES proves to be the efficient tool for comparative investigation of different variants of mapping parallel program and data onto high-performance computational system up to future exaflops supercomputers [25], [26]. Prior simulation of these algorithms allows choosing their parameters for improvement performance of their real execution and predicting performance for future runs on more powerful supercomputers.

The simulation model have been calibrated based on a real data obtained by profiler when running real computational program (by the PARMONC). Important information for configuring the model includes a diagram of the computation algorithm and temporal characteristics of the stages of computation.

For simulating large scale computations by the Monte-Carlo method, a computational core with an algorithm running on it had chosen as an elementary unit. That is, the same agent simulates the complete behavior of the computational core and the communication of the hardware. For this model, two types of agents are designed:

- *MonteCarlo* agent involved in direct simulation of computations;
- *CentralMC* agent that simulates aggregation of calculation results.

The simulation model works according the following steps:

1. All functional agents are initialized and prepared for work.
2. Agents *MonteCarlo* start simulating calculations of realizations of the Monte Carlo algorithm. After completing each L realizations, data with results of these calculations are sent to the agent *CentralMC*.
3. Agents *CentralMC* collect data with results of calculations and process them periodically, saving resulting information to the disk (for analysis of simulation results).
4. The criterion for stopping the simulation is achieving the desired accuracy of calculations, in other words the number of realizations simulated by agents *MonteCarlo*.

Thus, *CentralMC* counts the total number of performed operations and at achieving given threshold sends to the AGNES a command to complete the simulation run.

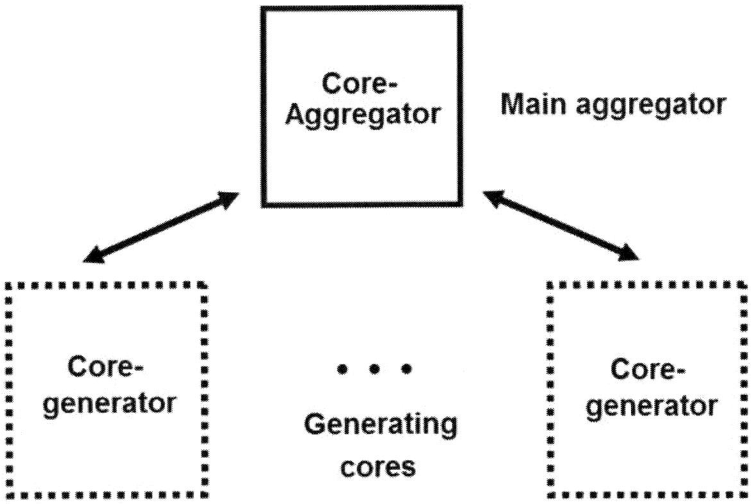

Figure 4. Basic simulation scheme of the Monte-Carlo method.

The model have been calibrated based on a real data obtained by profiler when running real computational program (by the PARMONC). Important information for configuring the model includes a diagram of the computation algorithm and temporal characteristics of the stages of computation. Results of the simulation run include the following reports generated by AGNES:

- General report contains information about the total model time spent for achieving given accuracy, resource usage, as well as service information.
- Report about realizations contains couples: a unique name for each agent *MonteCarlo* and a number of realizations which it had simulated.
- Report about times of realizations simulation. It allows obtaining and checking the statistics of calculations.
- Report on the intensity of the incoming data to the agent *CentralMC*. That is, agent *CentralMC* counts the number of messages received by it during regular intervals.

In the early stages of the simulation experiments, the model consisted of a large number of agents *MonteCarlo* and one agent *CentralMC* (see Figure 4). This allowed us to see the effect of overloading the agent *CentralMC* and its inability to handle the large amount of packets coming to it. In this regard, the model was modified in such a way, that one main *CentralMC* and several common *CentralMC* are created. Last agents collect information from *MonteCarlo* and in aggregated mode transfer it to main *CentralMC* (see Figure 5).

Lets us define a speed-up of parallelization in the following way:

$$S_L(M) = T_L(1)/T_L(M),$$

where $T_L(M)$ is computer time to simulate L realizations using M computational cores, M_{min} is minimal numbers of computational cores that was used (in our computations $M_{min} = 48$).

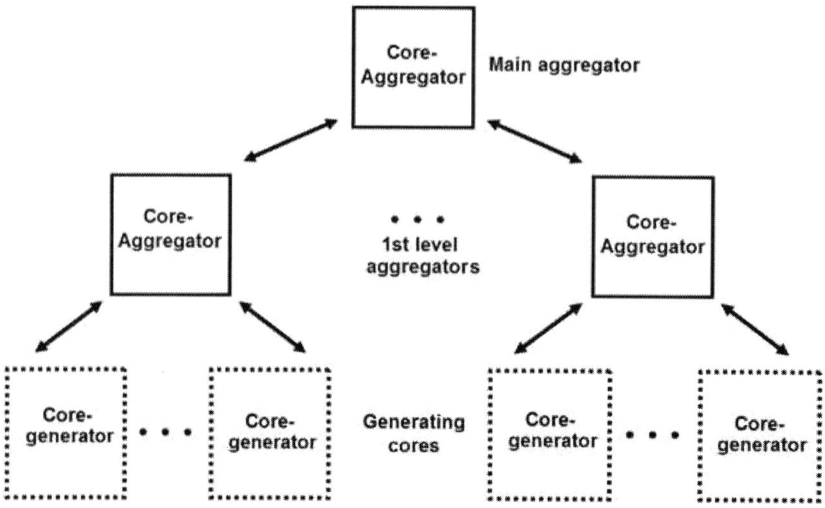

Figure 5. Modified simulation scheme of the Monte-Carlo method.

Figure 6 shows the speed-up of modeled algorithm and impact of the number of agents *CentralMC* on it. We can see that adding of several common *CentralMC* agents-aggregators minimize an effect of main *CentralMC* agent overloading. One can say that the result, which is overloading of a single aggregator, is obvious. However, by simulation we find the optimal number of aggregators and their distribution by levels.

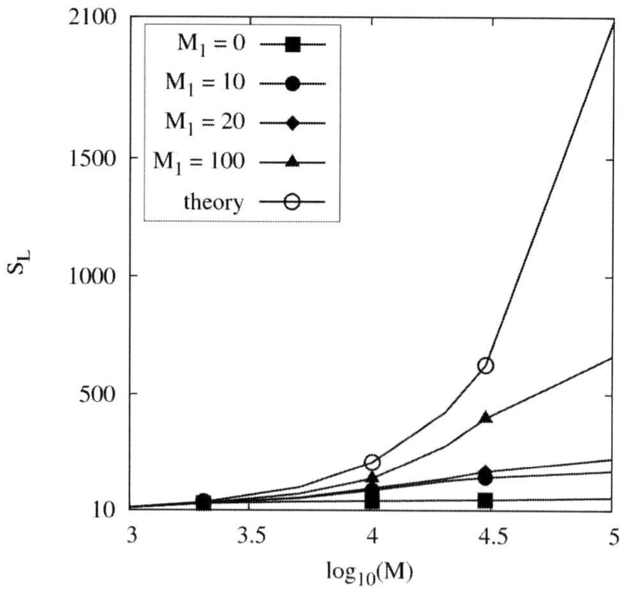

Figure 6. Comparison of modeled scalability of Monte-Carlo algorithm between theory and simulation modeling for $48 - 10^5$ cores range. Here M is number of cores used for calculations, M_1 is a number of *CentralMC* functional agents on the intermediate level.

Figure 7 shows dependence of the acceleration of calculations on the number of the aggregators M_1 on the intermediate level when $M = 10^6$ cores are used for calculations (simulation results).

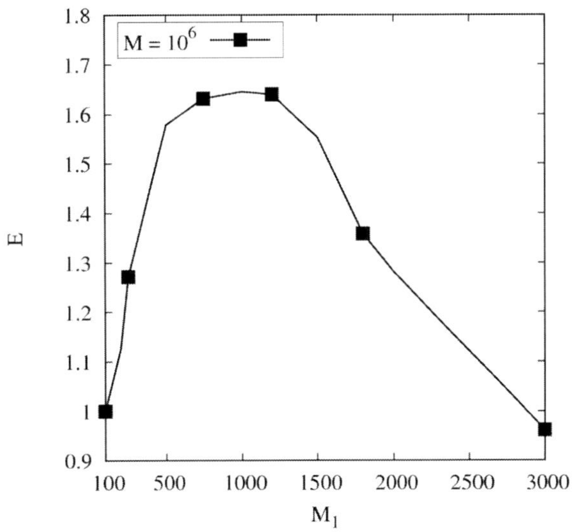

Figure 7. Dependence of the acceleration of calculations on the number of the aggregators M_1 on the intermediate level when $M = 10^6$ cores are used for calculations.

We also used the AGNES to simulate supercomputers workload for other kinds of algorithms [26].The results of simulation are in a good accordance with real run tests on supercomputer. We can state that such simulation is very useful forpreliminary tuning and even modifying algorithms before their executing on real supercomputers so saving time and money. Such simulation is also very important in projects aiming ondesigning algorithms and software for non-existent supercomputers of future generations at their design stage. Future development of AGNES concerns improvement of its interface abilities and implementing new algorithms for its own scalability, thus allowing high-performance simulation of really large systems. Another goal of the project is development of a number of object-oriented libraries of agents, specially designed for simulating promissory new supercomputer architectures.

4. Stochastic Simulation of Electron Avalanche Evolution

Gas discharges are of great interest to physicists and engineers in a number of fields. The primary element of the often very complicated breakdown process is the *electron avalanche*, which develops in the gas when a strong enough electric field is applied to it. An avalanche begins with a small number of "seed" electrons that appear accidentally (it can even be triggered by a single electron). An electron picks up energy in the electric field. Having reached energy somewhat greater than the ionization potential, the electron ionizes a molecule, thereby losing its energy. The result is the production of two slow electrons. They are again accelerated in the field, ionize molecules, thereby producing four electrons, and so forth [27].

The Monte Carlo method is often used for simulation of electron avalanches in gases (see, e.g. [28] – [32]). Corresponding probabilistic models are detailed enough and enable one to get adequate description of the avalanche evolution. Using the Monte Carlo simulation, one can also take into account important fluctuations in the state of the avalanche to estimate specific physical characteristics (effect of runaway electrons, e.g.). The main problem of the Monte Carlo method is the value of its computational cost: the number of transitions and multiplications in the avalanche may be quite large and therefore the number of particles may be great too.

In our research paper [33], a three-dimensional parallel algorithm of the Monte Carlo method (named ELSHOW) is developed for simulation of electron avalanches in gases. The parallel implementation is performed with the use of the PARMONC, which accelerates the calculations of such integral characteristics as the number of particles in an avalanche, the coefficient of impact ionization, the drift velocity, and the others, as well as ways to select an appropriate size of the time step using the technique of dependent statistical tests.

The PARMONC was used to run the ELSHOW in parallel on the cluster NKS-30T with the massive parallel architecture [34]. Nevertheless, the value of computational cost of the stochastic simulation forces us to seek new ways to speed up computations. For this goal, we developed the new version of the ELSHOW code adapted for clusters with hybrid architecture, namely with Intel Xeon Phi coprocessors.

4.1. Probabilistic Model of Electron Avalanche Evolution

Our goal is simulation of the initial stage of the breakdown process when the total electric field of electrons and ions in the avalanche is negligible in comparison with the external electric field.

Below, we briefly describe a mathematical model of the electron avalanche evolution. The model is based on the use of branching stochastic processes. We call a *particle tree* a realization of the branching process. To traverse the particle tree, the so called "lexicographical scheme" is used [35]. It helps to use the computer memory effectively.

We consider a three-dimensional open system with external electric field which strength $\mathbf{E} = (0, 0, -E_z)$ is considered to be constant. A gap between electrodes is filled with a gas with concentration C and pressure p. At the initial time moment $t = 0$, at the point $\mathbf{r} = (x, y, z) = (0, 0, 0)$ on the cathode n_0 electrons (or model particles) with zero energy are emitted. To represent a single electron we need to store six parameters in computer's memory, namely, its position and velocity components: (x, y, z, V_x, V_y, V_z).

We simulate each electron path until the maximum time moment t_{max}. For this goal, time steps of equal size Δt are made. In a time step, an electron with the energy T_{i-1} moves from the point $\mathbf{r}_{i-1} = (x_{i-1}, y_{i-1}, z_{i-1})$ to the point $\mathbf{r}_i = (x_i, y_i, z_i)$, where i is the number of the time step. As a result, its position and velocity change in the following way:

$$\mathbf{r}_i = \mathbf{r}_{i-1} + \mathbf{V}_{i-1}\Delta t - \mathrm{e}\mathbf{E}(\Delta t)^2/(2m_0), \qquad \mathbf{V}_i = \mathbf{V}_{i-1} - \mathrm{e}\mathbf{E}\Delta t/m_0,$$

where $\mathbf{V}_i = (V_x, V_y, V_z)$, e is the charge of the electron, m_0 is its mass. An acceleration of the electron is also taken into account in this formula.

At the end of free path, the incoming electron may collide with a neutral molecule of the gas. Thus, a collision event is simulated which probability is as follows:

$$P = 1 - \exp\Big(-\sigma_{tot}(T_i)C|\mathbf{r}_i - \mathbf{r}_{i-1}|\Big),$$

where $\sigma_{tot} = \sigma_{tot}(T)$ is a full microscopic cross-section of interactions. Then, if the collision event occurs, we randomly choose a type of collision:

- elastic collision (scattering) of the electron, or
- inelastic collision of the electron (leads to excitation of the atom), or
- ionization of the atom (leads to creation of a new electron).

Here, probabilities of collision types depend on the energy of incoming electron and are defined in accordance with the corresponding values of the cross-sections which are taken from experimental databases or defined by theoretical formulas [27], [33]. To simulate the random choice of the collision type effectively, it is desirable to use the "majorant frequency" method [36] which is the most effective computational approach for such kind of problems.

The elastic collision does not change the energy of the electron and its new moving direction is defined by the special differential cross-sections [27], [37]. Inelastic collision with the molecules changes the energy of the electron and its new moving direction is defined in the same way as for the elastic collision. The ionization leads to the inception of a new secondary electron which gets its energy from the incoming electron (its energy is reduced after ionization), the moving directions of the two electrons are defined by analogy. Thereby, these interactions form a single avalanche realization, i.e. the realization of the particle tree.

At the end, we are interested in evaluating some physical characteristics at given time moments $t_i, i = 1, 2, \ldots$:

- the number of electrons $n(t_i)$,
- the center of mass $\mathbf{r}_c(t_i) = (<x>, <y>, <z>)$, where

$$<x> = \sum_{k=1}^{n} x_k(t_i)/n(t_i), \quad <y> = \sum_{k=1}^{n} y_k(t_i)/n(t_i), \quad <z> = \sum_{k=1}^{n} z_k(t_i)/n(t_i),$$

- the velocity of the center of mass $V_c(t_i) = <z>/t_i$,
- the average velocity $<V_z> = \sum_{k=1}^{n} V_{z,k}(t_i)/n(t_i)$,
- the average kinetic energy $\epsilon_{aver} = \sum_{k=1}^{n} T_k(t_i)/n(t_i)$,
- coefficients of longitudinal and transverse diffusion D_L and D_T,
- coefficient of impact ionization α,
- collision frequency ν,

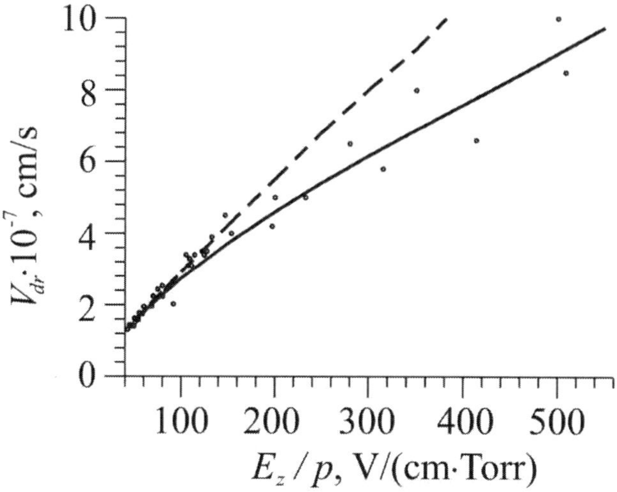

Figure 8. Dependence of the drift velocity V_{dr} and avalanche average speed V_c on E_z/p: solid line – $< V_z >$; dotted line – V_c; points – experimental data from [38].

and so on. In these formulas, the summation is made over all particles in the avalanche at time t_i. The mean-square errors of the functionals estimators are evaluated simultaneously.

Also, special precise computations were made to select an appropriate size of the time step $\triangle t$ using the technique of dependent statistical tests [33].

In our numerical experiments, the number of time steps reached up to 10^{10} by an order of magnitude and the total number of particles in the avalanche - up to 10^9 particles. For that reason, the requirements for computational resources are serious enough and the use of supercomputers with large memory and sufficient number of parallel processor is desired.

We compared results of our simulations with known experimental and numerical data [33]. Some results of the comparison are presented in Figure 8:, namely, dependence of the estimated drift velocity $V_{dr} =< V_z >$ and the avalanche average speed V_c on E_z/p are provided, experimental data is taken from [38]. In our calculations, we chose the value of E_z/p within the range $50 \leq E_z/p \leq 650$ V/(cm · Torr). The value of the relative stochastic error of the estimators is 2.6%.

4.2. Implementation of Parallel Monte Carlo Simulation on Different Supercomputer Architectures

To simulate the electron avalanches with large number of particles, we implemented several parallelization techniques. For this goal, we used either supercomputers with massive parallel architecture (i.e. without any accelerators or coprocessors) or hybrid supercomputers with the coprocessors such as Intel Xeon Phi.

We call a *coarse-grained parallelization* the above-mentioned technology of parallel Monte Carlo simulation (see Section 2.1). Most part of computations based on the coarse-grained parallelization were made on the massive parallel cluster NKS-30T of the Siberian Supercomputer Center of the Siberian Branch of the Russian Academy of Sciences [34]. For distributed stochastic simulation, we used in parallel up to 1200 cores of the cluster.

Also, up to 8 Gb of the main memory were available for each realization of the avalanche. But the value of the computational cost for the stochastic simulation is still quite large: the simulation of each realization takes a plenty of time (up to several hours, in some cases) [33].

A possible way to reduce the computational cost is to use a higher degree of parallelism in the course of the simulation of the particle trees. Namely, assume that sufficient number of computational cores is available for simulation of each realization. We start simulation of the realization on some core and do it till the moment when necessary number of particles is simulated (this number is greater or equal to the number of free cores). Then the conditionally independent branches which take origin from these particles may be simulated independently on different cores.

When the simulation of the avalanche starts on CPU, it is advisable to simulate generations of particles sequentially (here the generation of particles is the set of all particles at the specific time moment t_i). Simulation on each core uses the "lexicographical scheme" to simulate the particle trees, as described above.

Here, the technology of the distributive random numbers generation described above may also be used for the simulation of new branches. This parallelization technique is suitable for implementation on computers with many-core coprocessors, such as GPUs or Intel Xeon Phi accelerators.

In order to get much effect in comparison with the coarse-grained parallelism, it is possible to combine the above-mentioned techniques on hybrid supercomputers. Namely, it is reasonable to use the cores of the CPU and the coprocessor simultaneously in the following way:

- on each node of the cluster, all the CPU's cores (with the exception of the CPU's cores "attached" to coprocessor) are loaded with simulation of the independent realizations of the avalanche using the coarse-grained parallelism;
- the co-processor and the "attached" CPU's core are loaded with simulation of a single realization of the avalanche using the higher degree of parallelism.

In the last case it is possible to exchange "redundant" particles between the memory of the CPU's core (namely, the main memory on the node) and the memory of the coprocessor. This technique enables one to use the computational resources effectively.

To implement the combined technique, we used the hybrid supercomputer MVS-10P of the Joint Supercomputer Center of the Russian Academy of Sciences equipped with the Intel Xeon Phi coprocessors [39]. There a number of the hybrid nodes on the cluster, hardware resources of each node being as follows:

- there are two Intel Xeon E5-2690 CPUs and two Intel Xeon Phi 7110X coprocessors per node,
- each Intel Xeon processor (CPU) consists of 8 cores,
- each Intel Xeon Phi coprocessor consists of 61 cores,
- main memory on the node is 64 Gb,

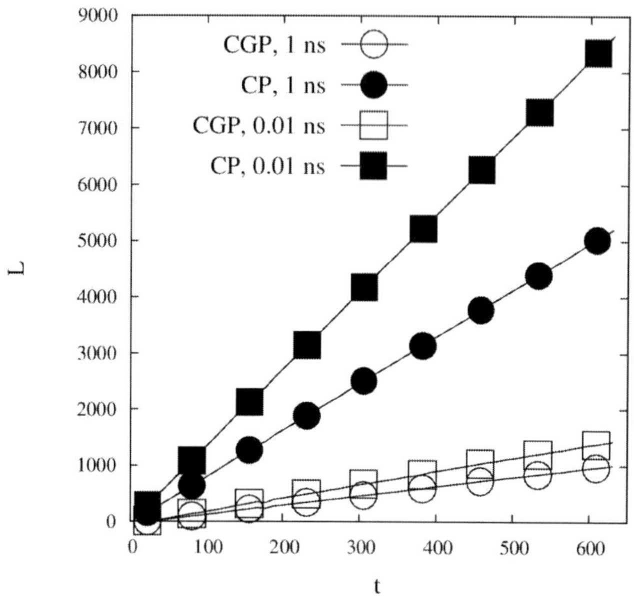

Figure 9. Comparison of efficiency of two parallelization techniques for two values of t_{max} (0.01 ns and 1 ns): technique of the coarse-grained parallelism (CGP) and the combined parallelization technique (CP). Here x-axis: computer time in seconds, y-axis: number of realizations.

- main memory on the Intel Xeon Phi coprocessor is 6 Gb.

The results of comparison of the efficiency of the coarse-grained parallelism (CGP) and the above-mentioned combined technique (CP) are presented in Figure 9. In our numerical experiments, we chose a particular set of physical parameters for the problem [33]. For different parallelization techniques, we compare graphs of the function $L = L(t)$ which is a total number of realizations L of the avalanche that are simulated by the computer time t. We also investigate this curves for two values of t_{max}: 0.01 ns and 1 ns. It is made in order to understand what happen when the number of particles in the avalanche is quite great (this is the case for the bigger value of t_{max}) and how the exchange of "redundant" particles between CPU and coprocessor affects the efficiency of computations.

It is clear from Figure 9 that the use of the combined parallelization technique is more effective than the technique of the coarse-grained parallelism. Namely, using it we can evaluate more realizations by the given time moment. The combined technique also enables effective use of computer memory to store the model particles of the avalanche.

5. Conclusion

In the chapter, we presented effective computational approaches for distributed stochastic simulation on supercomputers. First of all, the technology of parallel random numbers generation was given. In particular, it enables one to get correlated results of different Monte-Carlo computations. The RNG presented in the chapter satisfies very rigorous statistical requirements.

These approaches are implemented in the software library PARMONC, developed for a wide range of applications of the Monte Carlo method. The PARMONC effectively launches stochastic simulation on supercomputers with different architectures. Also, we presented results of studying of scalability of distributed stochastic simulation from current supercomputers to more powerful ones (up to future exaflop supercomputers).

We applied the developed approaches to simulate evolution of electron avalanches in gases and presented the technique of deep parallelization which enhance the efficiency of stochastic simulation. We performed Monte Carlo simulation on hybrid supercomputer using the central processors and coprocessors on each computational node simultaneously.

Acknowledgments

This research was supported by the Russian Foundation for Basic Research (RFBR), grants No. 12-01-00034, 12-01-00727, 13-01-00746 and 13-07-00589; Interdisciplinary Integration Projects of the Siberian Branch of Russian Academy of Sciences No. 39, 126 and 130; Program of Fundamental Research of the Presidium of the Russian Academy of Sciences No. 1.

References

[1] Gentle, J.: *Random Number Generation and Monte Carlo Methods*, 2 ed., Springer-Verlag (2003).

[2] *Applications of Monte Carlo Method in Science and Engineering*. Edited by Shaul Mordechai, 950 pages, Publisher: InTech http://www.intechopen.com/books/applications-of-monte-carlo-method-in-science-and-engineering (2011).

[3] Martin W.R.: Advances in Monte Carlo Methods for Global Reactor Analysis. *Invited lecture at the M&C 2007 International Conference*, April 15-19, 2007, Monterey, CA, USA (2007).

[4] Brown F.B., Martin W.R., Mosteller R.D.: Monte Carlo - Advances and Challenges. Workshop at PHYSOR-2008, Interlaken, Switzerland, 14-19 September 2008, *Report LA-UR-08-05891*, Los Alamos National Laboratory, http://www.physor2008.ch/documents/Workshop_I/PHYSOR08-WorkShopI.pdf (2008).

[5] Rubinstein, R. Y. , Kroese D. P.: *Simulation and the Monte Carlo Method*, 2 ed, New York: John Wiley & Sons (2007).

[6] Marchenko, M.A., Mikhailov, G.A.: Distributed Computing by the Monte Carlo Method. *Automation and Remote Control*, vol. 68, issue 5, pp. 888–900 (2007).

[7] Brent, R.: Fast and Reliable Random Number Generators for Scientific Computing. In: *Dongarra*, J., Madsen, K., Wasniewski, J. (Ed.) LNCS, vol. 3732, pp.1–10 (2006).

[8] Matsumoto, M., Nishimura, T. Mersenne Twister: A 623–dimensionally Equidistributed Uniform Pseudorandom Number Generator. *ACM Trans. on Modeling and Computer Simulation*, 8(1), pp. 3–30 (1998).

[9] Marsaglia, G. Xorshift RNGs. *Journal of Statistical Software* Vol. 8(14), pp. 1–6 (2003).

[10] L'Ecuyer, P. Uniform Random Number Generators. *International Encyclopedia of Statistical Science*, Lovric, Miodrag (Ed.), Springer-Verlag (2010).

[11] Barker, E., Kelsey, J. *Recommendation for Random Number Generation Using Deterministic Random Bit Generators*. NIST SP800-90A (2012).

[12] Manssen, M., Weigel, M., Hartmann, A.K. Random number generators for massively parallel simulations on GPU. *Eur. Phys. J. Special Topics* 210 (1), pp. 53–71 (2012).

[13] Sait, M., Matsumoto, M. Variants of Mersenne Twister Suitable for Graphic Processors. *Transactions on Mathematical Software*, 39, 12:1–12:20 (2013).

[14] Dyadkin, I.G., Hamilton, K.G.: A Study of 128-bit Multipliers for Congruential Pseudorandom Number Generators. *Comput. Phys. Comm.*, vol. 125, issues 1-3, pp.239 – 258 (2000).

[15] Marchenko, M.A., Mikhailov, G.A. Parallel Realization of Statistical Simulation and Random Number Generators. *Russian Journal of Numerical Analysis and Mathematical Modelling*. Vol. 17, 1, pp. 113–124 (2002).

[16] Marchenko, M.A.: Parallel Pseudorandom Number Generator for Large-scale Monte Carlo Simulations. In: *Malyshkin*, V. (Ed.) PaCT 2009. LNCS, vol. 4671, pp.276–282 (2007).

[17] Page of the *128-bit Parallel Congruential Random Number Generator*. Department of Stochastic Simulation in Physics of the Institute of Computational Mathematics and Mathematical Geophysics in Novosibirsk, Russia, http://osmf.sscc.ru/ mam/generator_en.htm

[18] Marchenko, M.: PARMONC - a Software Library for Massively Parallel Stochastic Simulation. In: *Malyshkin*, V. (ed.) PACT-2011. LNCS, vol. 6873, pp. 302–316 (2011).

[19] Page of the PARMONC on the Web Site of Siberian Supercomputer Center, http://www2.sscc.ru/SORAN-INTEL/paper/2011/parmonc.htm

[20] Link to a Full Documentation to the PARMONC, http://www2.sscc.ru/SORAN-INTEL/paper/2011/parmonc.pdf

[21] Mendes, B., Pereira, A.: Parallel Monte Carlo Driver (PMCD) - a Software Package for Monte Carlo Simulations in Parallel. *Comput. Phys. Comm.*, vol. 151, issue 1, pp.89–95 (2003).

[22] Badal, A., Sempau, J.: A Package of Linux Scripts for the Parallelization of Monte Carlo Simulations. *Comput. Phys. Comm.*, vol. 175, issue 6, pp.440–450 (2006).

[23] Slawinska, M., Jadach, S.: MCdevelop - a Universal Framework for Stochastic Simulations. Comput. Phys. Comm., vol. 182, issue 3, pp.748–762 (2011)

[24] Podkorytov, D., Rodionov, A., Choo, H.: Agent-based Simulation System AGNES for Networks Modeling: Review and Researching. *Proceedings of the 6th International Conference on Ubiquitous Information Management and Communication (ACM ICUIMC 2012)*, ISBN 978-1-4503-1172-4, Paper 115 ACM, 4 pages (2012).

[25] Glinsky, B., Rodionov, A., Marchenko, M., Podkorytov, D., Weins, D.: Scaling the Distributed Stochastic Simulation to Exaflop Supercomputers. *Proceedings of the 14th IEEE International Conference on High Performance Computing and Communication & 9th IEEE International Conference on Embedded Software and Systems*, HPCC-ICESS 2012, Liverpool, United Kingdom, June 25-27, 2012, IEEE Computer Society 2012 ISBN 978-1-4673-2164-8, pp. 1131–1136 (2012).

[26] Chernykh, I., Glinskiy, B., Kulikov, I., Marchenko, M., Rodionov, A., Podkorytov, D., Karavaev, D.: Using Simulation System AGNES for Modeling Execution of Parallel Algorithms on Supercomputers, *Proceedings of the 2014 International Conference on Systems, Control, Signal Processing and Informatics II*, Prague, Czech Republic, April 2-4, pp. 66–70 http://www.europment.org/library/2014/prague/SCSI.pdf (2014).

[27] Raizer, Yu.P.: *Gas discharge physics*, Springer-Verlag, (1991).

[28] Dolgos, D.: *Full-band Monte Carlo Simulation of Single Photon Avalanche Diodes*, http://www.iis.ee.ethz.ch/ schenk/theses/dolgos.pdf (2011).

[29] Donko, Z., Rozsa, K., Tobin, R.C.: Monte Carlo Analysis of the Electrons' Motion in a Segmented Hollow Cathode Discharge. *J. Physics D: Applied Physics*. Vol. 29, pp. 105-113 (1996).

[30] Pruchova, H., Franek, B.: 3-Dimensional Simulation of Electron Avalanches in Low Pressure Wire Chambers and Proportional Counters. *ICFA Instrumentation Bulletin*, 13, http://www.slac.stanford.edu/pubs/icfa/fall96/paper1a.html (1996).

[31] Settaouti, A.: Monte Carlo Simulation of Avalanche Formation and Streamer Discharge. *Electrical Engineering*. Vol. 92, No 1, pp. 35–42 (2010).

[32] Xiao, D.: Monte Carlo Simulation of Insulating Gas Avalanche Development. *Applications of Monte Carlo Method in Science and Engineering*, Publisher: InTech http://www.intechopen.com/books/applications-of-monte-carlo-method-in-science-and-engineering/monte-carlo-simulation-of-insulating-gas-avalanche-development (2011)

[33] Lotova, G.Z., Marchenko, M.A., Mikhailov, G.A., Rogazinskii, S.V., Ukhinov, S.V., Shklyaev, V.A.: Numerical statistical modelling algorithms for electron avalanches

in gases. *Russian Journal of Numerical Analysis and Mathematical Modelling*. Vol. 29, Iss. 4, pp. 251–263 (2014).

[34] Supercomputer Center of the Siberian Branch of the Russian Academy of Sciences, http://www2.sscc.ru/

[35] Sobol, I. M.: *A Primer for the Monte Carlo Method.* CRC Press, Boca Raton, FL (1994).

[36] Ivanov, M.S., Rogasinsky, S.V.: Analysis of numerical techniques of the direct simulation Monte Carlo method in the rarefied gas dynamics. Soviet *Journal of Numerical Analysis and Mathematical Modeling.* Vol. 3. No. 6, pp. 453–465 (1988).

[37] Hagelaar, G.J.M., Pitchford, L.C.: Solving the Boltzmann equation to obtain electron transport coefficients and rate coefficients for fluid models. *Plasma Sources Sci. Technol.* Vol. 14, pp. 722 - 733 (2005).

[38] Lisovskiy V., Booth, J.-P., Landry, K. et. al. Electron drift velocity in argon, nitrogen, hydrogen, oxygen and ammonia in strong electric fields determined from rf breakdown curves. *J. Phys. D: Appl. Phys.* Vol. 39, pp. 660–665 (2006).

[39] Joint Supercomputer Center of the Russian Academy of Sciences, http://www.jscc.ru/

In: Parallel Programming
Editor: Mikhail S. Tarkov

ISBN: 978-1-63321-957-1

Chapter 6

LATTICE GAS CELLULAR AUTOMATA FOR A FLOW SIMULATION AND THEIR PARALLEL IMPLEMENTATION

Yury G. Medvedev*
Supercomputer Software Department,
Institute of Computational Mathematics
and Mathematical Geophysics SB RAS, Novosibirsk, Russia

Abstract

This chapter presents some directions of the development of gas flows cellular automata models. The transitions from Boolean to integer models, from two-dimensional to three-dimensional models, and from the gas-stream to flow models in multiphase media are traced. A software implementation of a two-dimensional model of gas-powder flow with integer alphabet FHP-GP is proposed. A mechanism for parallel execution of the model on a cluster using the library MPI is described. The need for dynamic load balancing of cluster cores in the implementation of models with integer alphabet is shown. A diffusion balancing implemented for this model is argued. Also, some results of computational experiments on modeling the flows obtained using the above software are presented. A problem of dynamic load balancing application for gas and fluid flows simulation by lattice gas automata (LGA) is considered. The choice of a diffusion balancing method is justified. The results of testing both balanced and imbalanced cases are presented. The efficiency of the realizations for LGA simulation is presented and the PIC-method is compared.

Keywords: cellular automaton, flows simulation, LGA, parallel program, dynamic balancing

1. Introduction

One of the perspective directions of physical processes simulation is simulation by cellular automata. Cellular-automaton models of flows called the Lattice-Gas were suggested

* E-mail address: medvedev@ssd.sscc.ru

in the seventies of the last century [1] and, since then, they have been promptly advanced. These models are discrete; their ground is the Boolean algebra. It allows one to construct efficient programs and to minimize computer time usage.

But the Lattice-Gas simplicity superimposes some limitations in the area of their application. Here are some of them: the superior limit of the Reynolds number amounts some hundreds, boundary conditions allow one to set only the immovable walls; transonic velocity simulation causes result distortion. In this chapter, an attempt is made to solve these problems and a new kind of the Lattice-Gas model is proposed, which is called FHP-MP (multiparticle) cellular automaton. It is a generalization of the classical FHP (Frish, Hasslacher, Pomeau) model on Boolean vectors [2]. In the new model, it is enabled more than one particle in a cell with equal velocity vectors. Attempts to use miscellaneous mass particles in the Lattice-Gas had been made before [3], but, for different reasons, they were not successful.

In this chapter, the new FHP-MP model is featured and the results of its experimental research are given, such as two-dimensional approximation of a flow between two plains, a flow with a flat valve and a flow of a circular obstacle. In these examples, a correlation in the corresponding variety of a flow velocity and flow pressure rates between the FHP-MP and the FHP-I models is demonstrated. The Poiseuille flow for a new model is obtained. Swirls were obtained and the Kármán vortex street is visible in the presence of a valve or a circular obstacle, it points to the possibility of a flow turbulent properties simulation.

2. Specification Statement of the FHP-MP Model

2.1. The Basic Definitions

As a cellular automaton, the FHP-MP model is denoted by a triplet (W, A, N), where $W = \{w_1, w_2, \ldots, w_i, \ldots\}$ is the set *of cells* allocated in the corresponding sites in some discrete space. Each cell $w \in W$ is associated with a finite state machine (FSM) A called *the elementary FSM*. Its states are given by an integer-valued vector, as distinct from a Boolean vector in the classical FHP model. Each cell $w \in W$ is correlated with some coordinates $x(w)$ and $y(w)$ on the Cartesian plain. Therefore, between any two cells $w_1 \in W$ and $w_2 \in W$, it is possible to calculate distance $d(w_1, w_2)$ easily.

For each cell $w \in W$ an ordered set $N(w) = \{N_i(w)\colon N_0(w) = w, N_i(w) \in W \;\&\; d(w, N_i(w)) = 1, (i = 1, 2, \ldots, b)\}$ is determined. Its members belong to *a neighborhood* with the cell w and they are called its *neighboring cells* or *neighbors*. Constant b characterizes an amount of nonidentical neighbors of each cell $w \in W$. The cells are neighbors to each other. There is a correspondence between the elementary automaton A outputs in a cell $w \in W$ and the inputs of the neighbors of this cell and vice versa. Thus, the structure of the cellular automaton cells set W is a graph in which the vertexes are cells, and the edges from the set is the neighborhood relation. This graph has a regular lattice and the degree of its vertices equal to b. The cell state is represented by a vector with integer-valued components. A set of states $s(w)$ of all cells $w \in W$ in the same instant t is called *global state* $\sigma(t) = \{s(w_1), s(w_2), \ldots, s(w_i), \ldots\}$ of the cellular automaton.

2.2. The Neighbourhood Relation

Each cell in the classical FHP model has 6 neighbors (b = 6) (Figure 1). In some modifications of the model, each cell is a neighbor to itself (possibly several times), as well that stipulates the possibility of the presence of the rest particles. A ground of the FHP-MP model is the FHP model with one rest particle. In Figure 1 cell w, and its neighbors $N_i(w)$, i = 0, 1, ..., 6 are represented. Thus, the amount of neighbors of each cell w of the FHP-MP model is equal to seven, one of the neighbors is cell w, i.e., $N_0(w) = w$.

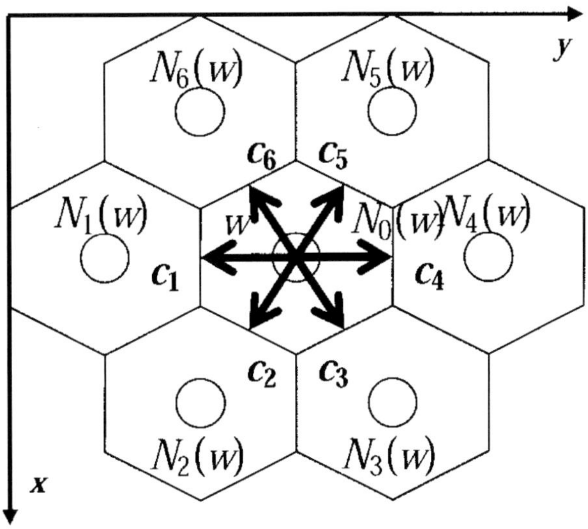

Figure 1. Particles velocity vectors. Neighbors numbering.

Unlike the FHP, in the FHP-MP model, components $s_0(w)$, $s_1(w)$, ..., $s_6(w)$ of state vector $\boldsymbol{s}(w)$ are not Boolean, but integer. Thus, the particles mass in cell w is equal to

$$m(w) = \sum_{i=0}^{b} s_i(w), \tag{1}$$

where $b = 6$ is an amount of the possible velocity vector directions, s_i is the i-th component of states vector $\boldsymbol{s}$. A physical interpretation of the vector $\boldsymbol{s}(w)$ components values is the following: s_i defines an amount of unit mass particles with the velocity vectors $\boldsymbol{c}_i$ directed towards neighbors $N_i(w)$.

Model momentum $\boldsymbol{p}$ in cell $w \in W$ is the total of all momentums directed to all neighbors $N_i(w)$, where i = 0, 1, ..., b, and b = 6:

$$\vec{p} = \sum_{i=1}^{b} s_i \vec{c}_i , \tag{2}$$

From (1), due to Figure 1, it is easy to compute the total momentum $\boldsymbol{p}$ projections p_x and p_y onto Cartesian axes Ox and Oy.

$$p_x = \frac{\sqrt{3}}{2}\left(s_2 + s_3 - s_5 - s_6\right), \tag{3}$$

$$p_y = s_4 - s_1 + \frac{1}{2}\left(s_3 + s_5 - s_2 - s_6\right), \tag{4}$$

where s_i is the sum of all particles velocity vectors in the cell w directed to neighbor $N_i(w)$.

2.3. Behavior of the Cellular Automaton

We introduce three types of cells $w \in W$. As *conventional* cells $w_c \in W_c$ we will call the cells in which both the mass and momentum conservation laws are satisfied. *Wall cells* $w_w \in W_w$ are the cells in which the mass conservation law is satisfied, but the momentum conservation law can be violated. And, at last, *source cells* $w_s \in W_s$ are the cells in which both the law of mass conservation and the law of momentum conservation can be violated. Sets of conventional cells W_c, of wall W_w, and of sources W_s do not intersecte pairwise ($W_c \cap W_w = \varnothing$, $W_c \cap W_s = \varnothing$, $W_w \cap W_s = \varnothing$). These sets integration coincides with a set of all automaton cells ($W_c \cup W_w \cup W_s = W$). The behavior of walls and sources specifies the boundary conditions of cellular automaton.

In the FHP-MP model, the cellular automaton with a synchronous operation is used. On each cycle, there is a replacement of states $\boldsymbol{s}(t)$ in all cells by states $\boldsymbol{s}(t+1) = \delta(\boldsymbol{s}(t))$, where $\delta(\boldsymbol{s}(t))$ is the next-state function of elementary FSM A. The cellular automaton, thus, changes its global state $\sigma(t)$ by a new global state $\sigma(t+1)$.

Each cycle of the cellular automaton processing has two phases: *propagation* and *collision*. So, the next-state function of elementary FSM consists of a composition of functions propagation δ_1 and collision δ_2:

$$\delta(\boldsymbol{s}) = \delta_2(\delta_1(\boldsymbol{s})). \tag{5}$$

Each of functions δ_1 and δ_2 should satisfy the laws of mass conservation

$$\sum_{w \in W} \sum_{i=1}^{b} \delta_j\left(s_i(w)\right) = \sum_{w \in W} \sum_{i=1}^{b} s_i(w), j \in \{1, 2\}, \tag{6}$$

and momentum

$$\sum_{w \in W} \sum_{i=1}^{b} \delta_j\left(s_i(w)\boldsymbol{c}_i(w)\right) = \sum_{w \in W} \sum_{i=1}^{b} s_i(w)\boldsymbol{c}_i(w), j \in \{1, 2\}. \tag{7}$$

In accordance with the fluid flow dynamics, the presence of these two phases is interpreted as follows. Collisions implement diffusion in fluids, and propagation matters for the transport process in a flow. These further two phases are featured explicitly.

2.4. Propagation Phase

In the propagation phase in each cell w ∈ W, each particle specified by components $s_i(w)$, at i = 1, ..., 6, propagates to the neighboring cell $N_i(w)$ corresponding to its velocity vector $\mathbf{c}_i$. The rest particles, correspondent to s_0, remain in the cell w. Thus, the i-th component $s_i(w)$ of the state vector **s**(w) of cell w after propagation acquires the value

$$\delta_1\left(s_i\left(w\right)\right)=\begin{cases} s_i\left(N_{((i+2)\bmod 6)+1}\left(w\right)\right), & \text{for } i=1,2,\ldots,b; \\ s_i\left(w\right), & \text{for } i=0. \end{cases} \tag{8}$$

In spite of the fact that at propagation the particles mass and momentum in a single cell are changed; within the whole cellular automaton, they are maintained, i.e., the requirements (6) and (7) are fulfilled.

2.5. Collision Phase

In the collision phase there is a veering of particles velocity vectors directions according to some collision rules which are not dependent on the states of the neighboring cells, i.e., δ_2 depends only on the state of its own elementary FSM. In the FHP-MP model, function δ_2 is probabilistic. The collision rules for all types of cells described above (conventional cells, walls and sources) are as follows.

Conventional cells. In conventional cells $w_c \in W_c$, function δ_2 is selected from such ones that mass $m(w)$ and momentum $\boldsymbol{p}(w)$ of particles in a cell were conserved:

$$\sum_{i=0}^{b}\delta_2\left(s_i\left(w_c\right)\right)=\sum_{i=0}^{b}s_i\left(w_c\right),\ \forall\ w_c\in W, \tag{9}$$

$$\sum_{i=0}^{b}\delta_2\left(\boldsymbol{c}_i\left(w_c\right)\right)=\sum_{l=0}^{b}s_i\left(w_c\right)\boldsymbol{c}_i\left(w_c\right),\ \forall\ w_c\in W \tag{10}$$

One of the possible values obeying (9) and (10) should be chosen with an equal probability. A fulfillment of (9) and (10) implies a fulfillment of (6) and (7).

Walls. In the cells $w_w \in W_w$ which are walls, the particles are "mirrored" backwards, violating, thus, the momentum conservation law:

$$\delta_2\left(s_i\left(w_w\right)\right)=\begin{cases} s_{((i+2)\bmod 6)+1}\left(w_w\right), & \text{for } i=1,2,\ldots,b, \\ s_i\left(w_w\right), & \text{for } i=0. \end{cases} \tag{11}$$

Since the number of particles in a cell is not changing, the requirements (9) and, therefore, (6) are satisfied. It is not so for (7), because the directions of particles velocity vectors $\boldsymbol{c}$ are changing, but it is admitted by boundary conditions. Such particles behavior in wall cells simulates the requirement of the flow zero speed on obstacles borders.

Sources. Each cell-source $w_s \in W_s$ sustains the given particles concentration $n_0(w_s)$. For this purpose, it generates the particles with any possible direction of the velocity vector when the current concentration of particles $n(w_s)$ is less than $n_0(w_s)$. The amount of generated particles is equal to the difference between the given concentration $n_0(w_s)$ and a current one $n(w_s)$. It is possible to construct various obstacles by source cells. For example, having placed them in one line (usually they are skirting a cellular array), we can obtain a source of a steady particle flow with the given concentration. Single source cell simulates an injector. Naturally, at generating new particles neither mass $m(w_s)$ nor momentum $\boldsymbol{p}(w_s)$ are conserved. Boundary conditions in cells-sources enable a breach of conditions (6) and (7).

2.6. Averaged Values

At flows simulation, the cellular automaton *microlevel* parameters, such as mass $m(w)$ and particles $\boldsymbol{c}_i(w)$ velocity in each cell $w \in W$, do not have practical significance. But *the averaged values* of their velocities $\langle \boldsymbol{u} \rangle$ and concentrations $\langle n \rangle$ over some *averaging vicinity* $Av(w)$, including all cells $w_j \in W$ placed not farther from a cell w than some distance r called *the averaging radius*, are worth much more. An averaged velocity is the total of all particles velocity vectors in averaging vicinity $Av(w)$, divided by the cardinal number of the averaging vicinity:

$$\langle \boldsymbol{u} \rangle(w) = \frac{1}{|Av(w)|} \sum_{w_j \in Av(w)} \sum_{i=0}^{b} s_i \boldsymbol{c}_i , \tag{12}$$

where $|Av(w)|$ is an amount of the cells situated in $Av(w)$, $\boldsymbol{c}_i$ is the unit velocity vector corresponding to the i-th digit of state vector $\boldsymbol{s}(w_j)$, and s_i is the magnitude of the i-th digit of state vector $\boldsymbol{s}(w_j)$ of cell $w_j \in Av(w)$.

An averaged concentration of particles $\langle n \rangle$ is evaluated in the same vicinity $Av(w)$ as follows:

$$\langle n \rangle(w) = \frac{1}{|Av(w)|} \sum_{w_j \in Av(w)} \sum_{i=0}^{b} s_i . \tag{13}$$

Averaged values of the particles velocity and concentration are called model velocity and model pressure, respectively. They correspond to the velocity and pressure values of a simulated fluid and are *macrolevel* arguments.

We will note that the average model velocity and the model concentration values will match their physical analogs only in the case when averaging vicinity $Av(w)$ consists exclusively of conventional cells $w_w \in W_w$, otherwise we will consider values $\langle \boldsymbol{u} \rangle$ and $\langle n \rangle$ as indefinite. This requirement does not allow calculating values $\langle \boldsymbol{u} \rangle$ and $\langle n \rangle$ for the cells with a distance to walls and sources less than averaging radius r.

3. Experimental Study of the FHP-MP Model

For validation of the proposed model, its program realization was constructed. It allows one to carry out the computing experiments both on single-processor computers and on multiprocessor and multicomputer systems. The code is written in C, the parallelism is implemented by means of the MPI library. The computing experiments performed with the FHP-MP model are described below. Qualitative behavior of a simulated flow is obtained.

3.1. Two-Dimensional Approximating of a Fluid Flow between Two Parallel Planes

This experiment, which has become already classical, allows us to check out our model on the correspondence to physics. Its essence is in the fact that a longitudinal flow velocity (the flow moves lengthways Oy in a positive direction) should be described by the parabolic law along direction Ox, when boundary velocity $\langle \boldsymbol{u} \rangle_b$ is zero. The cellular automaton used in this computing experiment has the size of 100×2000 cells (along Cartesian axes Ox and Oy accordingly). The cells with coordinates in the interval [(2, 1), (99, 1)] are sources. The cells with coordinates in spacing [(1, 1), (1, 2000)] and [(100, 1), (100, 2000)] are walls. The remaining ones are conventional cells. This 2D-construction is a cutting of a parallelepiped of the infinite width (lengthwise axis Oz) and it is an approximation of a three-dimensional flow between two parallel planes.

The projection of flow velocity $\langle \boldsymbol{u} \rangle_y$ onto axis Oy in a flow cross-section (lengthways Ox) is shown in Figure 2. The curve with markers illustrates results of numerical simulation. It is approximated by the parabola equation (in Figure 2 it is a curve without markers):

$$\langle \boldsymbol{u} \rangle_y (r) = -0.0008 r^2 + 2, \tag{14}$$

where r is the spacing interval between the middle of the bisecting point and an observed point of the cross-section.

Curve (14) is the inferential parabola of Poiseuille. It is one of few analytical solutions of the Navier-Stokes equation and it looks like the equation

$$\langle \boldsymbol{u} \rangle_y (r) = \frac{dP}{4\eta l}\left(R^2 - r^2\right), \tag{15}$$

where dP is a pressure drop on a part of a pipe with length l, η is fluid dynamic viscosity, R is the pipe radius (in a two-dimensional case it is a spacing interval between the plains).

The amount of iterations, after which one average is spent, is T = 20000. The averaging radius is r = 15 cells. According to the constraints imposed on (12) and (13), the averaged values cannot be obtained in the cells which are at a distance from the walls less than r = 15 cells. Therefore, idealized and experimental curves over the range, shown in the picture, are not declined to the zero point.

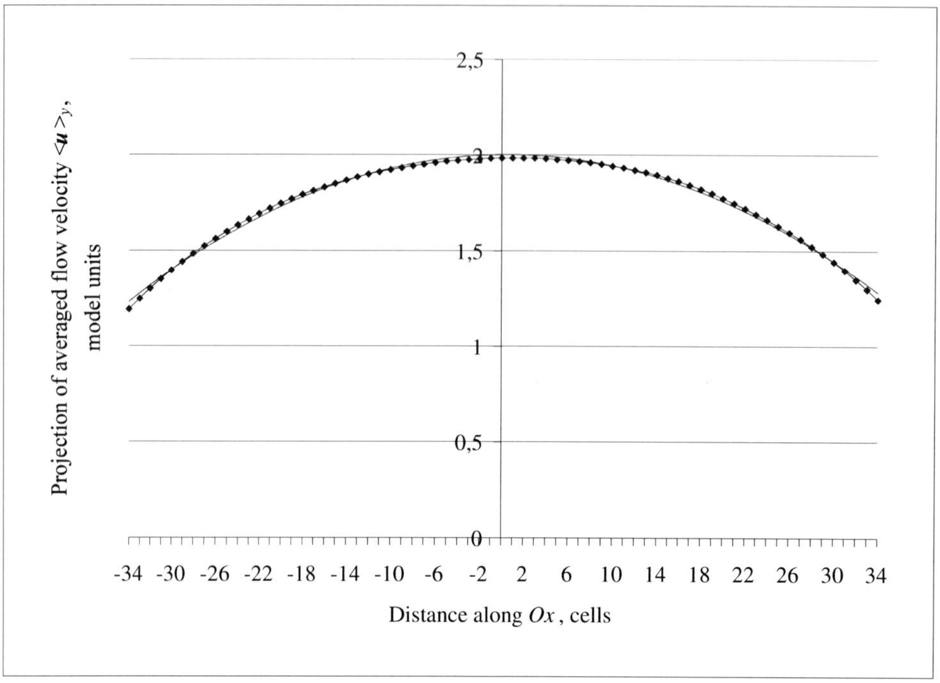

Figure 2. Flow velocity projection.

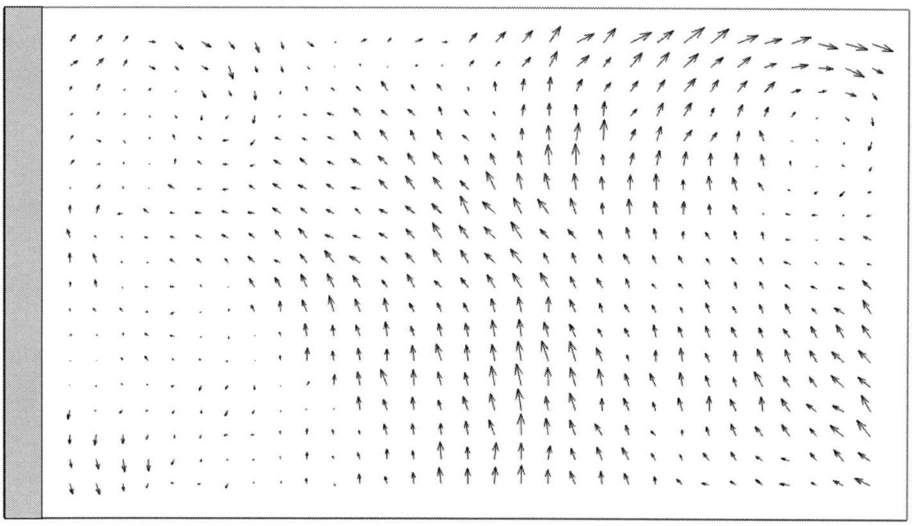

Figure 3. Flow velocity field with a valve as an obstacle. Fragment behind the valve.

The maximum flow velocity in the carried out experiment, apparently from Figure 2, was obtained equal to two, that is a little more than in the classical FHP model. But it is not the maximal velocity; in the proposed multiparticle model, it is possible to increase the concentration provided by sources, obtaining the flow velocity considerably superior than the obtained one.

The results of this experiment demonstrate, that the FHP-MP model correctly reproduces the processes in a flow and corresponds to physics.

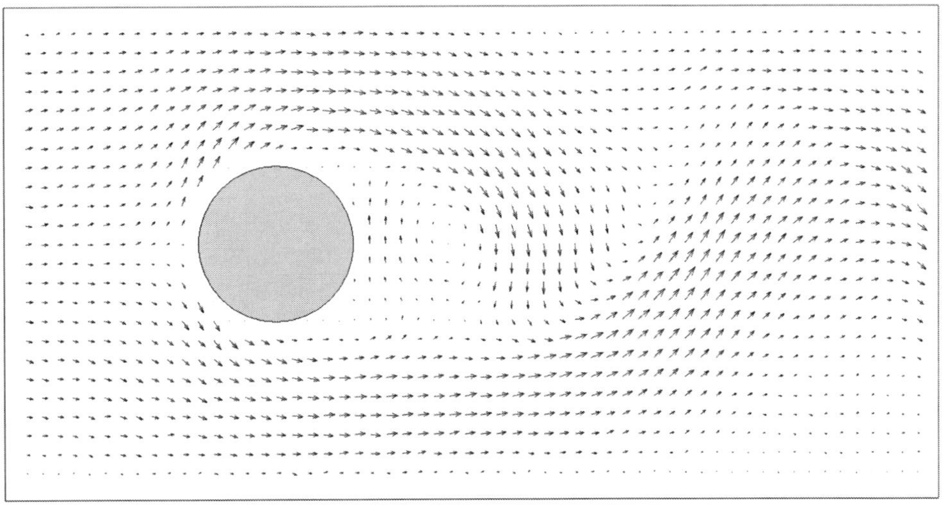

Figure 4. Flow velocity field with a circular obstacle.

3.2. Flow with a Valve

The following computing experiment was carried out with a research objective to study the flows with obstacles. For this purpose, an additional boundary condition as a valve-shaped obstacle was added to the cellular automaton being in the previous experiment. The valve was placed at the distance from the source line, equal to one-third part of the pipe length, perpendicularly to the flow propagation direction and has the pipe splitted in half. The obtained velocity field resembles a streamline of the valve by the flow. Unfortunately, at the small-sized image scale encompassing the whole cellular automaton, the flow high-velocity parts are visible only. It is necessary to discern a low velocity, such as the velocity behind the valve. In Figure 3, a fragment of the automaton, which is directly behind the valve, is given in a larger scale. The direction of each arrow in the figure coincides with a streamline on its basis, and its length is proportional to the flow velocity in that point. The flow is directed from the left side to the right one, the valve is figured in the left-hand part of the figure. The flow vortexes are clearly visible in the painted fragment.

3.3. Streamlining of a Circular Obstacle

One more experiment was carried out with a circular obstacle. It also demonstrates the flow vortices. In the initial cellular automaton a circle-shaped obstacle has been added. The obtained velocity field of this automaton is shown in Figure 4. Behind the obstacle an eddy is fetched away and the "S-turn" is visible. This "S-turn" is obviously alternative to the Kármán vortex street for a too small spacing interval to flow planes skirting.

4. Dynamic Load Balancing for Lattice Gas Simulations on a Cluster

4.1. Features of the Multi-Particle Models

It is not in all tasks that the traditional LGA [4] with the Boolean alphabet yields a good simulating effect. So, it is impossible to use them for simulating processes with the heavy pressure (for example, for detonation) gradients. Also, they cannot simulate the flows with moving obstacles. These limitations are absent in the multi-particle model [5, 6]. Since its state is represented by an integer vector, a cell has a huge number of possible various states. It is impossible to find all the states conserving the particles mass and momentum in a cell at each collision execution. Therefore, one has to compute a new state ad-hoc. From the above, it follows that the multi-particle LGA has the following properties:

1. The collisions take up more time than in Boolean case;
2. The collision functions runtime depends on a cell state essentially;
3. If the program is run on a cluster, there may be a load imbalance.

4.2. Parallel Program Implementation

In the LGA parallel implementation the domain decomposition method is used. The cellular array is divided into stripes along axis i. It is enough, for a good performance, to use one dimension cuts in this case. A stripe is assigned to any of p cores ($0 \le rank < p$) for processing which consists of several lines $i_A(rank) \le i < i_B(rank)$. The stripes boundaries are related by the following ratios:

$$i_A(rank + 1) = i_B(rank), \text{ for } 0 \le rank < p - 1,\ i_A(0) = 0,\ i_B(p) = I.$$

In the absence of balancing, the stripes have equal widths (exactly within integer rounding, $\lfloor x \rfloor$ denotes floor x):

$$i_A(rank) = \lfloor rank \cdot I / p \rfloor, \text{ for } 0 \le rank < p - 1,$$

$$i_B(rank) = \lfloor (rank + 1) \cdot I / p \rfloor, \text{ for } 1 \le rank < p.$$

Iteration consists of the following three stages:

1. Collisions.
2. Exchange of boundary cells states.

The core with the number *rank* sends:

to the core $rank - 1$ the line $i_A(rank)$, for $1 \le rank < p$,
to the core $rank + 1$ the line $i_B(rank) - 1$, for $0 \le rank < p - 1$.

The core with the number *rank* receives:

from the core *rank* – 1 the line $i_A(rank) - 1$, for $1 \leq rank < p$,
from the core *rank* + 1 the line $i_B(rank)$, for $0 \leq rank < p - 1$.

The received values are used at the third stage.

3. Propagation. For boundary cells in a stripe, the set of its neighbors includes those ones, whose states are just received from adjacent cores.

5. Load Balancing Algorithm

From the variety of balancing algorithms [7], we selected the diffusion algorithm for the following reasons.

The algorithm has high efficiency of parallel implementation on a cluster with the size of thousands of cores, as distinct from the centralized algorithms, where such size brings significant overheads.

The place of the cellular array section does not influence the amount of the data sent for each iteration.

The adjacent cores, as well, exchange their boundaries for each iteration.

The load imbalance increases slowly (except for in the tasks with an explosive wave).

5.1. Initial Balancing

Before the simulator starts, one test iteration is performed for every line i ($0 \leq i < I$). At this iteration, the collision function runtime in the lines is computed as follows:

$$t_0(i) = \sum_{j=0}^{J-1} t(i,j),$$

where $t(i,j)$ is the collision function runtime in cell (i,j). The propagation stage requires less time than the collision one and is not taken into account; hence, the averaged core time is computed as follows:

$$\bar{t} = \sum_{i=0}^{I-1} t_0(i) \Big/ p.$$

Now, for all cores ($0 \leq rank < p$), stripe boundaries $i_A(rank)$ and $i_B(rank)$ may be calculated. The lower boundary i_A is selected so that the following conditions are satisfied:

$$\sum_{i=0}^{i_A(rank)} t_0(i) \leq rank \cdot \bar{t}, \quad \sum_{i=0}^{i_A(rank)+1} t_0(i) > rank \cdot \bar{t}.$$

The choice of the upper boundary i_B should be made as follows:

$$\sum_{i=0}^{i_B(rank+1)} t_0(i) \le rank \cdot \bar{t}\ , \quad \sum_{i=0}^{i_B(rank+1)+1} t_0(i) > rank \cdot \bar{t}\ .$$

That is, the cells located between the lower and the upper boundaries, are processed at the same time $\bar{t}$. Let us remind that, as before $i_A(0) = 0$, $i_B(p) = I$. This method allows setting, precisely enough, the initial balancing in conditions when the cell processing time dependence on its state is unknown.

5.2. Dynamic Balancing

The three iteration stages are described in section 4.2. The first and third stages with balancing remain without modifications. The second stage has three small differences relative to the case without balancing.

1. The boundaries are doubled in thickness. It leads to a little less than twofold magnification of the transfer time since the transfer is carried out by one portion.

The core with the number *rank* sends:

to the core $rank - 1$ the lines $i_A(rank)$ and $i_A(rank) + 1$, for $1 \le rank < p$,
to the core $rank + 1$ the lines $i_B(rank) - 2$ and $i_B(rank) - 1$, for $0 \le rank < p - 1$.

The core with the number *rank* receives:

from the core $rank - 1$ the lines $i_A(rank) - 2$ and $i_A(rank) - 1$, for $1 \le rank < p$,
from the core $rank + 1$ the lines $i_B(rank)$ and $i_B(rank) + 1$, for $0 \le rank < p - 1$.

2. Together with the states of boundary cells, the runtime of the just completed collisions stage $t^{(k)}(rank)$ is transmitted, where k is the iteration number.
3. After the transfer, an adjustment of the stripes boundaries in each core is performed.

$$\mathrm{i_A}^{(k+1)}(\mathrm{rank}) = \mathrm{i_A}^{(k)}(\mathrm{rank}) - 1, \text{ if } \mathrm{t}^{(k)}(\mathrm{rank}) / \mathrm{t}^{(k)}(\mathrm{rank} - 1) < \mathrm{b}, \text{ for } 1 \le \mathrm{rank} < \mathrm{p},$$
$$\mathrm{i_A}^{(k+1)}(\mathrm{rank}) = \mathrm{i_A}^{(k)}(\mathrm{rank}) + 1, \text{ if } \mathrm{t}^{(k)}(\mathrm{rank} - 1) / \mathrm{t}^{(k)}(\mathrm{rank}) < \mathrm{b}, \text{ for } 1 \le \mathrm{rank} < \mathrm{p},$$
$$\mathrm{i_B}^{(k+1)}(\mathrm{rank}) = \mathrm{i_B}^{(k)}(\mathrm{rank}) - 1, \text{ if } \mathrm{t}^{(k)}(\mathrm{rank} + 1) / \mathrm{t}^{(k)}(\mathrm{rank}) < \mathrm{b}, \text{ for } 0 \le \mathrm{rank} < \mathrm{p} - 1,$$
$$\mathrm{i_B}^{(k+1)}(\mathrm{rank}) = \mathrm{i_B}^{(k)}(\mathrm{rank}) + 1, \text{ if } \mathrm{t}^{(k)}(\mathrm{rank}) / \mathrm{t}^{(k)}(\mathrm{rank} + 1) < \mathrm{b}, \text{ for } 0 \le \mathrm{rank} < \mathrm{p} - 1,$$

where b is movement borders threshold ($0 \le b \le 1$). Argument b defines the value of the time imbalance between the adjacent cores, above which the boundary drifts are performed in the direction of the less loaded core. At $b = 0$, we have a static balance case. At $b = 1$, the response sensitivity is the highest.

Test Results*

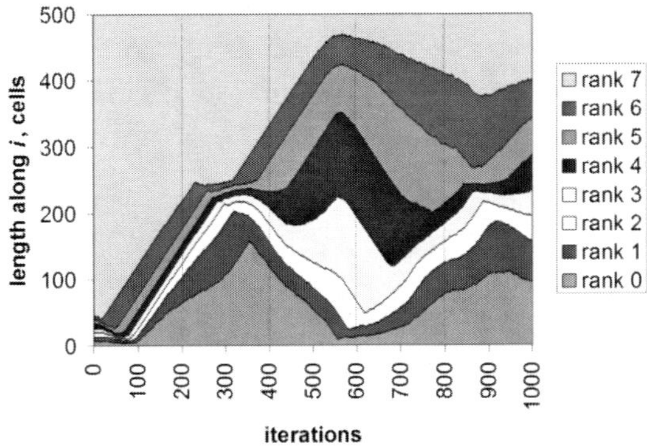

Figure 5. Cores load dynamics.

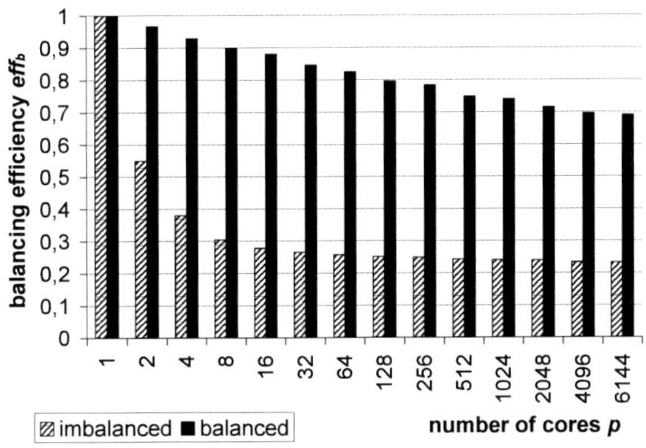

Figure 6. Dynamic balancing efficiency.

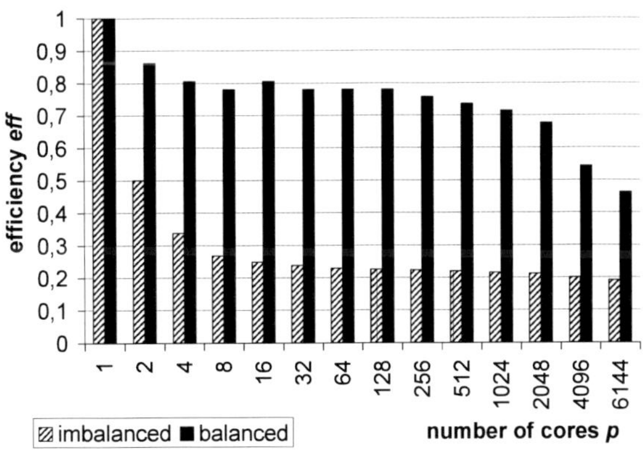

Figure 7. Parallel realization efficiency.

It should be noted that, in our implementation, the overhead for the dynamic diffusion balancing is minimal for two following reasons.

* Tests have been performed on MVS100K — JSCC Cluster, Moscow.

1. Data transfer is carried out only to the adjacent cores. Hence, the increase of cores number does not lead to the efficiency saturation as it takes place in the centralized balancing.
2. There are no additional transfers in comparison with the unbalanced case. Only the size of a single transmitted data package increases. This does not lead to a substantial increase of the transfer time.

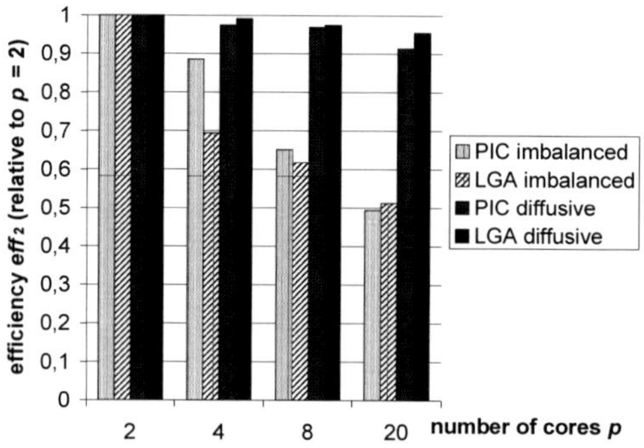

Figure 8. Comparison with the PIC method.

5.3. An Example of Explosion Simulation. Dynamics of the Cellular Array Distribution among Cores

An explosion in a closed camera is simulated. The cellular array has the size of $I = 500$, $J = 200$. The camera walls are allocated on the cellular array margins. Also, the obstacles are present in the middle of the array: [(250, 0), (250, 66)] and [(250, 133), (250, 199)]. The cellular array density at $i \leq 50$ is equal to 82 particles per cell. The density in the rest of the array (at i>50) is equal to 14 particles per cell. The cores number is $p = 8$. 1000 iterations were completed. The initial balancing is fulfilled according to the method in section 3.1. At each of 8 cores, the boundaries of stripes $i_A(rank)$ and $i_B(rank)$ were updated at each iteration.

The process goes as follows. In the beginning, the dense gas moves along the cellular array to its middle part and hit against the obstacles. A part of the flow passes through the hole between the obstacles. The other part is reflected from the obstacles. After that, the reflected flow goes backward, it is reflected from the bottom boundary of the cellular array again, and goes up to the obstacles. The part of the flow which passed through the hole is shaped in two vortexes above the obstacles. The amount of the particles is changed along i quite intensively. Therefore, it is difficult to achieve the acceptable balancing efficiency.

The chart of the stripe width, allocated on each core, is given in Figure 5. The efficiency (Figure 6) also does not remain steady; therefore, for its estimate, the next test with a quieter flow was performed.

5.4. An Example of a Quiet Flow. Comparison of the Efficiency

In the second test, the program was launched on $p = 1, 2, 4... 4096$ and 6144 cores with two conditions: with and without balancing. The cellular array sizes are equal to $I = 100 \cdot p$, J

= 10. Size I is taken depending on the number of cores p in order to eliminate harmful influence of the hardware over the runtime. Size J is selected tiny to diminish the test execution time. At the initial state, the particles density is invariable along j and is arranged linearly in lengthways i from 70 particles per cell (at $i = 0$) to 7 particles per cell (at $i = I - 1$). These boundary conditions are provided throughout the whole simulation process. Hence, the flow escapes along i in the positive direction. Special boundary cells [(0, 0), (0, 9)] and [(I – 1, 0), (I – 1, 199)] provide the required particles density. The walls [(0, 0), (I – 1, 0)] and [(0, 9), (I – 1, 9)] flanking the cellular array keep the flow inside.

Figure 6 shows the balancing efficiency (averaged over 100 iterations):

$$eff_b = \sum_{rank=0}^{p-1} t(rank) \Big/ p \cdot \max\left\{t(rank) : rank = \overline{0, p-1}\right\},$$

where $t(rank)$ is the total collision functions runtime at the cells with $i_A(rank) \le i < i_B(rank)$, $(0 \le rank < p - 1)$. This efficiency indicates only the cores loading imbalance, not including the communication overhead.

Figure 7 shows the parallelization efficiency of the program with the communication overhead (also averaged over 100 iterations): $eff = t_1 / t_p$, where t_1 is the executive time of the program on one core, t_p is the executive time of the program on p cores. Due to the fact that cellular array size I is proportional to the number of cores p, factor p in the denominator is missing.

Analysis of Figure 6 and Figure 7 leads to the following conclusions:

1. Without balancing the execution time, as expected, is greater than with balancing.
2. The efficiency remains acceptable even for a large number of cores.
3. With balancing the time, the loss of dependence on the cores number is logarithmic.
4. Communications between the cores bring an additional overhead of execution time, which is increased with increasing the number of cores.
5. For a great number of cores ($p > 2000$), the decrease of performance due to communications predominates the decrease generated by the loading imbalance. This shows the applicability of the diffusion balancing algorithm to any number of cores. With the increase of the cores number, the share of losses due to the imbalance is reduced and the share of communication losses is increased.

5.5. Comparison of the Implementation Efficiency for the LGA and the PIC-Method

In [8], the diffusion algorithm of balancing for the method of particles in cells (PIC) is considered. There, in particular, a program runtime is given for a different number of cores with and without balancing. The amount of particles used there is changed up to 800 thousand. We made the test in which 800 thousand of cells were used, and compared the efficiencies. Unfortunately, in [8] there is no data on runtime on one core, therefore, the efficiency was computed in relation to the runtime on two cores: $eff_2 = 2 \cdot t_2 / p \cdot t_p$, where t_2 is the program runtime on two cores, and t_p is the program runtime on p cores.

Figure 8 shows, that the efficiency of the diffusion algorithm of balancing used in the LGA is comparable to that used in the PIC-method.

Conclusion

In this chapter, a new cellular-automaton flow FHP-MP model, in which more than one particle is enabled in a cell with equal velocity vectors, is proposed. The computing experiments were carried out with this model; they demonstrate a correlation of the new model with the classical FHP model and with the physical laws. Experimentally, the obtained velocity field matches the Poiseuille parabola. The maximum flow velocity in the experiments is a little larger than the velocity in the FHP model. In the new model, it is possible to augment the initial concentration of particles. The obtained flow velocity is considerably superior than that for the classical model. Therefore, we hope that the FHP-MP model allows us to simulate a turbulent flow. The experiments with a valve and a circle-shaped obstacle are plausible to us, because the flows with whirls were obtained in the experiments and the Kármán vortex street behind the obstacle is in sight.

Our investigations show that, when simulating the flow using multi-particle LGA, the dynamic load balancing is not only necessary, but it can also be successfully used. With the acceptable efficiency, the number of used cores is limited by the communication speed rather than the load imbalance. In comparison with balancing by the PIC method, balancing by the LGA shows reasonable results. It is worth noting, that in the future LGA models, the transitions rules will be more complicated, more imbalanced and the balancing will be more urgent.

References

[1] Hardy, J., Pomeau, Y., de Pazzis, O., (1973). 2D Lattice-Gas Model, *J. Math. Phys.*, 14, 1746.

[2] Frisch, U., Hasslacher, B., Pomeau, Y., (1986). Lattice-Gas Automata for Navier-Stokes Equations, *Phys. Rev. Lett.*, 56, 1505.

[3] Rothman, D. H., Zaleski, S., (1997). *Lattice-Gas Cellular Automata: Simple Models of Complex Hydrodynamics*, Cambridge University Press.

[4] Bandman, O.L., (2005). Cellular-Automata Models of Spatial Dynamics. *System Informatics*, 10, 57–113 (in Russian).

[5] Medvedev, Yu., (2008). The FHP-MP model as multiparticle Lattice-Gas. *Bulletin of the Novosibirsk Computing Center. Series: Computer Science*, 27, 83–91.

[6] Medvedev, Yu., (2009). Cellular-Automaton Simulation of a Cumulative Jet Formation. *LNCS*, 5698, 250–259.

[7] Hu, Y.F., Blake, R.J., (2000). Load Balancing for Unstructured Mesh Applications. http://www.research.att.com/~yifanhu/PROJECT/pdcp_siam/pdcp_siam.html.

[8] Kraeva, M.A., Malyshkin, V.E., (2001). Assembly Technology for Parallel Realization of Numerical Models on MIMD-Multicomputers. *International Journal on Future Generation Computer Systems*, 17, 6, 755-765.

In: Parallel Programming
Editor: Mikhail S. Tarkov

ISBN: 978-1-63321-957-1

Chapter 7

PARALLEL SIMULATION OF ASYNCHRONOUS CELLULAR AUTOMATA

Konstantin Kalgin*
Institute of Computational Mathematics and Mathematical Geophysics,
SB RAS, Novosibirsk, Russia

Abstract

Overview and experimental comparative study of parallel algorithms of asynchronous cellular automata simulation is presented. The algorithms are tested for the model of physicochemical process of surface CO + O2 reaction over the supported Pd nanoparticles on different parallel computers. For testing we use shared memory computers, distributed memory computers (i.e. clusters), and graphical processing unit. Characterization of these algorithms in respect of methods of parallelism maintenance is given. A new domain specific language CACHE and its translator into C and Processing are presented, where the domain is a set of cellular automata models of physicochemical processes.

Keywords: asynchronous cellular automata, parallel algorithm, domain specific language

1. Introduction

Asynchronous cellular automata (ACA) are used for simulation of physical and chemical processes on molecular level, for example, to study oscillatory chemical surface reactions [1, 2], absorption, sublimation and diffusion of atoms in the epitaxial growth processes [3]. Simulation of natural processes requires huge cellular space and millions of iterative steps for obtaining the real scene of the process. Therefore, it requires a lot of computing power. Unfortunately, ACA can not be parallelized so easily as synchronous cellular automata (SCA). As distinct to SCA, ACA functioning is a sequential application of transition rule to randomly selected cells. The cells are selected with equal probabilities and irrespective of the process history.

*E-mail address: kalgin@ssd.sscc.ru. The author was supported by the Grant of the President of the Russian Federation for Young Russian Researchers (project no. MK-3644.2014.9).

Parallelization of the ACA is performed by domain decomposition method: each process hosts its own domain of cells and stores the copies of boundary cells of neighboring processes. A parallel algorithm simulation should preserve the behavioral properties of ACA: **I**ndependence, **F**airness, **C**orrectness, and **E**fficiency. Independence means independent selection of cells during simulation. Fairness means that different cells are selected with equal probabilities. Correctness means deadlock-absence and coherence of boundary cell states and corresponding copies in different processes. Efficiency implies that T_k is less then T_1 for some k. Here T_k is the total time of parallel algorithm execution on k processors, and T_1 is the total time of sequential algorithm execution on one processor.

There are several parallel algorithms of ACA simulation on computers with different architectures. In [4] an algorithm suitable for shared memory computers only is proposed. Parallel algorithms for distributed memory computers are presented in [5, 6]. In addition, [7] and [8] describe a practical approach to parallel simulation of ACA. Where the given ACA is transformed into a synchronous one, called block-synchronous cellular automata (BSCA), that approximates its evolution and also provides easy parallelization.

In this chapter we present comparative study of the mentioned above parallel algorithms and their efficiency on computers with different architectures. All tested combinations of computer architectures and parallel algorithm implementations are presented at Table 1. We do not present results for the algorithm given in [5] as far as additional costs of the parallel computations maintaining are too large for the model under consideration.

Table 1. Tested combinations of computer architectures and parallel algorithm implementations

	Shared memory	Distributed memory	Graphical processing unit
[4]	+	–	–
[6]	+	+	–
[7,8]	+	+	+

Taking into account the diversity of computer architectures, we can see that the following versions of implementation may be required by researchers:

- serial implementation with ability to visualize the process interactively,
- parallel implementation on a multicore computer with shared memory,
- parallel implementation on a cluster,
- parallel implementation on GPUs.

To satisfy the above requirements an attempt is made: a new domain specific language CACHE (Cellular Automata for CHEmical models) and its translator into C and Processing [15] is presented. The domain is a set of cellular automata models of physico-chemical processes. The language and the translator are intended for studying such processes. The translator allows to obtain both serial (C, Processing) and parallel (C+MPI, C+POSIX Threads) implementations of a cellular automata model. Additionally, one can easily visualize the process interactively, create movie, and publish Java-applet in the Internet using Processing.

2. Asynchronous Cellular Automata

2.1. Formal Representation of CA

Cellular automaton is specified by the following tuple:

$$CA = \langle Z^d, A, \Theta, M \rangle \tag{1}$$

where Z^d is a finite set of *cell coordinates*, A is an *alphabet*, i.e. a finite set of cell states, Θ is a *local transition rule*, and M is an *iteration mode*.

Further we use two dimensional rectangular space Z^2:

$$Z^2 = \{(i,j) \mid 1 \le i \le N_x,\ 1 \le j \le N_y\} \tag{2}$$

with periodic boundaries. A pair $(\mathbf{x}, a) \in Z^2 \times A$ is called a *cell*, where $a \in A$ is a cell state, $\mathbf{x} \in Z^2$ is its coordinates. Set of cells $\Omega = \{(\mathbf{x_i}, a_i)\} \subset Z^2 \times A$ is called a *cellular array* if there does not exist a pair of cells with equal coordinates and $\{\mathbf{x} \mid (\mathbf{x}, a) \in \Omega\} = Z^2$. Since between the cells in a cellular array and their coordinates there exists a one-to-one correspondence, we further identify each cell with its coordinates.

The *local transition rule* Θ is a probabilistic function:

$$\Theta : A^{|B_\Theta|} \times A^{|C_\Theta|} \xrightarrow{p} A^{|B_\Theta|}, \tag{3}$$

where the *base template* B_Θ and the *context template* C_Θ are lists of *naming functions* $\phi : Z^2 \to Z^2$, $B_\Theta = \{\phi_1^B, \phi_2^B, \ldots, \phi_{|B_\Theta|}^B\}$, $C_\Theta = \{\phi_1^C, \phi_2^C, \ldots, \phi_{|C_\Theta|}^C\}$. These templates determine *base* and *context neighborhoods* of a cell $\mathbf{x}$:

$$B_\Theta(\mathbf{x}) = \{\phi_1^B(\mathbf{x}), \ldots, \phi_{|B_\Theta|}^B(\mathbf{x})\}, \quad C_\Theta(\mathbf{x}) = \{\phi_1^C(\mathbf{x}), \ldots, \phi_{|C_\Theta|}^C(\mathbf{x})\}. \tag{4}$$

Additionally, context and base templates should meet the following condition:

$$\forall \mathbf{x} \in Z^2 \ : \ B_\Theta(\mathbf{x}) \cap C_\Theta(\mathbf{x}) = \emptyset. \tag{5}$$

Further the following neighborhoods are used:

$$T_{13}(\mathbf{x}) = \{\mathbf{x} + \mathbf{v_0}, \mathbf{x} + \mathbf{v_1}, \ldots, \mathbf{x} + \mathbf{v_{12}}\}, \tag{6}$$

$$T_9(\mathbf{x}) = \{\mathbf{x} + \mathbf{v_0}, \mathbf{x} + \mathbf{v_1}, \ldots, \mathbf{x} + \mathbf{v_8}\}, \tag{7}$$

$$T_5(\mathbf{x}) = \{\mathbf{x} + \mathbf{v_0}, \mathbf{x} + \mathbf{v_1}, \ldots, \mathbf{x} + \mathbf{v_4}\}, \tag{8}$$

$$T_1(\mathbf{x}) = \{\mathbf{x} + \mathbf{v_0}\}, \tag{9}$$

where $V = \{\mathbf{v_0}, \mathbf{v_1}, \ldots, \mathbf{v_{12}}\} = \{(0,0), (0,1), (1,0), (0,-1), (-1,0), (1,1), (1,-1), (-1,1), (-1,-1), (0,2), (2,0), (0,-2), (-2,0)\}$ (Fig. 1).

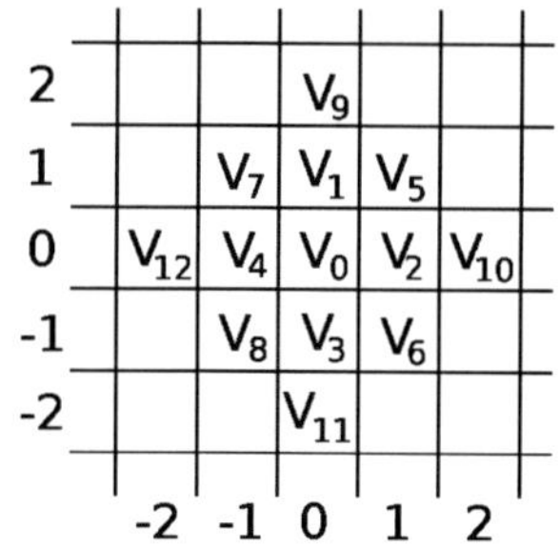

Figure 1. Neighborhood $T_{13}(6)$.

An *application of the local transition rule* (3) *to a cell* $\mathbf{x}$ results in replacing states of cells from the base neighborhood $B_\Theta(\mathbf{x})$ with next states $\Theta(S_\Theta)$, $S_\Theta(\mathbf{x})$ being a list of states of cells from $B_\Theta(\mathbf{x}) \cup C_\Theta(\mathbf{x})$.

Simulation process of CA is split into *iterations*. An iteration comprises $|Z^2| = N_x \cdot N_y$ local transition rule applications. The iteration mode M defines the order of Θ application. There are many iteration modes. Here we use three of them: synchronous, asynchronous, and block-synchronous modes. In *synchronous* mode a local transition rule is applied simultaneously to all cells, this means that all cell states depend only on states from previous iteration. In *asynchronous* mode a local transition rule is sequentially applied $|Z^2|$ times to randomly chosen cells. To define *block-synchronous* mode we have to define a partition $\{S_0, S_2, \ldots, S_{w-1}\}$ of the set of cell coordinates Z^2 with additional condition to be met by each subset S_k:

$$\forall \mathbf{x}_1, \mathbf{x}_2 \in S_k \, : \, B_\Theta(\mathbf{x}_1) \cap C_\Theta(\mathbf{x}_2) = \emptyset. \tag{10}$$

In block-synchronous mode each iteration consists of w stages. At each stage a local transition rule is simultaneously applied to all cells from randomly chosen subset S_k.

2.2. Formal Representation of Local Transition Rule

Usually, local transition rules of CA models of physico-chemical processes are expressed as a *composition of elementary substitutions* [16], where each elementary substitution corresponds to elementary physico-chemical process (diffusion, adsorption, desorption, reaction, etc.). The composition of elementary substitutions is called a *composed substitution*. Before formal definition of composed substitution let us define the *elementary substitution*.

Elementary substitution Θ_{sub} is a probabilistic function $\Theta_{sub} : A^{|B_{\Theta_{sub}}|} \times A^{|C_{\Theta_{sub}}|} \xrightarrow{p} A^{|B_{\Theta_{sub}}|}$ with its own base and context templates, which is written in the following form:

$$\Theta_{sub} : \{a_1, a_2, \ldots, a_m\} \xrightarrow[cond]{p} \{a'_1, a'_2, \ldots, a'_{m'}\}, \tag{11}$$

where $m = |B_{\Theta_{sub}}| + |C_{\Theta_{sub}}|$, $m' = |B_{\Theta_{sub}}|$, $a_1, \ldots, a_m$ are current states of cells from base and context neighborhood, and $a'_1, \ldots, a'_{m'}$ are next states of cells from the base neighborhood. Application of Θ_{sub} to a cell $\mathbf{x}$ results in changing the states of cells $B_{\Theta_{sub}}(\mathbf{x})$ with probability p only if condition $cond(a_1, a_2, \ldots, a_m)$ satisfied. Here probability p and states a'_i may be functions of current states, $p = p(a_1, a_2, \ldots, a_m)$, $a'_i = f_i(a_1, a_2, \ldots, a_m)$.

Let us return to the definition of a *composed substitution*. A composed substitution is a set of several elementary and/or other composed substitutions combined by composition rules. The most used rules of composition are *random execution* (R), *sequential execution* (S), and *randomly ordered sequential execution* (RS). These rules are given by

$$\Theta_R = R(\Theta_1, p_1; \Theta_2, p_2; \ldots, \Theta_n, p_n), \tag{12}$$

$$\Theta'_R = R(\Theta_1, \Theta_2, \ldots \Theta_n), \tag{13}$$

$$\Theta_S = S(\Theta_1, \Theta_2, \ldots \Theta_n), \tag{14}$$

$$\Theta_{RS} = RS(\Theta_1, \Theta_2, \ldots \Theta_n). \tag{15}$$

Additionally, for each Θ_i, $i = 1 \ldots n$, a cell to which Θ_i is applied should be defined by a function $\varphi_i : Z^2 \to Z^2$:

$$B_{\Theta_R}(\mathbf{x}) = B_{\Theta'_R}(\mathbf{x}) = B_{\Theta_S}(\mathbf{x}) = B_{\Theta_{RS}}(\mathbf{x}) = \bigcup_{i=1}^{n} B_{\Theta_i}(\varphi_i(\mathbf{x})), \tag{16}$$

$$C_{\Theta_R}(\mathbf{x}) = C_{\Theta'_R}(\mathbf{x}) = C_{\Theta_S}(\mathbf{x}) = C_{\Theta_{RS}}(\mathbf{x}) = \bigcup_{i=1}^{n} C_{\Theta_i}(\varphi_i(\mathbf{x})) \setminus \bigcup_{i=1}^{n} B_{\Theta_i}(\varphi_i(\mathbf{x})). \tag{17}$$

The result of Θ_R application to $\mathbf{x}$ coincides with result of Θ_i application to $\varphi_i(\mathbf{x})$ with probability $\frac{p_i}{\sum_{k=1}^{n} p_k}$. If p_i are all equal then they may be omitted (13). The result of Θ_S application to $\mathbf{x}$ coincides with sequential applications of $\Theta_1, \Theta_2, \ldots, \Theta_n$ to $\varphi_1(\mathbf{x}), \varphi_2(\mathbf{x}), \ldots, \varphi_n(\mathbf{x})$, respectively. The result of Θ_{RS} application to $\mathbf{x}$ coincides with sequential applications of randomly ordered $\Theta_{\tau_1}, \Theta_{\tau_2}, \ldots, \Theta_{\tau_n}$ to $\varphi_{\tau_1}(\mathbf{x}), \varphi_{\tau_2}(\mathbf{x}), \ldots, \varphi_{\tau_n}(\mathbf{x})$, , respectively.

Sometimes it is useful to define templates of a substitution Θ' on a group of cells, rather than on a single one:

$$T_{\Theta'}(\mathbf{x}_1, \ldots, \mathbf{x}_m) = \{\phi'_1(\mathbf{x}_1, \ldots, \mathbf{x}_m), \ldots, \phi'_{|T_{\Theta'}|}(\mathbf{x}_1, \ldots, \mathbf{x}_m)\}, \tag{18}$$

where $\phi'_i : \underbrace{Z^2 \times \ldots \times Z^2}_{m} \to Z^2$. Definition of elementary and composed substitutions, and its applications can be easily modified according to this template form. Further the following templates are used:

$$T_2(\mathbf{x}_1, \mathbf{x}_2) = \{\mathbf{x}_1, \mathbf{x}_2\}, \tag{19}$$

$$T_4(\mathbf{x}_1, \mathbf{x}_2, \mathbf{x}_3, \mathbf{x}_4) = \{\mathbf{x}_1, \mathbf{x}_2, \mathbf{x}_3, \mathbf{x}_4\}, \tag{20}$$

$$T'_5(\mathbf{x}_1, \ldots, \mathbf{x}_5) = \{\mathbf{x}_1, \ldots, \mathbf{x}_5\}. \tag{21}$$

3. Parallel Algorithms

In papers [4, 5] ACA is defined as a discrete event model that evolves in continuous time. Transition rule applications at different cells occur asynchronously at random times. These applications form a Poisson process for each cell. For different cells these Poisson processes are independent, and the application rate is the same for each cell. Parallelization of the ACA model is performed by domain decomposition: each process hosts its own domain of cells and the copies of boundary cells of neighboring processes. For correct simulation of Poisson process for each cell, every computing process controls its own local time. The *process' local time* is the next time of transition rule application to a newly selected cell from its domain. A process increments its own local time by an exponentially distributed pseudorandom number after each transition rule application.

In [4] an algorithm suitable for shared memory computers is proposed. Each process repeats the following steps while its own local time is less than predefined T_{max}: (1) selects a random cell from its domain, (2) waits for the situation when minimal local time of neighboring processes is greater than its own local time for the cells belonging to the domain boundary, (3) applies transition rule to the cell, and (4) increments its own local time according to Poisson distribution. **I**ndependence and **F**airness of the algorithm are provided by independence and fairness of random cell selection from the domain and the way of local time incrementing. **C**orrectness is provided by the synchronization based on domain's local time briefly described in step (2). **E**fficiency is provided by the property that boundary cells are selected infrequently in large domains.

In [5] a modified Time Warp algorithm is presented. Time Warp [10] is an optimistic parallel algorithm for simulation of any discrete event model on distributed memory computers. The main idea of the parallel Time Warp algorithm is as follows. In contrast to the previous algorithm, application of the transition rule and computing new local time are performed without waiting for neighboring processes (each process "hopes" that neighboring processes will not change boundary cell states). If a process changes a boundary cell state, then it sends a message to its neighbors called a *positive message*. When a process receives a positive message "from the future" (i.e., its own local time is less than that of the sender) it saves the message for the future processing. A situation when process receives a positive message "from the past" is called *causality error*. In this situation a recovery mechanism should be initiated. Recovery from the prematurely executed steps results in two things to be rolled back: the cellular array and the messages sent to the other processes. Rolling back the cellular array is accomplished by periodically saving updated cell states and restoring boundary cell states valid for the rolled back local time. Rolling back previously sent positive messages is accomplished by sending *anti-messages*. If a process receives an anti-message that corresponds to an unprocessed positive message, then these two messages annihilate each other and the process proceeds. If there arrives an anti-message that corresponds to a positive message already processed, then the process has made an error and is to be also rolled back. A consequence of the recovery mechanism is that more anti-messages can be sent to other processes recursively. **I**ndependence and **F**airness of the algorithm are provided in the same way as in the previous algorithm. **C**orrectness is provided by recovery mechanism from causality errors (for detail see [5]). In few words, **E**fficiency is provided by optimistic behavior of processes. However, there are some costs for saving the history of message sendings and updatings of boundary cell states. If the costs are large (with respect to effective work), then efficiency of the algorithm decreases. Also efficiency significantly depends on the following two parameters of the transition rule [5]: amount of work to be performed for the rule computing and average number of actually changed cell states after application of the rule.

In [6] an algorithm suitable for distributed memory computers is presented. ACA is defined as described in Section 2. Let us consider a sequence of randomly selected coordinates $X = \mathbf{x_1}, \mathbf{x_2}, \ldots, \mathbf{x_n}$ for an iteration. According to the decomposition of the cellular array into domains $d_1, d_2, \ldots, d_p$, we can divide the sequence X into $2p$ parts: for each domain d_k we take its internal I_k and boundary B_k subsequences. The subsequences I_k and B_k can be formed by use of uniform, exponential, and binomial pseudorandom number generators. The algorithm is based on the stochastic properties of I_k and B_k, and on planning the order of interactions between processes. The main idea of the parallel algorithm is as follows. Firstly, a process k (hosting a domain d_k) forms the pair (I_k, B_k) independently of other processes. Secondly, each process avoids unnecessary synchronizations because it is informed about neighbors' subsequences $B_{k'}$. It means that the process waits only for those new boundary cell states that will be actually used by it. Note that in the first [4] algorithm process has to wait in any case. **I**ndependence and **F**airness of the algorithm are provided by the method in which I_k and B_k are formed, for detail see [6]. **C**orrectness is provided by means of synchronization based on B_k. **E**fficiency is provided by avoiding of unnecessary synchronizations.

In [7, 8] a practical analogue of ACA is described. This model is called Block-Synchronous Cellular Automata due to the ways of asynchronism reduction. Iteration of BSCA is a sequence of m stages. On each stage the transition rule is synchronously applied to all cells from a randomly selected set $S_i \subset \Omega$, where $\{S_1, S_2, \ldots, S_m\}$ is a partitioning of cellular array Ω with the following properties:

$$\bigcup_{i=1}^{m} S_i = \Omega \tag{22}$$

$$\forall i\ \forall j : S_i \cap S_j = \emptyset \tag{23}$$

$$\forall i\ \forall j : |S_i| = |S_j| \tag{24}$$

$$\forall i\ \forall a \in S_i\ \forall b \in S_i : T(a) \cap T(b) = \emptyset \tag{25}$$

Such a reduction of asynchronism (at the expense of **I**ndependence) results in very simple parallel algorithm. In this algorithm processes have to synchronize each with other (send and receive new boundary cell states) only between stages. High **e**fficiency of the algorithm is provided by rare process synchronizations. **C**orrectness and **F**airness are provided by properties (25) and (22-24), respectively.

4. Computers Architecture Overview

For testing the algorithms given above, we use computers with three types of architecture: multicores and multiprocessors with shared memory, a cluster with distributed memory and graphical processing unit (GPU). Parameters of computers with shared memory *Core-i7* and *SMP-8* are given at the Table 2.

Cluster *MVS-100k* consists of SMP-8 nodes connected through Infiniband.

GPU *GTX-280* consists of a 240-core processor and 2Gb off-chip *global memory*. The cores are grouped in 8-core *multiprocessors*. Each multiprocessor has its own 16Kb on-chip *shared memory* and 32Kb *register file*. Note, that multiprocessor belongs to SIMD (Single

Table 2. Multicores' and multiprocessors' parameters

	Processors	GHz	Total cores	Memory controller
Core-i7	1×Intel Core i7	2.6	4	integrated
SMP-8	2×Intel Xeon 5140	2.3	8	separate

Instruction Multiple Data) class in Flynn's taxonomy: at each clock all eight cores perform the same instruction but using different arguments.

Parallel program intended for running on GTX-280 consists of thousands of threads grouped in *blocks*. Each block consists of not more than 512 threads. One block of threads can be run on one multiprocessor only. But one multiprocessor can manage up to 8 blocks. Threads of the same block can communicate all to all through the shared memory of multiprocessor and synchronize. But threads from different blocks can not communicate and can not synchronize in the same way.

Unfortunately, one can not directly implement parallel algorithms of ACA simulation mentioned above with exception to BSCA. The reason is in SIMD architecture of multiprocessor and impossibility of synchronization of threads belonging to different blocks.

5. Surface Reactions on Palladium

The model of oscillatory dynamics of the $CO+O_2$ reaction over the supported Pd nanoparticles is described in [2]. This model is a combination of the model for the $CO + O_2$ reaction over the Pd(110) single crystal [11] and the stochastic model for the imitating the supported nanoparticle with dynamically changing shape and surface morphology [12]. The model consists of the following processes: CO adsorption $(\Theta_1, \Theta_2, \Theta_6)$, CO desorption $(\Theta_3, \Theta_4, \Theta_7)$, O_2 adsorption (Θ_9^i), CO diffusion $(\Theta_{11}^i, \Theta_{12}^i, \Theta_{13}^i)$, Pd's atoms diffusion (Θ_{14}^i), subsurface oxygen O_{ss} formation (Θ_5), $CO + O$ and $CO + O_{ss}$ reaction $(\Theta_8, \Theta_{10}^i, \Theta_{15}^i)$. In terms of ACA this model can be described as follows.

State a of a cell $\mathbf{x}$ is written as $[n, \alpha]$, where n is the number of Pd atoms, $n \in \{0, 1, 2, \ldots\}$, and α is the state of the Pd surface, $\alpha \in \{\emptyset, CO, O, O_{ss}, CO.O_{ss}\}$.

$$A = \{0, 1, 2, \ldots\} \times \{\emptyset, CO, O, O_{ss}, CO.O_{ss}\}$$

$$\Theta = R(\Theta^1, \Theta^2, \Theta^3, \Theta^4)$$

$$\Theta^i = S\left(R\left(\Theta_1, p_1; \ldots \Theta_8, p_8; \Theta_9^i, p_9; \Theta_{10}^i, p_{10}; S\left(\Theta_{11}^i, \ldots \Theta_{14}^i\right), p_{11}\right) \Theta_{15}^i\right)$$

$$\Theta_{15}^i = RS\left(\Theta_{15}^{1,0}, \ldots, \Theta_{15}^{5,0}, \Theta_{15}^{0,1}, \ldots, \Theta_{15}^{0,5}, \Theta_{15}^{1,i}, \ldots, \Theta_{15}^{5,i}, \Theta_{15}^{i,1}, \ldots, \Theta_{15}^{i,5}\right)$$

$$T_\Theta(\mathbf{x}) = T_{\Theta^i}(\mathbf{x}) = T_{13}(\mathbf{x})$$

$$T_{\Theta_j}(\mathbf{x}) = T_1(\mathbf{x})$$

$$T_{\Theta_j^i}(\mathbf{x}) = T_1(\mathbf{x}) \cup T_1(\mathbf{x} + \mathbf{v_i}), \quad j = 9, 10, 11, 12, 13$$

$$T_{\Theta_j^i}(\mathbf{x}) = T_5(\mathbf{x}) \cup T_5(\mathbf{x} + \mathbf{v_i}), \quad j = 14, 15$$

$$T_{\Theta_{15}^{k,m}}(\mathbf{x}) = T_1(\mathbf{x} + \mathbf{v_k}) \cup T_1(\mathbf{x} + \mathbf{v_m})$$

$$\Theta_1 : \{[n, \emptyset]\} \to \{[n, CO]\}$$

$$\Theta_2 : \{[0, \emptyset]\} \to \{[0, CO]\}$$

$$\Theta_3 : \{[n, CO]\} \to \{[n, \emptyset]\}$$

$$\Theta_4 : \{[0, CO]\} \to \{[0, \emptyset]\}$$

$$\Theta_5 : \{[n, O]\} \to \{[n, O_{ss}]\}$$

$$\Theta_6 : \{[n, O_{ss}]\} \to \{[n, CO.O_{ss}]\}$$

$$\Theta_7 : \{[n, CO.O_{ss}]\} \to \{[n, O_{ss}]\}$$

$$\Theta_8 : \{[n, CO.O_{ss}]\} \to \{[n, \emptyset]\}$$

$$\Theta_9^i : \quad \{[n, \emptyset], [n, \emptyset]\} \to \{[n, O], [n, O]\}$$

$$\Theta_{10}^i : \quad \{[n, CO], [n, O_{ss}]\} \to \{[n, \emptyset], [n, \emptyset]\}$$

$$\Theta_{11}^i : \quad \{[n, CO], [m, \emptyset]\} \to \{[n, \emptyset], [m, CO]\}$$

$$\Theta_{12}^i : \quad \{[n, CO], [m, O_{ss}]\} \to \{[n, \emptyset], [m, CO.O_{ss}]\}$$

$$\Theta_{13}^i : \quad \{[n, CO.O_{ss}], [m, O_{ss}]\} \to \{[n, O_{ss}], [m, CO.O_{ss}]\}$$

$$\Theta_{14}^i : \quad \{[n+1, \emptyset], a_1, \ldots, a_4, [m, \emptyset], a_6, \ldots, a_9\} \xrightarrow{p'} \{[n, \emptyset], a_1, \ldots, a_4, [m+1, \emptyset], a_6, \ldots, a_9\}$$

$$\Theta_{15}^{k,j} : \quad \{[n, CO], [n, O]\} \to \{[n, \emptyset], [n, \emptyset]\}$$

Here for Θ_{14}^i the states a_i are $a_i = [n_i, \alpha_i]$, and the probability p' is the probability of actual Pd atom movement, which depends on changing of total energy of atoms connections ΔE, $p' = exp(-\Delta E/kT)$. The probabilities p_i depend on rates of processes k_i, $p_i = k_i/\sum_{j=1}^{11} k_j$. For concrete values $k_1, k_2, \ldots, k_{11}$ and concrete energies of atoms connections see [2].

The algorithm [4] is implemented as a multithreaded program using POSIX Threads. Each thread controls its own local time and hosts a part of the cellular array (domain). The algorithm [6] is implemented using MPI (Message Passing Interface). For sending short messages containing new cell states MPI_Bsend (buffered mode) is used. The algorithm [7, 8] is implemented using MPI and OpenMP. In each SMP-8 node one process with eight threads is executed. Using of OpenMP reduces the number of actually executed processes and therefore, also reduces communication costs. For GTX-280 the algorithm [7, 8] is implemented using CUDA [9]. Each thread deals with the neighborhood of a particular cell. First, it loads states of the neighboring cells to the shared memory. Then the thread computes new states for the neighborhood. After that the thread puts new states back to the global memory.

Results of testing on shared memory computers, cluster and GPU are presented at Fig. 2, Fig. 3, and Table 3, respectively. All tests are performed with several cellular array sizes ($1000 \times 1000, 2000 \times 2000, 4000 \times 4000, 8000 \times 8000$). As usuall, the efficiency of parallelization is $E_p = T_1/(pT_p)$.

6. CACHE Language

In the CACHE language the following concepts are to be defined: iteration mode, type of cell state, several parameters, local transition rule, several counters, initialization function,

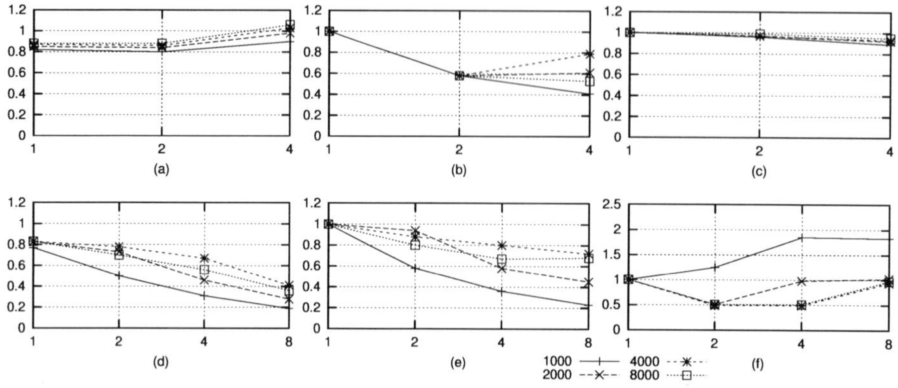

Figure 2. Efficiency of the parallel algorithms ((a, d) for [4], (b, e) for [6], and (c, f) for [7,8]) for Core-i7 (a, b, c) and SMP-8 (d, e, f). Along x-axis are the numbers of used cores, along y-axis efficiency is shown.

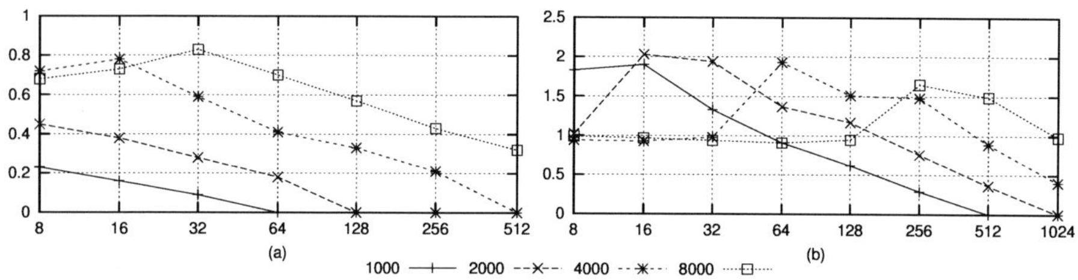

Figure 3. Efficiency of the parallel algorithms ((a) for [6], and (b) for [7,8]) for MVS-100k. Along x-axis are the numbers of used cores, along y-axis efficiency is shown.

and color determination function. Description syntax of initialization function and color determination function is not considered here.

6.1. Iteration Mode

Cellular automata iteration mode M is defined by one line:

Ex.1: `iteration : asynchronous(K)`

Here `K` may be a natural number or an arithmetic expression which means that each iteration of the model comprises `K` iterations as defined in Section 2. The following modes now are supported: `asynchronous`, `synchronous`, `blocksynchronous5`, `blocksynchronous9`, `blocksynchronous13`, `blocksynchronous25`. Each mode `blocksynchronousW`, where `W` is one of `5`, `9`, or `13`, corresponds to the template T_W (6-8) . For the block-synchronous modes the sets S_k (10) are defined as follows:

Table 3. Acceleration of the [7,8] algorithm implemented on GPU in comparison with that on Core-i7

	1000	2000	4000	8000
GTX-280	25	31	34	35

$$S_{k=0...4}^{blocksynchronous5} = \{(i,j) : i + 3j = k\,(mod\,5)\}, \quad (26)$$

$$S_{k=0...8}^{blocksynchronous9} = \{(i,j) : i - \left\lfloor \frac{i}{3} \right\rfloor + 3(j - \left\lfloor \frac{j}{3} \right\rfloor) = k\,(mod\,9)\}, \quad (27)$$

$$S_{k=0...12}^{blocksynchronous13} = \{(i,j) : i + 5j = k\,(mod\,13)\}, \quad (28)$$

$$S_{k=0...24}^{blocksynchronous25} = \{(i,j) : i - \left\lfloor \frac{i}{5} \right\rfloor + 5(j - \left\lfloor \frac{j}{5} \right\rfloor) = k\,(mod\,25)\}. \quad (29)$$

6.2. Type of Cell State

Cell state is of primitive, set, or structure type. A primitive type is one out of: `byte`, `int` or `float`. In the case of set type, a set of possible cell state values is defined by a list of identifiers. The structure type is a list of fields, where each field has a name and a type. A field is also of primitive, set, or structure type. Several examples of cell state type definition:

Ex.2:
```
cell : int;
cell : set{ empty, stable, movable };
cell : struct{
  h : int;
  a : set{ CO, O, Oss, CO_Oss, Empty };
};
```

6.3. Parameters

Description of a parameter starts from `'param'`. Parameter is a variable of primitive type visible among all arithmetico-logical expressions in cellular automata definition. Value of parameter by default is to be written in the text as follows:

Ex.3:
```
param float probCOdes = 0.2;
param float probO2ads = 0.1;
```

In addition to user-defined parameters, there are two built-in integer parameters `N` and `M`: sizes of cellular array N_y and N_x, respectively. Default value for `N` and `M` is `100`.

The default value of a parameter can be changed by program arguments:

Ex.4:
```
./ca -probCOdes 0.5 -N 1024 -M 128
```

6.4. Elementary Substitution

In the language base and context templates of elementary substitution (11) are

$$B_{\Theta_{sub}}(\mathbf{x}_1, \ldots, \mathbf{x}_m) = \{\mathbf{x}_1, \ldots, \mathbf{x}_{m'}\}, \quad (30)$$
$$C_{\Theta_{sub}}(\mathbf{x}_1, \ldots, \mathbf{x}_m) = \{\mathbf{x}_{m'+1}, \ldots, \mathbf{x}_m\}. \quad (31)$$

Template of a composed substitution is automatically computed according to (16) and it is not given directly in the text of cellular automata definition.

Description of an elementary substitution starts from `'sub'`. Two lists including initial and next cell states enclosed in square brackets are separated by `'->'`. Structured state is written as a list of field values enclosed in round brackets. In the case of states of structure/primitive type each field/state is stated as a concrete value, or as a designator, or as any-value expression. A concrete value is defined by arithmetic expression. A designator is an identifier not defined as parameter or as element of a set type. The any-value expression is written as a dot. The any-value expression in the list of initial cell states means "this value is not important", and in the list of next cell states means "do not change this value". Probability of actual state changing is represented by arithmetic expression which follows the symbol '`%`'. Condition of actual state changing of the elementary substitution is represented by an explicit and an implicit part. The explicit part of the condition is written in round brackets of `if` statement. The implicit part is derived from designators and concrete values/states listed in the list of initial cell states.

Consider some examples of elementary substitution definition:

Ex.5:
```
sub stabilization:  [ movable, a, b, c, d ]->[ stable ] %0.1
                    if( a==stable||b==stable||c==stable||d==stable )
```

Here `stabilization` is the name of the elementary substitution. Base template of the substitution is T_1 (9), and context template is $T_5' \backslash T_1$ according to (30,31). In the first square brackets, `movable` is a concrete value of the first cell state, `a`, `b`, `c` and `d` are designators of other four cell states. In the second square brackets next concrete state `stable` of the first cell is indicated. The last four cell states are not changed by application of the substitution. Implicit part of condition is represented by indicating the concrete value `movable` in the first square brackets: it means that state of the first cell is to be `movable`.

Ex.6:
```
sub ads02:  [ (n>0 , Empty), (n, Empty) ] -> [ (., 0), (., 0) ]
```

Base template of the substitution is T_2' (19), and context template is empty according to (30,31). Here two occurrences of `n` means that values of the first fields of two structured cell states is to be equal. It is the second way to specify implicit part of condition. The third way to specify implicit part of condition is using `A B C` expressions, where `A` is a designator of the value, `C` is an arithmetic expression, and `B` is one of `>`, `<`, `>=`, or `<=`.

6.5. Composed Substitution

Description of a composed substitution starts from '`csub`', which is followed by its name and a list of identifiers in round brackets. These identifiers are designators of cells to which the substitution are applied. To compose several substitutions one is to write the name of a composition rule (`random` for *random execution*, `seq` for *sequential execution*, and `random_order` for *randomly ordered sequential execution* rule) and then a list of rule names with arguments. A comma-separated list of rule names is enclosed in curly brackets. A comma-separated list of arguments is enclosed in round brackets. The arguments determine cells the substitution is to be applied to. Probabilities for substitution executions, which may be omitted in `random` composition rule, are represented by arithmetic expression after '`%`' symbol.

Ex.7:
```
csub rule( x )  :  random{
        ads02(x, x+T5(1)) %0.25,
        ads02(x, x+T5(2)) %(0.5/2.0),
        ads02(x, x+T5(3)) %(1.0/4.0),
        ads02(x, x+T5(4)) %0.25
}
```

Here an expression `x+T5(i)` determines i'th neighboring cell from $T_5(\mathbf{x})$ (8). In the language neighborhood functions `TW(i)`, where `W` is on of `5`, `9`, `13`, `and 25`, are also implemented. For this example the base template of the composed substitution `rule` is T_5, and context template is empty according to (16) and (30,31).

6.6. Local Transition Rule

In the language the local transition rule is a composed substitution named `rule` with base and context templates on one cell (4).

6.7. Counters

Counter is a variable of integer type. Value of a counter equals to the number of cell states with certain properties in the cellular array. Values of all defined counters are printed at each iteration. Counters are very useful to analyse the modeling process in dynamics.

Description of counter starts from `'counter'` followed by its name, cell state and logical expression. The logical expression determines the explicit part of the condition of counter incrementing. The implicit part of the condition is represented in cell state description like it is represented in cell state description of elementary substitution (Sec. 6.4).

Ex.8:
```
counter howManyStableStates:  [ stable ]
counter countAds0: [(h , CO)] if( h > 0 )
```

7. Translator

The translator allows to obtain both serial (C, Processing) and parallel (C+POSIX Threads for multicores, C+MPI for clusters) implementations of a cellular automata model. Parallel algorithm for asynchronous cellular automata simulation is described in [17]. Techniques for efficient parallel implementation of synchronous and block-synchronous cellular automata on multicore and cluster are considered in [18].

A generated file consists of three parts:

- header (global variables definition and main function),
- implementation of local transition rule,

- implementation of iteration function.

The generated code for the first two parts depends quite slightly on target language and computer architecture. Differences are only in functions declaration, and cellular array declaration and allocation. Generation of the last part, which implements the iteration function, depends on iteration mode, target language and target computer architecture, not depending on the first two parts. All variants of iteration implementation ($iteration\, mode \times target\, language \times computer\, architecture$) are included in the translator. During the generation process the translator copies appropriate implementation to the output file.

8. Conclusion

Results of testing show that efficiency of the algorithm [4] is high on modern multicore computers (Core-i7) even for relatively small cellular arrays. The algorithm [6] delivers good efficiency only for large cellular arrays but can be run on cluster with several nodes. The reason is in additional costs of MPI sendings and receivings. Further improvement of the algorithm should be focused on multithread extensions to reduce the costs of communications. The algorithm [7, 8] shows high efficiency for all sizes of cellular array and on all parallel architectures. The reason of such high performance is in reduction of asynchronism (at the expense of **I**ndependence). For some models it is shown [7, 8] that such reduction does not affect the simulation process. Nevetheless, for each new model one has to make sure that the model allows such reduction.

References

[1] R. Danielak, A. Perera, M. Moreau, M. Frankowicz, R. Kapral. *Surface Structure and Catalytic CO Oxidation Oscillations*. arXiv:chao-dyn/9602015v1, 13 Feb 1996.

[2] Elokhin, V.I., Latkin, E.I., Matveev, A.V., and Gorodetskii, V.V. Application of Statistical Lattice Models to the Analysis of Oscillatory and Autowave Processes on the Reaction of Carbon Monoxide Oxidation over Platinum and Palladium Surfaces. *Kinetics and Catalysis*, vol. 44 (2003), N5, 672-700.

[3] Neizvestny, I.G., Shwartz, N.L., Yanovitskaya, Z.Sh., and Zverev A.V. 3D-model of epitaxial growth on porous $\{111\}$ and $\{100\}$ Si surfaces. *Computer Physics Communications*, vol.147 (2002), 272-275.

[4] B.D. Lubachevsky. Efficient parallel simulations of asynchronous cellular arrays. *Complex Systems* 1, 6 (Dec. 1987), 1099-1123.

[5] Benno J. Overeinder, Peter M. A. Sloot. Extensions to Time Warp Parallel Simulation for Spatial Decomposed Applications. *Proceedings of the Fourth United Kingdom Simulation Society Conference* (UKSim 99), pp. 67-73.

[6] K.V. Kalgin. Parallel simulation of asynchronous Cellular Automata evolution. *Bull. Nov. Comp. Center, Comp. Science*, 27(2008), 55-63.

[7] S. V. Nedea, J. J. Lukkien, P. A. J. Hilbers, A. P. J. Jansen. *Methods for Parallel Simulations of Surface Reactions*. arXiv:physics/0209017v1, 4 Sep 2002.

[8] O.L. Bandman. Parallel Simulation of Asynchronous Cellular Automata Evolution. *ACRI* 2006, *LNCS* 4173, pp.41-47, 2006.

[9] *NVIDIA CUDA Programming Guide*. http://www.nvidia.com/object/cuda_get.html (accessed May 30, 2010)

[10] D.R. Jefferson. Virtual time. *ACM Trans. on Program. Lang. and Sys.* 7, 3(July 1985). 404-425.

[11] Latkin E.I., Elokhin V.I., Matveev A.V., Gorodetskii V.V. *J. Molec. Catal. A*, Chemical, 2000, 158, 161-166.

[12] Kovalyov E.V., Elokhin V.I., Myshlyavtsev A.V. *J. Comput. Chem.*, 2008, 29, 79-86.

[13] Talia, D., Naumov, L.: Parallel Cellular Programming for Emergent Computation. In: Alfons G. Hoekstra et al. (eds.) *Simulating Complex Systems by Cellular Automata, Understanding Complex Systems*. Springer, Heidelberg (2010).

[14] *WinALT system*, http://winalt.sscc.ru.

[15] *Processing*, http://processing.org.

[16] Achasova, S.M., Bandman, O.L., Markova, V.P., Piskunov, S.V.: *Parallel Substitution Algorithm. Theory and Application*. World Scientific, Singapore (1994).

[17] Kalgin, K.V.: Comparative Study of Parallel Algorithms for Asynchronous Cellular Automata Simulation on Different Computer Architectures. ACRI-2010, *LNCS*, vol. 6350, pp. 399-408, Springer, Heidelberg (2010).

[18] Kalgin, K.V.: Implementation of algorithms with a fine-grained parallelism on GPUs. *Numerical Analysis and Applications*, DOI 10.1134/S1995423911010058 (2011).

In: Parallel Programming
Editor: Mikhail S. Tarkov

ISBN: 978-1-63321-957-1

Chapter 8

XPU: A C++ METAPROGRAMMING APPROACH TO EASE PARALLELISM EXPRESSION: PARALLELIZATION METHODOLOGY, INTERNAL DESIGN AND PRACTICAL APPLICATION

Nader Khammassi* and Jean-Christophe Le Lann†
Lab-STICC UMR CNRS 6285, ENSTA-Bretagne, Brest Cedex, France

Abstract

The continuous proliferation of multicore architectures has placed developers under great pressure to parallelize their applications in order to take advantage of such platforms. Unfortunately, traditional low-level programming models exacerbate the difficulties of building large and complex parallel applications.

Consequently, programmers are facing a complex productivity performance trade-off where they should extract enough parallelism to justify the use of a dedicated parallel programming library. High-level parallel programming models are in high-demand as they reduce the burdens on developers significantly and provide enough abstraction to accommodate hardware heterogeneity.

In this chapter, we present a task-based parallel programming model named XPU which aims to ease parallelism expression without sacrificing performances. Contrary to many parallel programming models which introduce new languages, extend existing language or define compiler annotations and thus require specialized compilers, virtual machines or extra-hardware... XPU is a pure software technology entirely based on the traditional C++ language and requires nothing more than a standard C++ compiler to be used, and therefore, improves learning curve steepness and is easily portable to many systems.

We show how XPU exploits C++ metaprogramming techniques to ease expression of several types of parallelism including task, data and temporal parallelism at all levels of granularity inside a single structured and homogeneous programming model. We describe the XPU parallelization methodology and we show through a practical signal processing application how we can apply this methodology to parallelize a sequential program at the cost

* E-mail address: nader.khammassi@ensta-bretagne.fr; Address: Lab-STICC UMR CNRS 6285, ENSTA-Bretagne, 29806 Brest Cedex 9, France

† E-mail address: jean-christophe.le_lann@ensta-bretagne.fr.

of a little amount of parallel paradigms-related extra-code while reusing the sequential legacy code without significant alteration.

This case study demonstrates the ability of the XPU programming model to provide high programmability to improve programmer productivity while delivering high performances.

Keywords: Parallel programming model, structured parallelism, skeleton, execution patterns, parallel constructs, multicore

1. Introduction

1.1. Context

With the rise of the Chip Multicore Processor (CMP), parallel computing hardware is becoming widely available on many scales: from personal computers to embedded systems to high performance supercomputers... [5-8]. While concurrent programming is still distant from the average sequential programmers, this proliferation of multicore architectures has placed mainstream developers under a great pressure to parallelize their applications as much as possible to take advantage of these platforms. Parallel programming using the traditional thread-and-lock programming model remains a hard task for most of the programmers since it is time consuming, error prone and requires deep knowledge and skills.

Moreover, parallel hardware is becoming increasingly heterogeneous: a modern work station may include two or more multicore processors with several manycore GPUs. In order to target such architectures, a programmer must have a deep understanding of the target hardware and should often use several disparate programming models making parallel programming harder and resulting in poor productivity.

Exploiting software parallelism on these emerging heterogeneous multicore architectures has become a great design challenge which outlines the need for new technologies to make multicore processors more accessible to a larger community [22].

Due to this technological context, two major needs have emerged: on one hand, a *high hardware abstraction* to hide details of the underlying platform providing portability, scalability and accommodating its heterogeneity.

On the other hand, *programmability* improvement is in high-demand as it increases productivity and minimizes programming complexity. These two needs should be satisfied without sacrificing *performance and forward scalability*. Programmability is achieved by minimizing parallel development costs in term of time, complexity and required tools in order to remain as close as possible to traditional sequential development.

Parallel development overheads are mainly generated by programming paradigm-related routines such as synchronization, communication, shared memory management, and workload scheduling. These routines introduce a significant amount of extra-code related to parallel programming paradigms and not to the user application itself.

Additional effects such as hard debugging and difficult performance tuning are also induced.

1.2. Structured Parallel Programming

Skeleton-based programming, often referred to as "structured parallel programming" [14, 15], is a promising high-level approach which satisfies most of these requirements and attempts to replace the traditional low-level thread lock model with better abstraction and an easier way to express parallelism through a collection of recurrent parallel patterns [10, 13]. It aims mainly to provide a good trade-off between programmability, portability, reusability and performance enhancement in order to improve programmer productivity by letting him focus on algorithms instead of hardware architectures.

In previous work [1] we introduced the pattern-based parallel programming model named MHPM (Multiscale Hybrid Programming Model) that allows expression of both sequential execution and several types of parallelism, including task, data and temporal parallelism at many granularity levels inside a single homogeneous programming model.

XPU [38] is a C++ framework which exploits C++ meta-programming techniques to implement the MHPM, and tries to develop the structured parallel programming approach toward better productivity and higher performances. The philosophy behind XPU design is "Easing parallelism expression without sacrificing execution efficiency". In this Chapter, we describe XPU parallelization methodology, its programming interface and its different parallel execution patterns. We show how XPU exploits C++ meta-programming to promote reuse of sequential code and to offer a light weight programming interface. In order to illustrate the potential of the XPU programming model, we describe the progressive parallelization process of a signal processing application which implements the Quadrature Mirror Filter Bank technique and evaluate both programmability and performances of our approach.

2. Related Works

Structured parallel programming with deterministic patterns [10] is a high-level approach mainly based on a collection of recurrent parallel execution patterns, often referred to as algorithmic skeletons [13-15] or parallel constructs, which abstract program description and hide low-level multithreading details and many complexities inherent in parallelism from the programmers [20, 23]. These reusable patterns automate many parallel paradigm-related routines such as synchronization, communication, data partitioning or task scheduling and handle them internally. For instance, many task-based structured programming models such as Thread Building Blocks [11] and Cilk++ [12] offer a set of execution patterns which transparently handles task scheduling, data partitioning and load-balancing. Unified Parallel C (UPC) Task Library HotSLAW [9] abstracts concurrent task management details and provides transparent data communication and dynamic load balancing [9, 22]. Sequoia [24] is another task-based programming model which offers transparent data management in deep processor's memory hierarchy including data allocation and communication through the memory tree [22]. By decoupling the programming model from the underlying architecture, a pattern-based approach also offers a good hardware abstraction accommodating architecture heterogeneity, opening the path to more hardware support and allowing the programmer to focus on algorithms instead of hardware architecture.

For instance MIT-LL is developing the Parallel Vector Tile Optimization Library (PVTOL) [18] in order to expand parallel programming constructs in the Parallel Vector Library (PVL) [26] and VSIPL++ [16] to support both homogeneous and heterogeneous multicore architectures [22].

Despite their ability to express parallelism at the cost of a relatively little amount of programming effort, most task-based parallel programming models target specific application domains such as signal processing in the case of PVL, PVTOL and VSIPL++ and offer limited collection of execution patterns to express specific type of parallelism: for instance if Cilk++ allows easy expression of simple and nested task parallelism, it is much harder to use it to express temporal parallelism such as in the pipeline execution pattern, where verbose restructuring of the code is required [31]. Finally, in spite of their high hardware abstraction, most task-based programming models are not yet able to support heterogeneous multicore architectures requiring programmers to use one or more additional programming models: for example OpenCL [29] or CUDA [30] may be used to support GPGPU, in conjunction with another task-based programming model to exploit multicore CPU and SMP platforms and perhaps a third programming models such as MPI to support distributed memory architecture. This results in a heterogeneous programming model which is hard to use and maintain and requires multiple skills and deep understanding of different hardware and software components. These constraints result in a severe productivity loss and can be discouraging for the average sequential programmers.

Main-stream applications and general-purpose programs may expose varying amount of parallelism and different parallel-sequential ratios: many scientific simulations and signal processing problems are massively parallelizable however many other general-purpose applications are much less parallelizable and exhibit much more sequential execution constraints such as many video decoding algorithms [32] and compression algorithms [33].

This outlines the need to express both parallel and sequential execution in a single homogeneous hybrid programming model able to specify both sequential and parallel execution in order to provide a generic and non-domain specific programming model.

In addition, a program may contains several different types of parallelism which are often difficult to express using a single programming model so the programmer uses several disparate programming models inside the same application resulting in ineffective use of processor caches, poor load-balancing and potentially system overloading with many independent run-times.

The MHPM tries to bypass these limitations by allowing easy expression of both sequential execution and several types of parallelism at multiple levels of granularity inside a single homogeneous model, so a programmer can parallelize its application as much as possible by using a single flexible programming model. Since it allows the specification of parallel execution as well as sequential execution, the MHPM targets a wide range of programs from various application domains: from highly parallelizable applications to those which are much less parallelizable and remains valid even for those which are fully sequential. The MHPM is based on a powerful and rich intermediate program representation, named the *Hierarchical Task Group Graph* (HTGG). HTGG is the heart of the MHPM which specifies sequential execution and several types of parallelism at many levels of granularity disregarding the available amount of parallelism in the target program. The HTGG is built from an extendable collection of nestable execution patterns which can be used hierarchically inside each other allowing progressive parallelization, better granularity control and data, task and temporal parallelism integration inside a single homogeneous and highly structured programming model.

Since promoting productivity is one of our primary design goals, the MHPM handles many parallel programming paradigm-related routines implicitly, such as synchronization, communication and shared memory management and therefore, hides many complexities inherent in parallelism from users. The internal design of parallel and sequential patterns allows transparent extraction of valuable information on task-data dependencies enabling an intelligent run-time system to detect shared data between tasks and protect it transparently against conflictual accesses often referred as “race condition”.

3. Task Parallelization Methodology

Task-based programming is based on the decomposition of a program into a set of tasks which cooperates with each other to perform the main work of the application program. Task granularity can be controlled and specified by the programmer: a program is basically the main task which is split into several coarse-grain tasks which may be split, in turn, into finer-grain tasks, and so on... until we reach the finest-grain allowed by the host programming language (cf. Figure 1).

Each task of the application program performs a piece of work in which it may consume or produce data, i.e., read or write private or shared data.

In order to speedup program execution optimally on parallel computing architectures, we have to extract the maximum amount of parallelism. The ideal case, is the one in which all tasks, at the finest possible granularity level, do not display any data or control dependencies, so they can be executed simultaneously (cf Figure 2).

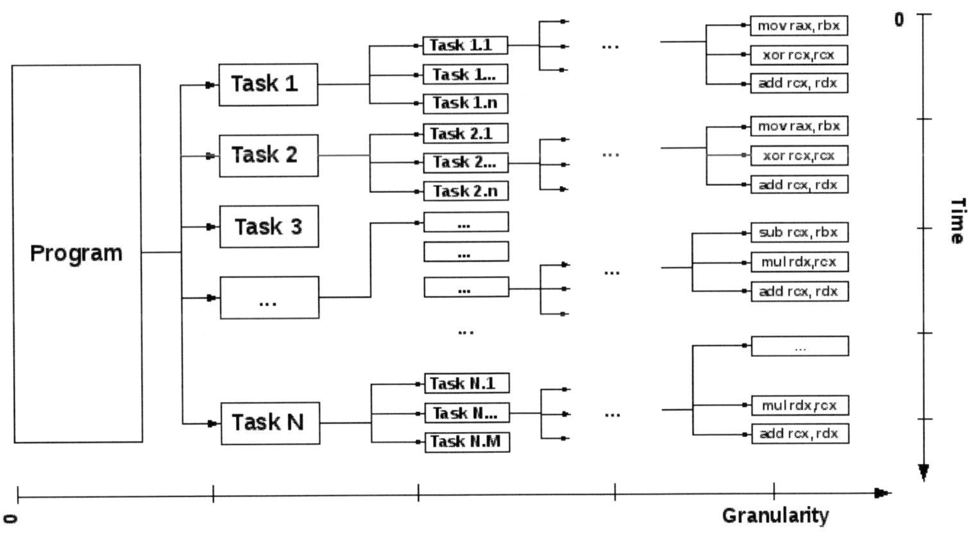

Figure 1. Program decomposition at many granularity levels.

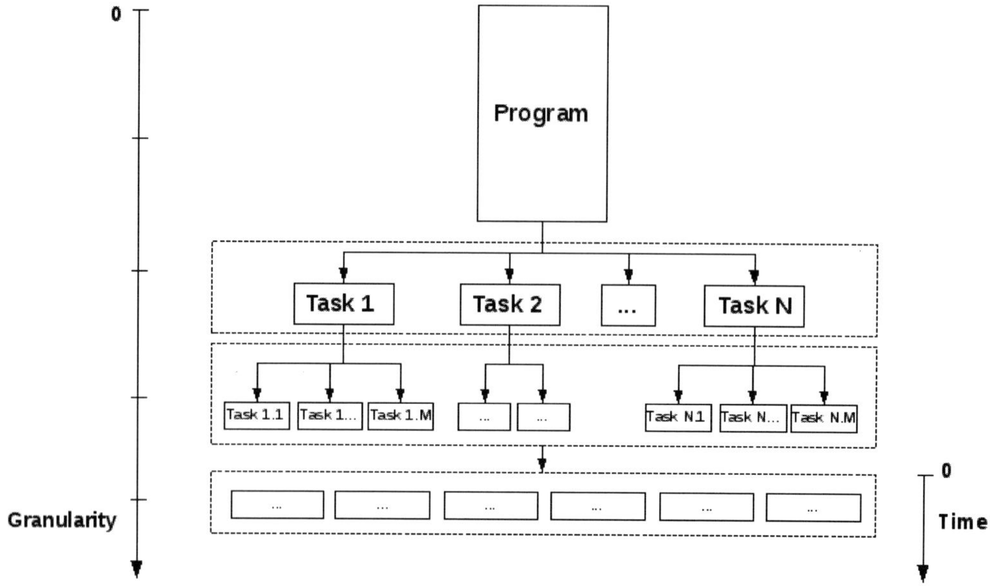

Figure 2. Ideal Parallel Program.

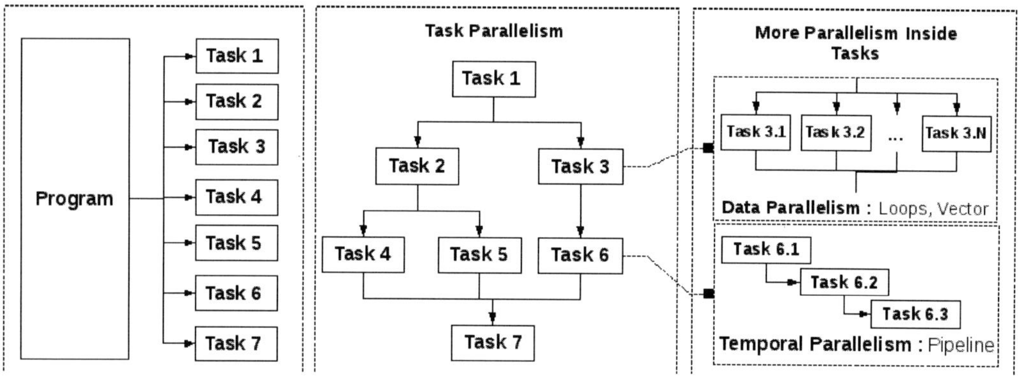

Figure 3. The Hybrid programming Model specifies sequential execution and several types of parallelism at all level of granularity.

Unfortunately, real world programs are "more-or-less" parallelizable depending on their natures: while many scientific simulations exhibit massive data parallelism and thus are highly parallelizable, many other general-purpose applications, which represent the vast majority in the software landscape, are much less parallelizable due to data and control dependencies and explicit task ordering. Indeed, these algorithmic constraints introduce the need for synchronization and ordering to preserve memory coherency and algorithmic consistency. Consequently, each subset of the tasks composing the program can be executed either in parallel or sequentially depending on these constraints which define thus the parallel-sequential code ratio or the available parallelism in the target program. At the end of the parallelization process, we obtain a hybrid execution graph containing both sequential and parallel sections (cf Figure 3). The available parallelism varies depending on the nature of application, but the model remains usable for either highly or weakly parallelizable programs and even for those which are fully sequential.

Tasks may locally exhibit several types of parallelism including nested task parallelism, data parallelism at thread level through parallel loops or instruction level through vectorization or temporal parallelism through pipelined execution. These execution configurations can be specified using a collection of execution patterns. For the sake of simplicity, we use interchangeably “execution pattern”, “construct” or “skeleton” to indicate a structure storing a set of tasks and specifying their execution configuration.

In order to accommodate heterogeneity of the execution patterns, so that they can fit into a single homogeneous structure representing the program, we define a common abstract construct named “task_group”. All our execution patterns implement this common interface for example “sequential_tasks” is a group of tasks scheduled to run sequentially while “parallel_tasks” is a group of tasks scheduled to be executed simultaneously (a basic fork and join pattern) and “pipeline” is a group of communicating tasks running as a chain of overlapping processing stages... etc. (cf. Figure 4).

These task group implementations can be easily extended to express more execution patterns and meet specific programmer needs in all application domains. We note the “Task” is also, by design, a “task_group” containing a single task. Consequently most provided constructs are nestable and can be used hierarchically inside each other.

The HTGG is a complex structure containing several heterogeneous constructs to express different execution patterns. It encapsulates not only the code of tasks but also specifies task execution ordering and contains many other pieces of information about task-data dependencies and shared memory and provides an interface to specify the task-processor mapping. In order to build this complex structure easily, we tried to exploit C++ Meta-programming capabilities to offer an intuitive interface to build the HTGG at the cost of a small amount of paradigm-related extra code and to promote reuse of sequential code with the lowest possible modification/alteration. The resulting programming interface is easy-to-use and do not display any template structure to the programmer.

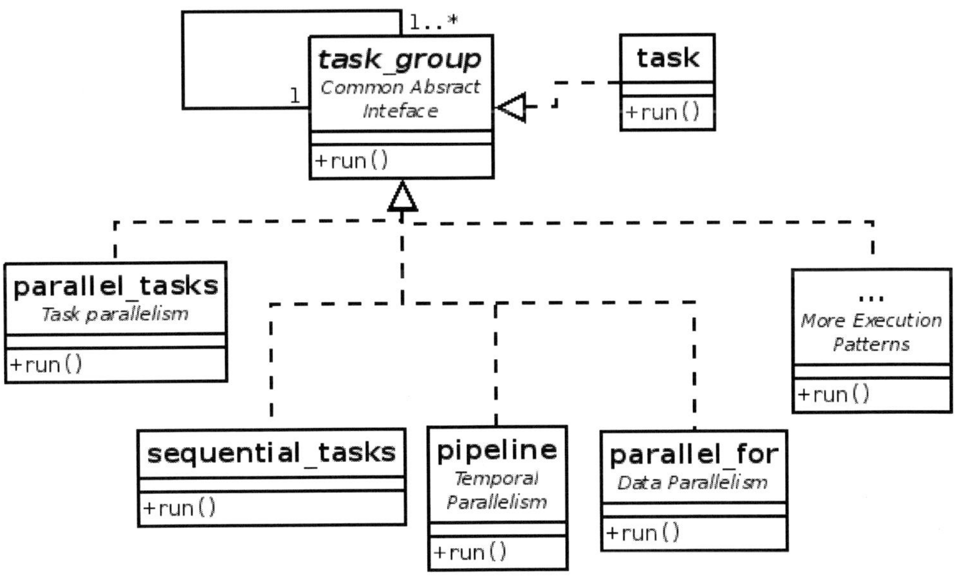

Figure 4. A Simplified overview of the internal software design accommodating constructs heterogeneity so that they can fit inside a single homogeneous and hierarchical structure: The HTGG.

4. XPU Overview

XPU [38] is a task-based library which exploits C++ meta- programming capabilities [27, 28] to ease parallelism expression. C++ Meta-programming techniques exploit the potential of standard C++ language without any extension and thus do not introduce any need to any particular tool other than a standard C++ compiler. Thus, XPU based programs are simply compiled like any C++ program. XPU provides a friendly and light weight programming interface which enable programmer to design parallel applications or parallelize those which are sequential at the cost of a little amount of extra-code.

XPU is a based on a set of reusable parallel constructs which specifies execution configuration of a group of tasks. In order to promote reuse of sequential legacy code without almost any alteration, these tasks are designed to encapsulate different pieces of code including functions, class method or lambda expression. As depicted in Figure 5, these tasks can be ordered by choosing the appropriate parallel construct to express task, data or temporal parallelism. Several types of parallelism can be implemented at different granularity levels through composing different skeletons in a hierarchical fashion. This allows progressive parallelization of a program starting from coarse-grain parallelism to finer grain parallelism.

The XPU execution patterns handle transparently many parallel-paradigms-related routines such as synchronization, communication or task scheduling. An intelligent run-time system exploits information, extracted transparently from both hardware system and used execution patterns (task ordering and task-data dependencies) to perform dynamically efficient execution on the underlying architecture through cache-aware and load-balanced task scheduling.

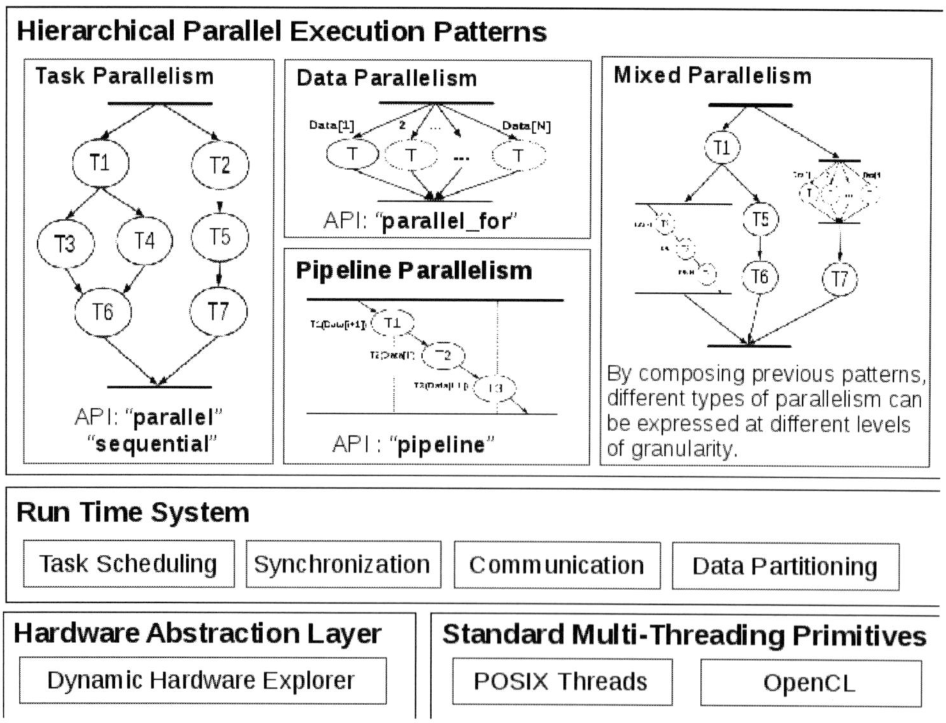

Figure 5. Overview of XPU Architecture.

5. Case Study: Implementation of the Quadrature Mirror Filter Bank

The Quadrature Mirror Filter Bank (QMFB) is a powerful signal processing technique that offers a fine spectral decomposition of a signal: a wide frequency band signal is decomposed into a set of narrow frequency sub-band. The QMFB is implemented as a set of band-pass filters that isolate each of these sub-bands. Several filter banks can be used as cascaded filtering stages to perform hierarchical spectral decomposition.

In this case, the main wide frequency band is decomposed into several narrow sub-bands, each of these sub-bands is then decomposed in turn into narrower sub-bands, etc... QMFB have many applications such as frequency spectrum analysis, audio equalization, signal compression or speech recognition.

Figure 6 gives an overview of a three-stage cascaded filter banks implementation. In the first stage, the input signal is decomposed into two sub-bands then these sub-bands are decomposed into four then eight narrower sub-bands respectively in the second and third stage. We note that decimation is performed after each filtering operation. For the sake of simplicity, decimation is not represented in the figure.

The QMFB has been implemented as a sequential C++ program within an industrial context. An experimental version has been derived from the industrial one. The later is still sequential and has smaller filter banks containing less filters. We used XPU to parallelize progressively the sequential QMFB code using different parallelism types at different granularity levels. As we present the different XPU parallelization techniques along this chapter, we use the QMFB application as a case study to evaluate XPU programmability and performance.

6. Task Definition

Decomposing a program into a set of pieces of code is the first step in the parallelization process in most parallel programming models. In low-level thread-lock programming model, these pieces of code are called callbacks, in higher level task-based programming models this piece of code is called task.

6.1. POSIX Threads Callbacks

In the traditional low-level thread-lock model, this piece of code is called "callback" and plays the role of tasks in task-based programming models and is the main component of multi-threaded applications. If we consider C++ language, the host-language of our programming model, sequential code is often greatly altered since the targeted piece of code has to meet the native callback prototype "void * function(void *)" which imposes many restrictions on the programmer when parallelizing applications or reusing sequential code: only static functions can be used as callback, the class method cannot be used directly. In addition, consumed and produced data should be stored in a common intermediate structure then extracted and restored to their original type through type casting.

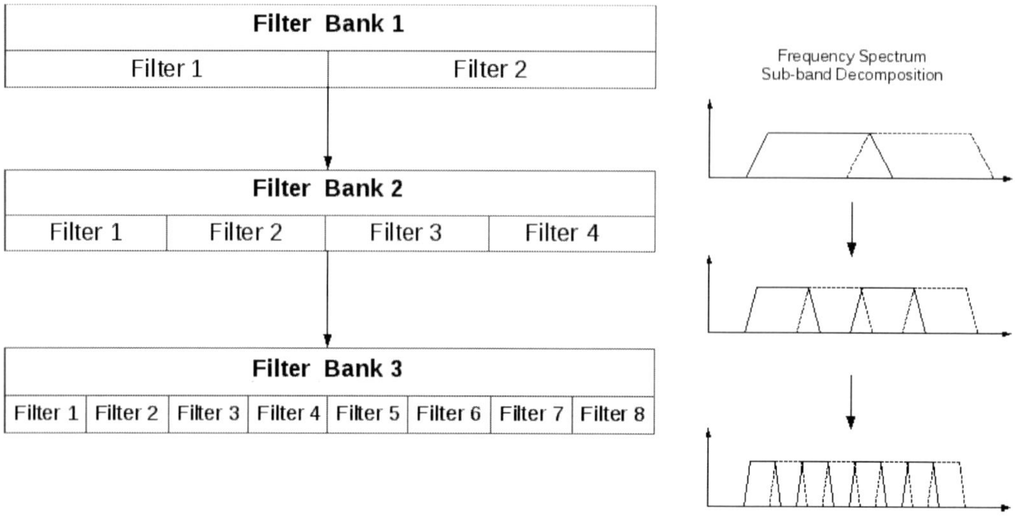

Figure 6. Overview of the QMFB Technique.

These constraints lead to many modifications of the sequential code, usually a lot of programming paradigm-related extra-code and thus make the code less readable, error-prone and difficult to maintain. This lack of flexibility and programmability amplifies the burden on the programmer dramatically and makes the reuse of sequential code difficult.

6.2. XPU Task

Since promoting the reuse of sequential code is one of the primary design goals of XPU, we tried to overcome the previously enumerated limitations through a more flexible task design. In the MHPM, by design, a task is basically an abstract callable piece of code which can be executed. This piece of code may consume or produce data. Data are passed in the form of arguments to each task.

Figure 7 shows how a task can be created from a function or a class method disregarding its argument count or type and its return type. We exploit C++ meta-programming capabilities to provide a friendly programming interface allowing simple and fast definition of tasks from existing code to promote reuse of code and improve programmer productivity.

At the same time, by combining polymorphism and several C++ template programming techniques we take advantage of compile-time compiler optimization to produce efficient code.

Moreover, meta-programming techniques allow us to investigate used data type, through Compile-Time Type Identification CTTI [27, 28], and therefore, detect transparently task-data dependencies at compile-time. This information is exploited to detect automatically concurrent accesses to shared data in the HTGG and protect them against potential race condition. In ongoing work, we are trying to exploit this same information to perform efficient execution on the underlying architecture dynamically by improving temporal and spatial data locality through cache-aware task scheduling.

When defining a task, data access is specified implicitly or explicitly through the passed argument.

C/C++
Function
	int load_input_stream(float * stream);
	int process_stream(float * in, float * out);
	
	int main()
	{
	task *load_stream_t*(load_input_stream, in_stream);
	task *process_stream_*t(process_stream, *__read_only*(in_stream), out_stream);
	
	load_stream_t.run(); // to run task
	// ...
	}

C++ Class Method	class signal
	{
	public:
	int filter(float low, float high);
	int decimate(...);
	...
	};
	int main( )
	{
	signal s(“samples.dat”);
	task sharpen_t(&s, &signal::filter, 1000, 1500);
	}

C++
Lambda Expression
(C++0x or later)
	int main( )
	{
	float * f;
	xpu::task low_pass([](float * samples, int freq);
	{...code... }, samples, 7000);
	}

Figure 7. Task definition from different pieces of code.

By default, arguments passed by value are considered as local read access data, arguments passed by pointer are considered as potentially shared data accessed in write mode, arguments passed through constant pointer are considered as potentially shared data accessed in “read only” mode (they can be explicitly specified using the *__read_only( )* macro or simply passed as a constant pointer argument), finally, the case of arguments passed by references is not yet treated due to value/reference ambiguity issue with some compilers. Internal task implementation relies on C++ meta-programming techniques and intensive use of template allowing compiler to perform many optimizations at compile-time providing thus efficient execution.

7. Task Parallelism

7.1. Parallelism Expression

After decomposing a program into tasks, dependencies between these tasks can be analyzed to extract task parallelism. A program may contains determines parallel and sequential tasks.

At the end of this task dependency analysis, we obtain a task dependency graph which specifies parallelism at different granularity levels. Figure 8 shows three different task graph configurations and their associated XPU code which enables the programmer to express the task parallelism specified by an arbitrary task graph:

- Configuration (a): All Tasks are sequential. The "*sequential*" keyword is used to specify sequential execution and is equivalent to traditional sequential execution of the functions encapsulated in the tasks.
- Configuration (b): All three Tasks are parallel. The "*parallel*" keyword allows programmer to specify parallel execution of a set of tasks.
- Configuration (c): There are both parallel and sequential tasks at different granularity levels and parallelism is specified through a more complex task graph. Combined use of the "*parallel*" and "*sequential*" keywords allows the specification of an arbitrary task graph.

1: void main() { 2: task t1(f1, data_1), t2(f2) ...; *// task definition* 3: task_group * program; 4: program = sequential(&t1, &t2, &t3); *// construct task graph* 5: program->run(); *// execute it* 6: }	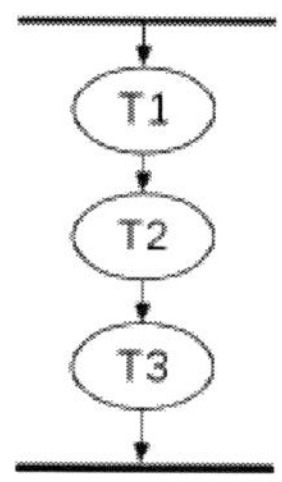 (a)
1: void main() { 2: task t1(f1, data_1), t2(f2) ...; *// task definition* 3: task_group * program; 4: program = parallel(&t1, &t2, &t3); *// construct task graph* 5: program->run(); *// execute it* 6: }	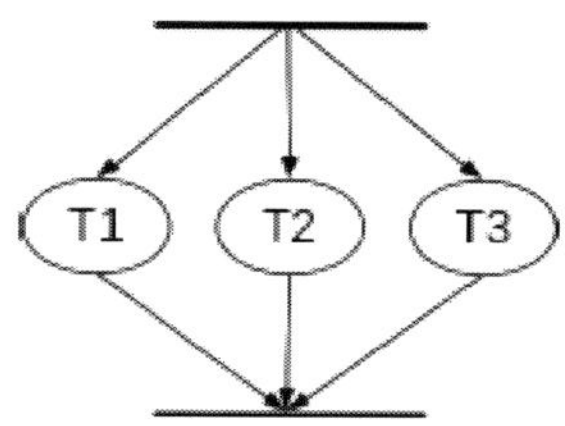 (b)
1: void main() { 2: task t1(f1, data_1), t2(f2) ...; *// task definition* 3: task_group * program; 4: program = parallel(sequential(&t1, *// construct task graph* 5: parallel(&t3, &t4), 6: &t6), 7: sequential(&t2,&t5,&t7)); 5: program->run(); *// execute it* 6: }	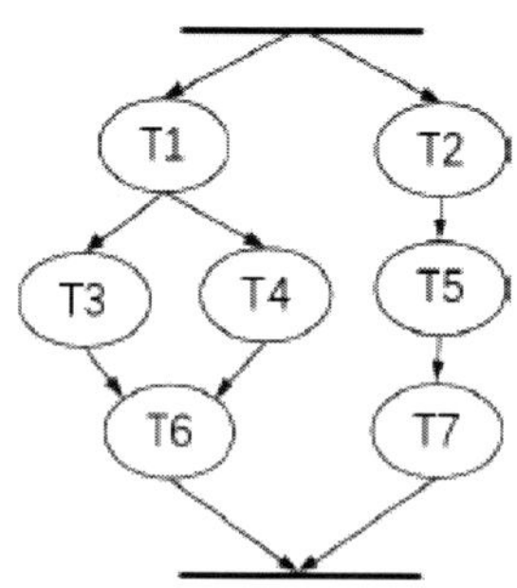 (c)

Figure 8. Task parallelism can specified using the XPU "sequential" or "parallel" keywords. Complex task graphs can be constructed by combining both of them.

7.2. Internal Implementations

The "*parallel*" and "*sequential*" programming interface build respectively two different kinds of Hierarchical Task Groups (HTG). Both of them can encapsulate a set of Tasks, a set of HTG or a mix of them. The difference is that "*parallel*" specifies that the produced set of tasks can be executed in parallel while "*sequential*" enforces sequential execution of this set of tasks.

Task is one implementation of the HTG among others, e.g., Task is an implementation of a task group containing one single task. Many other implementations exists in XPU including "parallel task group", "sequential task group", "pipeline", "parallel for " ... etc. This flexible design allows hierarchical composition of these task groups and thus allows the hierarchical specification of different types of parallelism at different levels of granularity.

7.3. Automatic Shared Data Detection and Protection

In the previous section, we discussed the ability of Tasks to detect their data dependencies providing thus valuable information. This feature is exploited by the XPU run-time system to detect shared data between tasks and protect them automatically and transparently against conflictual concurrent accesses often referred as "*race condition*". "*race condition*" is a recurrent problem in parallel programming which occurs when concurrent threads access and modify the shared data concurrently without using a mutual exclusion mechanism which guarantees exclusive access to the shared data and ensures synchronization between threads and atomicity of the performed operations on such data.

Shared data management is a time-consuming process which increases the complexity of parallel application and requires additional programming effort including identification of shared data and implementation of the mutual exclusion which translate into additional code. This additional code is related to the parallel-paradigms and not to the application algorithm itself and can result into verbose code which is difficult to understand and maintain. Consequently, shared data management is parallel programming routine which can contribute to reducing programmer productivity.

In order to improve programmer productivity, XPU relieve programmer from the hard task of managing shared data and mutual exclusion "manually" by providing the Automatic Shared Data Detection and Protection (ASDDP) capability. This mechanism allows XPU to detect shared data and protect it against race condition when required.

When building a task graph, the run-time system will dynamically check task-data dependencies to determine which task accesses which data and how they are accessed (write or read mode), then it will look for shared data in parallel sections at all granularity levels. Finally, if two or more concurrent tasks access shared data in write mode, these tasks will be transformed in critical sections by associating transparently a "lockable" (an abstraction of the mutual exclusion mechanism: mutex and spinlock are an example of implementations of the "lockable" interface) so the shared data will be protected against potential race-condition when executing the tasks. We note that this technique suppose no unsafe direct accesses from tasks to global variables since this type of accesses is out of the control of our run-time system which uses an arguments list to determine task-data dependencies.

Consequently, the programmer is invited to specify explicitly used data in his argument list when defining tasks and should not hide pointers to shared data inside complex structures.

Figure 9 shows and example of task graph implying concurrent read/write accesses to “data_5” by task 4 and 5. The final XPU program is executed safely without need to associating a “mutex” to the shared data: XPU is responsible of managing shared data transparently by running task 4 and 5 inside two critical sections which guarantees exclusive accesses to the shared data. When Task 4 and 5 are time consuming, executing them inside two critical sections can introduce a significant overhead which may annihilate parallelism in the worst case. In such case, an expert programmer may prefer handling shared data at finer grain by himself. In such case, the programmer can disable the ASDDP in XPU run-time system.

7.4. Application: Quadrature Mirror Filter Bank Implementation

In our signal processing application is based on a set of cascaded polyphase filter banks. The input signal is processed through the three processing stage.

The first processing stage applies a set of filters and resamples the signal to decompose it into several subbands. These sub-bands are decomposed in turn by the next stage into narrower subbands using another filter bank.

The same operation is reproduced by the last stage using more filters to reconstruct finally the signal while offering excellent frequency selectivity.

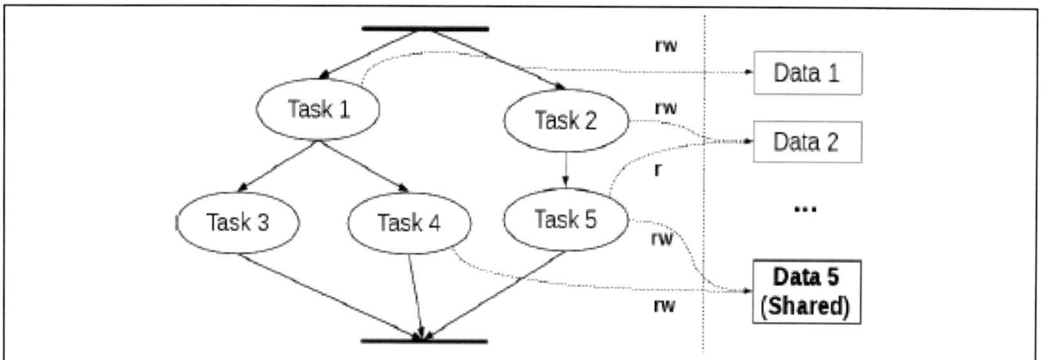


```
void main() {
task t1(f1),t2(f2),t3(f3)...; // task definition
task_group * program;
program = parallel(sequential(&t1, parallel(&t3,&t4)),
sequential(&t2, &t5));
program->run(); // shared 'data_5' protected automatically
return;
}
```

(r: read; w: write; rw: read/write).

Figure 9. While specifying task parallelism through a task graph, XPU detect shared data and protect it against potential race condition.

7.4.1. Task Graph

The signal processing application displays naturally data dependencies between its consecutive filtering/resampling stages: the data output of each stage is the input of the next stage. While dependent stages should be executed sequentially, each stage is composed of a set of independent filters that can be executed simultaneously.

Consequently available parallelism is can exploited inside each processing stages while these stages are executed sequentially. Figure 10 depicts the task graph that specifies the parallelism of the application. This figure has been simplified for clarity purpose: the original application has the same three-stage architecture but more filters at each stage.

7.4.2. Performance

As depicted in Figure 11, the implementation of task parallelism provides about 2.5x speedup over the original sequential version on the 4 Threads Intel Xeon E3-1220 platform. The 8 Threads Intel Core i7 and the 16 Threads Intel Xeon E5-2670 provide respectively about 1.8x and 2.6x speedup. The execution speedup and the application scalability are limited by the available coarse grain task parallelism in this version of the application. We note that the original industrial version of this application from which our current application is derived has a similar design but encapsulates much more filters in its stages: 5 Filters in the first stage, 20 Filters in the second stage and 80 Filters in the last stage providing thus much more task parallelism. In the next section, we show how we can exact more parallelism at both threat-level and instruction level using different XPU parallel constructs.

8. Data Parallelism

Data parallelism refers to scenarios in which the same operation is performed concurrently on elements of a data container [37]. Data parallelism can be specified at different levels of granularity and can be implemented at thread level (Thread Level Parallelism (TLP)) or at the instruction level (Instruction Level Parallelism (ILP)).

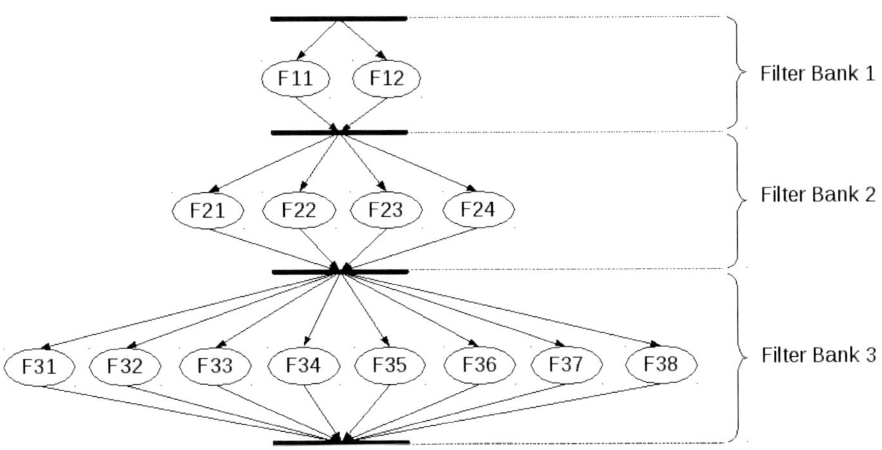

Figure 10. Polyphase Filter Bank application consists into three consecutive filtering stages. Each stage decomposes the signal produced by the previous stage into narrower subbands using a set of filters.

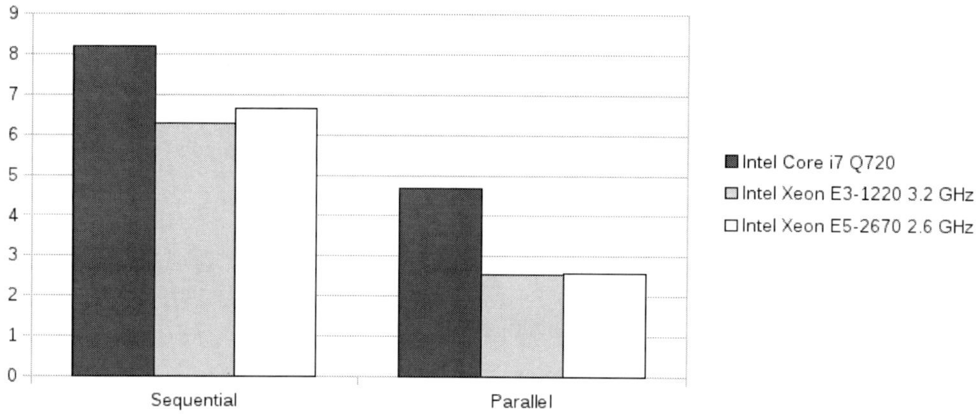

Figure 11. Execution time (sec) of the sequential and task parallel version on different multicore platforms.

In data parallel operations, data are partitioned so multiple threads can operate on different data partition concurrently. XPU enables the programmer to express data parallelism at thread level (TLP) through parallelized for loop and at instruction level (ILP) through a set of vectorized data types (SIMD) and at both through "parallel vector" interface [1].

8.1. Parallel for Loop

Parallel loop is one of the most used execution pattern since it can act as a great parallelism multiplier in data parallel applications while achieving an excellent scalability. It targets often "for loops" when processing large number of data items. "Parallel For" execution pattern is implemented in most of the popular parallel programming models such as OpenMP, TBB or Cilk++...

XPU provides a construct named "parallel_for" which enable the programmers to parallelize "for" loops easily: this "parallel_for" construct automates many routines which are related to the parallel loop implementation such as scalable data partitioning and workload scheduling. XPU use an efficient cache-hierarchy-aware scheduling algorithm named CHATS [4] and designed to provide both good load balancing and efficient use of recent multicore processor caches by improving spatial and temporal data locality and reducing inter-thread communication overhead. The internal implementation of the "parallel_for" has been detailed in previous dedicated work [4].

8.2. Vectorization

Most recent multicore and manycore processors implements thus ILP (Instruction Level Parallelism) by providing a set of SIMD (Single Instruction Multiple Data) instructions. Contrary to the traditional scalar operation where a single operation is performed on a single data, SIMD technologies allow performing a single operation simultaneously on multiple data. SIMD operations, often referred as "vectorization", can increase significantly computation throughput an improve processor use efficiency.

SIMD technologies are available in most recent monocore, multicore and manycore processors. Recent Intel and AMD processors implements the Streaming SIMD Extension (SSE) [39] which is a SIMD instruction set extension to the x86 architecture. SSE operates on 128 bits-wide registers and allows simultaneous SIMD operations on eight chars, four integers, four simple precision floats or two double precision floats.

While implementing data parallelism at thread level through the "parallel_for" construct, XPU provide instruction-level data parallelism at finer gain through a set of built-in vectorized types which are implemented in top of SSE to support SIMD. Traditional SSE programming can be a hard and time-consuming task since programmer is responsible of performing many low-level routines such as data loading, storing and computations in addition to ensuring data alignment in memory and organizing data structures for SIMD operations... XPU try to relieve programmer from these burdens by hiding these low-level details behind a set of built-in vectorized types that act almost like regular floating-point types in C/C++ language and handle internally many of these low-level routines. XPU provide the "vec3f" and "vec3f" vectorized types to allow simultaneous operations on respectively three and four single precision float and the "vec2d" to enable simultaneous operations on two double precision floats. Supported operations include basic arithmetic operations such as addition or multiplication natively supported by SSE in addition to more advanced functions such as trigonometric primitives, logarithm and exponential approximations... [1].

8.3. Application

The "parallel_for" construct has been used in several applications such as the "Black-Scholes" algorithm and the "Fluid Animation" problem from the PARSEC benchmark. The results of these benchmarks have been discussed in previous works [1, 4].

In our signal processing application, we used the vectorization capability of XPU to speedup the filtering process. At each processing stage (filter bank), each filtering operation implies uniform multiplication of large number of signal samples by the filter coefficients then the accumulation of their sum. Both signal samples and filter coefficients are stored as tables of floats. Vectorization can be naturally implemented by processing the regular float buffers as XPU "vec4f" buffers. This allows us to process four pairs of floats at once at each operation instead of one single pair float at a time.

As shown in Figure 12, the vectorized application performs about four times faster than the original sequential application on an 8 threads Inter Core i7 Q720 (Platform A). On the two others platforms running the Intel Xeon E3-1220 at 3.2 GHz and Xeon E5-2670 at 2.6 GHz packaging respectively 4 hardware (4 physical cores) threads and 16 hardware threads (8 physical cores), the vectorized application displays comparable speedup. We note that since our application implements only instruction level parallelism and do not introduce any thread parallelism, the number of cores does not give any advantage to the third platform over the second one: since the later run at higher frequency (3.2 GHz), it enables the application to perform the best execution time.

In the second experiment shown in Figure 13, the vectorized version of the filters is used in the task parallel version which we described in the previous section (Task Parallelism). Figure 13 shows that the vectorization of the task parallel version improve significantly its execution time and perform about twice faster.

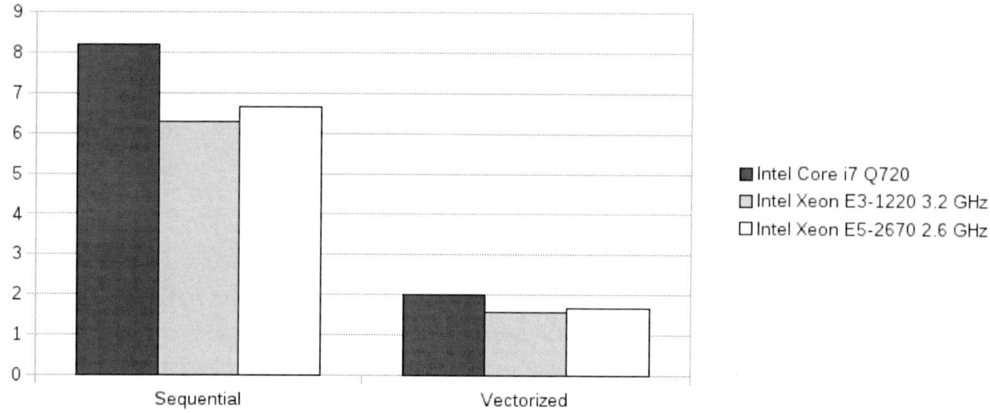

Figure 12. Vectorization effect on the execution time (sec) of the sequential version of the application.

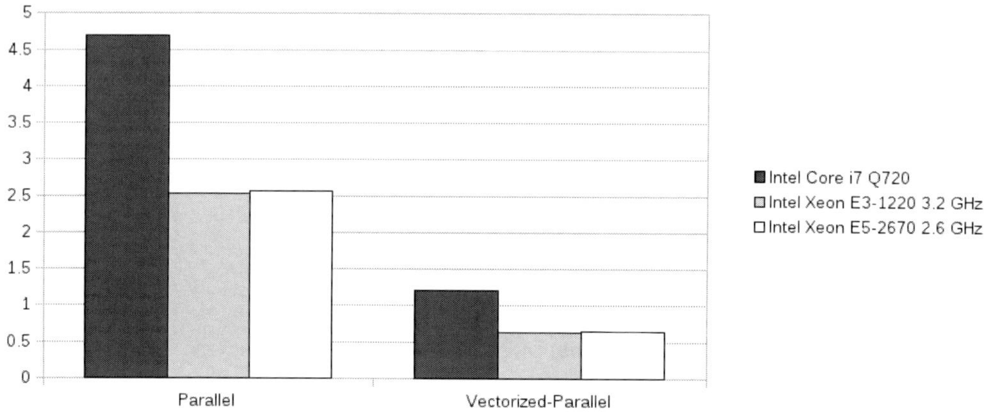

Figure 13. Vectorization effect on the execution time (sec) of the parallel version of the application.

Despite it has less cores than the third platform, the second platform provides comparable performance thanks to it higher clock frequency and due to the limited thread-parallelism in the application: for instance, the maximum amount of parallelism is available in the last processing stage where eight filters can be executed simultaneously (cf Figure. 10).

Extracting more thread-level parallelism is required to exploit the available processor cores and offer better scalability. In the next section, we show how pipeline parallelism can act as great parallelism multiplier.

9. Pipeline Parallelism

9.1. Pipeline Execution Pattern

Pipeline execution pattern is a recurrent execution configuration in many application domains involving stream processing such as digital signal processing, video encoding or data compression. Pipeline execution pattern follows a consumer/producer scheme similar to a production assembly line.

A pipeline is set of simultaneously active tasks called "stages" that communicate following a producer-consumer relationship: each stage is responsible of both consuming and producing data. Thus, each pair of adjacent stages forms a producer-consumer pair [40]. At the opposite of the serial execution pattern where completely dependent sequences of tasks are executed serially, pipeline stages are activated at the same time. However, in order to recover data coherency, sequentially dependent activities or "folds" are serialized and parallelism is exploited only on independent activities. Figure 14 shows the difference between conventional sequential execution and pipeline execution.

Pipeline parallelism can act as a great parallelism multiplier and can be very useful in many real-time applications where the main algorithm must process a data stream such as in our signal processing application. Unfortunately, low-level parallel programming models exacerbate the difficulties of expressing pipeline parallelism and require verbose restructuring of the code and complex scheduling techniques to perform efficient execution on modern multicore architectures. XPU provides a parallel construct named "pipeline" which aims to ease expression of pipeline parallelism [1-3]. As all the other XPU parallel construct, the pipeline is a particular configuration of a set tasks. Tasks are used as the stages of the pipeline. The "pipeline" construct handle internally synchronization between stages through and asynchronous event-based scheduling. Pipeline implementation details are discussed in previous publication [1, 3]. The XPU run-time system uses a cache-aware scheduling technique to perform efficient pipeline execution on multicore processor through efficient cache use and dynamic load balancing.

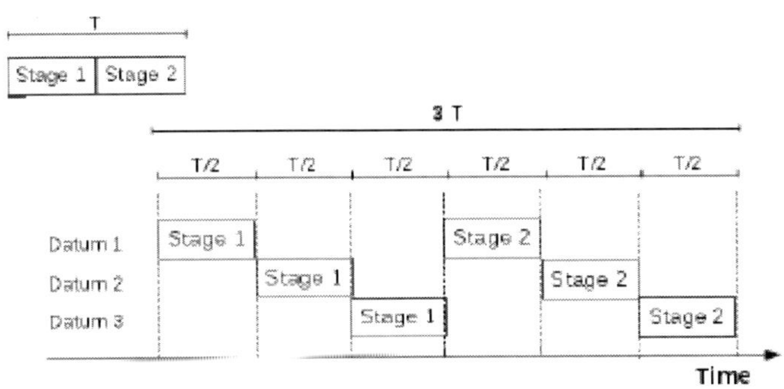

Figure 14. Traditional sequential execution.

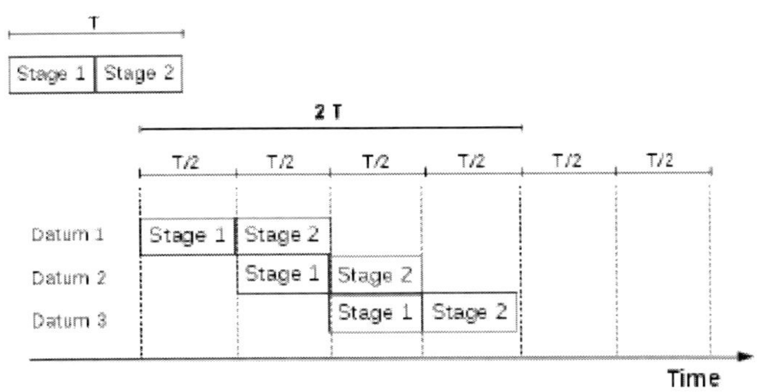

Figure 15. Pipeline execution serialize only dependent activities while exploiting parallelism on independent ones.

Several pipeline scheduling techniques has been implemented in XPU and are detailed and discussed in [3].

9.2. Pipeline Programming Interface

Figure 16 shows how pipeline parallelism can be expressed using the XPU programming interface. As in all the previous parallel constructs, tasks are defined first then used to build the "pipeline" construct. When invoking the "run" method the "pipeline" is executed and the run-time system is responsible of scheduling and synchronizing the pipeline stages.

We note that implementations of each stage can be parallelized using the task parallelism primitives such as in line 4.

9.3. Application

The three processing stages of our signal processing application can form a pipeline: each filter bank can be implemented as a stage of the pipeline.

We use the XPU "pipeline" construct with both the sequential version and the parallel version while enabling then disabling the vectorization.

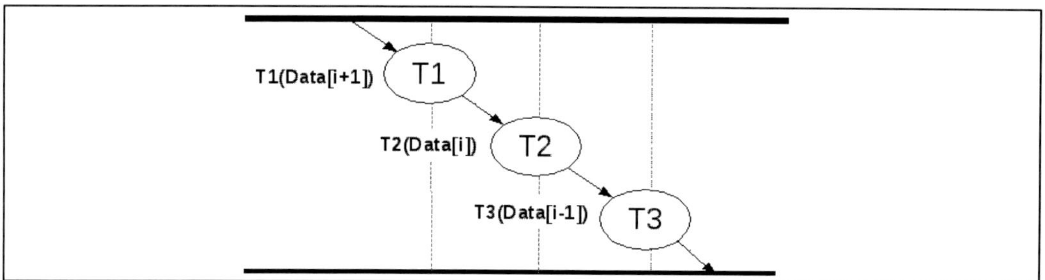


```
1: // pipeline stages implementations
2: int filter_bank_1(int i, float ** data, const float ** filters) {
3: // after defining tasks, execute the parallel filters on data "i"
4: xpu::parallel(&filter1, &filter2)->run();
5: }
6: int filter_bank_2(int i, float ** data, const float ** filters);
7: int filter_bank_3(int i, float ** data, const float ** filters);
8:
9: void main() {
10: // task definition
11: xpu::task fb1_t(filter_bank_1, 0, data, filters);
12: xpu::task fb2_t(filter_bank_1, 0, data, filters);
13: xpu::task fb3_t(filter_bank_1, 0, data, filters);
14: // pipeline construction
15: xpu::piepeline p(size, &fb1_t, &fb2_t, &fb3_t);
16: // pipeline execution
17: p.run();
18: }
```

Figure 15. Pipeline parallelism expression using XPU.

Figure 16 shows the achieved performances of these three versions on three different platforms. The achieved performances shows that pipeline execution pattern offer a speedup of about 16x in comparison to the previous sequential execution on the first 8 Threads platform.

Combination of pipeline parallelism with the task parallelism and vectorization speedups the pipeline-only execution with a factor of 5x in the second configuration (Intel Xeon E3-1220).

Conclusion

Along this chapter, we parallelized the target application progressively by expressing several parallelism types at different granularity levels starting from coarse grain tasks to finer grain ones. Use of both tasks, pipeline and data parallelism, enabled us to extract a significant amount of parallelism and to achieve high performance and good scalability.

We outline the programmability of the XPU programming model which allows the programmers to easily express several types of parallelism at the cost of a little amount of parallelism-related extra-code and in the same time, by enabling him to reuse most of the legacy sequential code without significant alteration. This programmability can improve significantly programmer's productivity.

The QMFB processing case study is a typical stream processing application which outlined both the programmability and performance aspect and showed that despite its emphasis on programmability, XPU can still provide good performances. Figure 17 gives a synthesis of the achieved execution times at the different parallelization steps.

The Final parallel version of the application execute more than 80 times faster than the original sequential application on an Intel Core i7 Q720.

Many algorithms and industrial applications can be parallelized following the same methodology used in the presented case study.

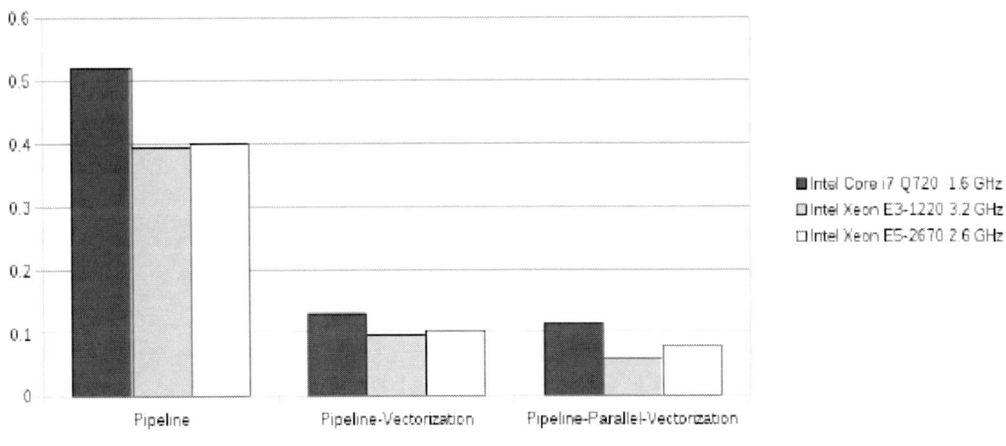

Figure 16. Execution time (sec) of different configurations of the pipelined version of the application: pipeline only, pipeline with vectorization and pipeline with vectroization and parallel filters.

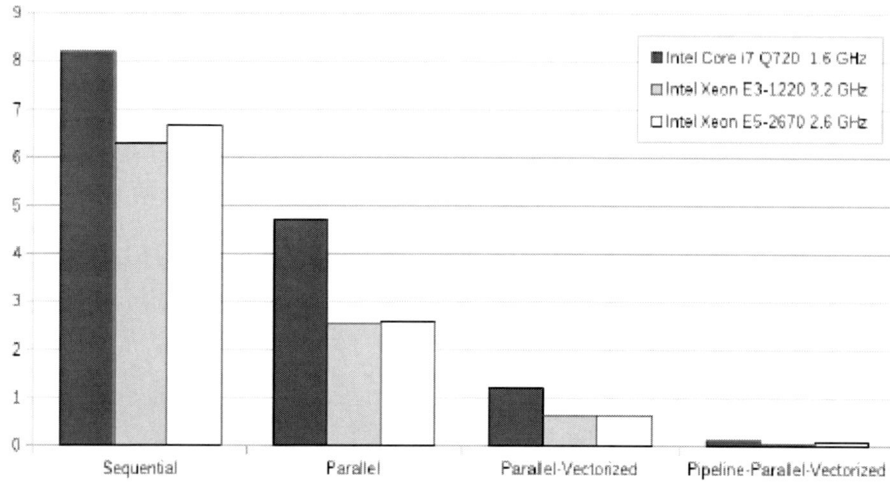

Figure 17. Synthesis of the achieved execution time (sec) of the sequential application and the different parallel versions during the parallelization process.

References

[1] Khammassi, N., Le Lann, J. C., Diguet, J. P., Skrzyniarz, A., (2012). MHPM: Multi-Scale Hybrid Programming Model: A Flexible Parallelization Methodology, *HPCC '12 Proceedings of the 2012 IEEE 14th International Conference on High Performance Computing and Communication*, Liverpool, UK, 71-80.

[2] Khammassi, N., Le Lann, J. C., (2014). Tackling Real-Time Signal Processing Applications on Shared Memory Multicore Architectures Using XPU, *Embedded Real Time Software and Systems ERTS 2014*, Toulouse, France.

[3] Khammassi, N., Le Lann, J. C., (2014). A High-Level Programming Model to Ease Pipeline Parallelism Expression On Shared Memory Multicore Architectures, *22nd High Performance Computing Symposium HPC 2014*, Tampa, FL, US.

[4] Khammassi, N., Le Lann, J. C., (2014). Design and Implementation Of A Cache Hierarchy-Aware Task Scheduling For Parallel Loops On Multicore Architectures, *Third International conference on Parallel, Distributed Computing Technologies and Applications PDCTA,* Sydney, Australia.

[5] Blake, G., Dreslinski, R. G., Mudge, T., (2009). A Survey of Multicore Processors, *IEEE Signal Processing,* 26, 6, 26-37.

[6] Karam, L. J., Alkamal, I., Gatherer, A., Frantz, G. A., Anderson, D. V., Evans, B. L., (2009). Trends in Multicore DSP platforms, *IEEE Signal Processing*, 26, 6, 38-49.

[7] Wolf, W., (2009). Multiprocessor System-on-Chip Technology, *IEEE Signal Processing*, 26, 6.

[8] Park, H., Oh, H., Ha, S., (2009). Multiprocessor SoC Design Methods and Tools, *IEEE Signal Processing*, 26, 6.

[9] Min, S.-J., Iancu, C., Yelick, K., (2011). Hierarchical Work Stealing on Manycore Clusters, *Fifth Conference on Partitioned Global Address Space Programming Models (PGAS11).*

[10] McCool, M. D., (2010). Structured Parallel Programming with Deterministic Patterns, *HotPar'10 Proceedings of the 2nd USENIX conference on Hot topics in parallelism.*

[11] *Threading Building Blocks Tutorial, rev. 1.6*, (2007). Intel Corporation, http://www.threadingbuildingblocks.org.

[12] *Cilk++ Programmer's Guides*, (2009). Cilk Art, Lexington, MA.

[13] Aldinucci, M., Danelutto, M. (2007). Skeleton-based parallel programming: Functional and parallel semantics in a single shot, *Comput. Lang. Syst. Struct.*, 33(3-4), 179-192.

[14] Cole, M., (1989). *Algorithmic Skeletons: structured management of parallel computations*, Pitman/MIT Press.

[15] Cole, M., (2004). Bringing Skeleton out of the closet: a pragmatic manifesto for skeletal parallel programming, *Parallel Computing*, 30(3), 389-406.

[16] Lebak, J., Kepner, J., Hoffman, H., Rutledge, E., (2005). Parallel VSIPL++: An open standard software library for high-performance parallel signal processing, *Proc. IEEE*, 93, 2, 313-330.

[17] Bienia, C., Kumar, S., Singh, J. P., Li, K., (2008). The PARSEC Benchmark Suite: Characterization and Architectural Implications, *Proc. of the 17th Int. Conf. on Parallel Architectures and Compilation Techniques.*

[18] Kim, H., Rutledge, E., Sacco, S., Mohindra, S., Marzilli, M., Kepner, J., Haney, R., Daly, J., Bliss, N., (2008). PVTOL: Providing Productivity, Performance and Portability to DoD Signal Processing Applications on Multicore Processors, *Proc. High Performance Computing Modernization Program Users Group Conf.* Seattle, WA, MIT Lincoln Lab., Lexington, MA, 327-333.

[19] Mohindra, S., Daly, J., Haney, R., Schrader, G., (2008). Task and conduit framework for multi-core systems, *Proc. High Performance Computing Modernization Program Users Group Conf.*, Seattle, WA, 506-513.

[20] González-Vélez, H., Leyton, M., (2010).A survey of algorithmic skeleton frameworks: high-level structured parallel programming enablers, *Software: Practice and Experience*, 40, 12, 1135-1160.

[21] Leyton, M., Piquer, J. M., (2010). Skandium: Multi-core Programming with algorithmic skeletons, *IEEE Euro-micro PDP* 2010.

[22] Kim, H., Bond, R., (2009). Multicore Software Technologies, *IEEE Signal Processing*, 26, 6, 80-89.

[23] Silva, L. M. E., Buyya, R., (1999). Parallel Programming Models and Paradigms, *Citeseer Cluster Computing*, 2, 4-27.

[24] Fatahalian, K., Knight, T. J., Houston, M., Erez, M., Horn, D. R., Leem, L., Park, J. Y., Ren, M., Aiken, A., Dally, W. J., Hanrahan, P., (2006). Sequoia: Programming The Memory Hierarchy, *Proc. Supercomputing*, Tampa Bay, FL.

[25] Hoberock, J., Bell, N., (2008). *Thrust*, http://code.google.com/p/thrust/

[26] Kepner, J., Lebak, J., (2003). Software technologies for high-performance parallel signal processing, *Lincoln Lab. J.*, 14, 2, 181-198.

[27] Singh, H., (2004). *Introspective C++*, Thesis, Virginia Polytechnic Institute.

[28] Koskinen, J., (2004). *Meta-programming in C++*.

[29] Munshi, A., (2011). *The OpenCL specification, version 1.1*, Khronos Group.

[30] *NVIDIA CUDA Programming Guide, Version 2.2.1*, (2009). NVIDIA Santa Clara, CA.

[31] Vandierendonck, H., Pratikakis, P., Nikolopoulos, D. S., (2011). Parallel Programming of General-Purpose Programs Using Task-Based Programming Models, *Proceeding*

HotPar'11 Proceedings of the 3rd USENIX conference on Hot topic in parallelism, USENIX Association Berkeley, CA, US.

[32] Lin, D., Huang, X., Nguyen, Q., Blackburn, J., Rodrigues, C., Huang, T., Do, M. N., Patel, S. J., Hwu, W. W., (2009). The Parallelization Of Video Processing, *IEEE Signal Processing*, 26, 6, 38-49.

[33] Klein, S. T., Wiseman, Y., (2000). Parallel Huffman Decoding, *Proceeding DCC '00 Proceedings of the Conference on Data Compression*, IEEE Computer Society, Washington, DC, US.

[34] *CLOC – Count Lines Of Code*, Northrop Grumman Corporation – IT Solutions, v. 1.53, http://cloc.sourceforge.net.

[35] Teijeiro, C., Taboada, G. L., Tourino, J., Fraguela, B. B., Doallo, R., Mallon, D. A., Gomez, A., Mourino J. C., Wibecan, B., (2009). Evaluation of UPC Programmability using class room, *Proc. of the 3rd Conf. on Partitioned Global Address Space programming Models*, ACM, New York, US.

[36] *PARSEC Benchmark Suite*, v. 2.1, http://parsec.cs.princeton.edu/

[37] *Microsoft Task Parallel Library*, http://msdn.microsoft.com/en-us/library/dd537608.aspx.

[38] Khammassi, N., *XPU Framework*, http://www.xpu-project.net/

[39] *Intel 64 and IA-32 Architectures Software Developer Manuals*, http://www.intel.com/content/www/us/en/processors/architectures-software-developer-manuals.html.

[40] Deloatch, C. *Pipeline Parallelism*.

In: Parallel Programming
Editor: Mikhail S. Tarkov

ISBN: 978-1-63321-957-1

Chapter 9

AN APPROACH TO THE CONSTRUCTION OF ROBUST SYSTEMS OF INTERACTING PROCESSES

Igor N. Skopin*

Institute of Computational Mathematics and Mathematical Geophysics
SB RAS, Novosibirsk State University, Novosibirsk, Russia

Abstract

The problems of distributed computing associated with the reliability of network interactions are discussed. Sequential solutions of some problems that are naturally interpreted as systems of interacted processes are considered. Descriptions of traditional problems solutions as systems of interacting processes are applicable for decomposition of computing task and increase the computations robustness.

Keywords: Robustness, reliability, parallel systems, errors and their diagnostic, processes interactions, parallel and concurrent processes, good cases of solving error problems

1. Introduction

The notion of *robustness* means a condition wherein the characteristics of the technology, the process or processes are not sensitive to the destabilizing factors [1]. This concept is directly related to the quality features such as system *reliability*. If reliability is understood as the external characteristic of the system, describing the degree of satisfaction of expectations under the system, the robustness should be considered as a package of actions to achieve the required reliability. These actions are envisaged and taken throughout the life cycle of the system development from its conception, design and construction, and then to a stop of using it. As applied to computer systems, general provisions on the robustness and reliability are

---

* E-mail address: iskopin@gmail.com.
The chapter presents the work that is supported by grant RF RSF № 14 – 11 00485 “High-performance methods and technologies of electrophysical processes and devices modeling”.

specified as follows. For computer systems, in processes which are executed in parallel, it is natural to consider all sorts of mistakes distorting, terminating with no results or hanging calculations as destabilizing factors. Errors must be diagnosed and, if possible, be neutralized. This should enable the users, the developers of the system processes, the operating system and hardware support service to take appropriate actions. The diagnosis should be targeted and undistorted information about the incident, and the neutralization should be minimizing losses from failures. However, all this is very difficult to achieve, in particular, because of non-determinism of a parallel computer system, excluding the detection of all the errors by testing. The main problem is the recognition of the hidden errors, which do not always manifest themselves even in situations that look as identical. An increase of the interacting processes robustness is possible by monitoring the effective processes implementation. Unfortunately, the use of this approach has its limitations.

A very promising solution of the problems of parallel computer systems is considered modeling the distributed processes interactions. One of the main problems of this approach is to define the process interface, the satisfaction of which would prevent the system (network) from falling into undesirable states: suspension, exceeding expectations, etc. When modeling, the processes are described as sending messages in a standard format, receiving them with detecting the errors, performing actions to neutralize errors in terms of their own functioning and the network computing stability. The existing network organizes the processes interaction and allows users to carry out their tasks.

It is often interpreted as an implementability of a formal process description. However, the undesirable conditions arise, much time is spent unproductively, and the network management of processes is a complex task which is bordered with art. Considerable efforts to standardize protocols and messages do not change the matter [2, 3].

Thus, the existing methods of improving the reliability of network interactions are not sufficient to get the desired level of parallel systems robustness. Along with their development, we need other methods and approaches that would be able to correctly diagnose and neutralize the errors, and would prevent complex situations involving errors. It seems appropriate to use and adapt the experience gained in other areas to the subject of parallel interacting processes. This problem is solved in the following sections.

Section 2 deals with the motivation of the approach and presenting ideas of the method used in the following sections. The main content of the material is presented in the form of the analysis of several examples in Section 3. Recommendations are given on how this or that method may be used in the systems development of interacting processes. To present the results of analysis, regardless of their motivation, these recommendations are highlighted in the text and numbered. In conclusion, the presented recommendations are discussed, and possible ways of the approach's development are outlined.

2. Communication between Processes: Good and Bad Cases

When modeling networks, it is usually assumed that to describe relevant process interactions, it is sufficient: 1) to operate with abstract messages and related concepts: sending, receiving, waiting for a message, reply, etc.; 2) use the messages to regulate the interaction of local pairs of processes: the source and recipient of messages.

The following example makes one doubt that the selected base is adequate to describe the network functioning.

Suppose that process *A* sends a message to process *B*, which, in turn, because of any external impacts and internal state, sends a message to process *C*. Let *C* detects an error, i.e., a mismatch of the received message to the expected one. It is unable to interpret the situation differently as an error of *B*. However, the actual error can occur when transmitting a message from *A* to *B*, but it was (for whatever reason) unnoticed, and as a result, process *B* sends a message to *C*. Process *C*, of course, can give a response message, which indicates the error, but *C* is unable to properly diagnose the error because there is no data for it.

In turn, the process *B* engaged its work, can not always respond adequately to the bug report. To do this, it should at least expect the response message. But this is not enough, since the source of the error could be not process *A*, but an earlier process or even a hardware failure. The reaction to error propagation requires an analysis that goes beyond the limits of local interactions between processes *A*, *B* and *C*.

There are more difficult cases with the expectation of messages that are capable of generating paradoxes of suspension (deadlock) type such as "pasta philosophers" [4].

The consideration of "bad" cases is useful when they show the direction of development. For computer networks they show it creating increasingly complex regulations and agreements that still do not provide a satisfactory solution for the problem. In this regard, it is useful to analyze the "good" situations when it is possible to overcome the avalanche growth of the size of local information used for decision-making. On this base, we can try to get an answer to the question of how to overcome the difficulties useful in certain situations, for example, when modeling networks. Good cases should be complex enough not to be in a situation of trivial solutions (like the "ban all sorts of interaction"). But, at the same time, it should be clear why, in the particular case, a solution is obtained. It does not matter from what area good cases are taken. It is only important that the conditions be similar.

The aim of this work is to analyze the solutions of some problems, methods which could be useful for proper adaptation to describe robust network interactions. To do this, we consider the possibility of presenting the solutions as processes interaction, which implementation lends itself to a reasonable robust scheme to support the network reliability.

3. Examples of Solutions by Processes

The proposed idea is demonstrated in a number of examples of solving the known problems:

- parsing as interaction of processes;
- exhaustive search in finding the shortest path in the graph;
- character transformations of structured strings and the model of computation in Refal.

Conventional solutions for these problems are converted into a form that can be represented as processes interaction. This representation allows one to figure out how to solve the problems of programs improper behavior in these examples. Common to all the problems in their process-representation is the use of meaningful information pledged to the algorithm.

However, the methods of information use are different. The analysis of these methods from the perspective of their applicability in more general cases is represented below.

3.1. Parsing

The process description of an analyzer comes from the usual convention that string to be parsed is viewed from left to right, character by character. Each character of the string is checked for a match with a terminal symbol of the product and if the result is affirmative, then it is a signal for moving the line forward. This promotion is accompanied by a generation of the process responsible for the analysis of the line remainder. We can assume that the input string is multiplied: each activated process gets your copy of the unread input string portion (it is enough to store and transfer to processes the copies of pointer to the next character and return the copies after the completion of the production process).

The analysis should distinguish between two types of completion:

- *inglorious conclusion*, when it turns out that the process was activated at the time in vain, that everything it did in the hope for a sequel, must be destroyed along with the memories of it;
- *completion with the hope for a sequel*, when there is an opportunity to find out that the completed process was carried out not in vain: the product is a member of the restored sequence of productions (i.e., at the time it participated in the inference).

The inglorious conclusion exactly corresponds to the metaphor of inglorious life of an individual who leaves a memory (here, on the absurd stack discipline, parents outlive their children). Also, in accordance with the metaphor, the hope for the continuation may be in vain: ingloriously terminated parent (grandparent) process makes all its children the same (no matter, already completed children or continue to exist).

The scheme can generate an infinite number of processes: when the grammar is left-recursive, the process generation is cycling. The situation is remedied if the condition of generation is complicated, but for the purposes of comparison of parsing and processes interactions, the left-recursive grammars can be excluded from consideration.

It is clear that the presentation of the scheme and its relationship with the processes of string generation is too high a price: avalanche growth of concurrent processes requires excessive resources.

Therefore, in practice, this scheme is rejected. Only the method of recursive descent clearly describes the idea of the string generation process. Here, from the outset, it is assumed the special case, where, at the first stage it can be solved for sure which of the productions was applied. This is true for LL(1) grammars [5] which are important in terms of the application but it does not cover all relevant practical cases.

It is instructive to note that, in the concept of object oriented design and programming, there is a trend of explicit description of recursive descent as the interaction of objects (processes) which represent the tree nodes of parsing the string. The activity of these objects, i.e., feasibility of autonomous generation of the processes seen in the following: built as part of the syntactic structure (nonterminal), the object activates the processes that are responsible for the analysis of each of the string, generated by it, and finish building the structure.

Availability of object methods for all generation variants, as well as the uniqueness of the choice of a variant by the first analyzed symbol, guarantees the correctness of such decentralized algorithm.

The object-oriented view of the structured text is productive not only in solving the problems of parsing. In particular, in connection with the structuring of texts, the concept of the document object model [6] was introduced. This concept declares the structural units of the text as its active components, i.e., objects capable of performing certain actions.

These actions are described as class methods that can be interpreted as processes. The process activities and interactions are controlled by the syntactic structure of the text.

The recursive descent method is interesting as one of the approaches to overcome the processes multiplicity:

1. **By external information, available to all processes (the current symbol of parsed string), it can be established exactly which processes need to be activated.**

Most practical schemes of bottom-up analysis are not described explicitly by defining interacting processes, but they can be treated as a reduction in the number of active processes by special techniques.

However, there is a scheme which clearly does not involve reduction of a set of active processes. This is the LR-analysis of D. Knut [7]. In LR-analysis

2. **The encoding of the set of all possible processes combinations by states of the automaton, as an approach to overcome processes reproduction, is opposed to processes avalanche.**

For the so called deterministic languages, this coding is efficiently feasible. Because the operating role of analyzing processes is negligible (they should be noted as final with the hope to continue), you can do without them, and the alignment of recovered productions sequences can be entrusted to the stage of convolution. Knut builds the states encoding processes–analyzers by grammatical tracking all possible lines sequels. He uses the look-ahead on the line to eliminate transitions ambiguities and hence the avalanche growth in the processes number.

The states encode the analyzing processes, but rather, the potential of their activation and completion. It turns out that the number of states of these processes and the transitions between states is finite and foreseeable. There is a technique of reducing the size of tables representing the transition diagrams, by which the Knut method becomes acceptable to all relevant practical purposes. This method has become the basis for building a number of technological systems for compiler construction (in particular, YACC [8]).

The main conclusion from the comparison of LR-methodology and process descriptions of the analysis that demonstrates the feasibility of overcoming the avalanche generation of processes, is the following:

3. **Complexity of the problem of multiplicity is completely controllable if we reject attempts to control the situation by the local transmission of information.**

In the task of analysis, the coding of processes is a key moment that is, essentially, a way of local interactions substitution by global distributed control. Coding solves the problem of increasing the processes number by gluing them.

All processes are glued in parsing. The glued processes split when a real separation of their actions is required. Splitting is possible in controversial points of continuation of the work where the conflicts, such as "shift – reduction", arise.

Usually, splitting is bypassed by attracting more information: peek strings are checked, precedence relationships are calculated, etc. So, there is an opportunity to continue exactly one process, and it turns out static.

In the real environment of interacting processes, it is usually impossible to build all the actions in a linear sequence. Therefore, the division of actions will require processes splitting. In such cases, the coding is not able to eliminate the generation of processes, but it may well help to curb the avalanche.

Parsing using the processes demonstrates another unpleasant possible event: *waiting for messages* (e.g., waiting for the completion of certain processes) *without assurances that they will go.* When encoding the parsing processes, this problem, as conflicts "shift - reduction", is solved by replacing local information to information about grammar in general. In any environment of interacting processes, such reception fails. As a generalization, it can offer

4. **The use of an external arbiter is chosen on the basis of some criterion of how long to wait for messages to arrive.**

A criterion for the process of analysis is the following agreement: if none of the processes is moving along the input line, it is a sign of possible suspension. Here, as in many cases, it is true that

5. **The local information transmitted between processes is insufficient. It should be replaced by a general information about the processes system.**

3.2. Exhaustive Search

The situation, when it is possible to cope with a multiplicity of processes, can be seen in the solution of the famous problem of searching the shortest path between the cities connected by a network of unidirectional roads. It is often considered in the study of iterative methods of programming when we want to emphasize that the results efficiency depends on the order of sorting (comparison of searches in depth and width). In terms of quality of learning, the solution is interesting if it is based on a system of interacting processes without considering the question of the implementation of this system on real (single- and multiprocessor) computers. When the process solution is mastered, it is advisable to show that iterative methods offer a way to map the solution in a real computing environment. This approach seems more natural for beginners. Sometimes they can offer it, even with errors typical of those who have not previously encountered the problems with processes synchronization. The approach prepares students for the development of methods of parallelism without regard to the extent to which their skill is deep in sequential programming [9][1]. The idea dates back to the approach of Dal and Hoare, who, on this task, demonstrated the capabilities of systems with discrete events of the language Simula 67 [10, 11].

Determination of the shortest distance between cities *A* and *B*, linked by a network of unidirectional roads on the base of a system of interacting processes, can be represented as a competition in speed of achieving a goal of a suitable number of active agents "wandering" on different roads. There are two classes of algorithms that implement the wandering: direct algorithms, when the overall process starts with *A*, and back algorithms starting from *B*. To discuss the overcoming of processes multiplicity, it is sufficient to consider only one of them (for other solutions see [12]).

The direct algorithm of dispersed agents up to the technical details can be described as the behavior of each agent according to the following scheme, which is specified for the agent location as a parameter:

1) If the agent is in *B*, then the goal is achieved. The traversed path is presented as a result which first contains only *A* and, as the agent moves from town to town, the path is updated (see below).
2) Otherwise, the agent copies are generated as many as the roads derived from the current city of the agent. The traveled distance is given as the local data of new agents. This is the distance of the parent agent from *A* to the current city (we can assume that, in this situation, the parent agent is destroyed, it ends with the hope to continue or it becomes a copy, but it is important that the accumulated local path is stored in each copy). If there are no roads from the current city, the agent is eliminated (its process ends ingloriously).
3) The action of each agent-copy delayed to move to its next point (since all copies are identical, the distance between the points can serve as measure of the time).
4) When the delay is over, the agent checks whether the destination is one of those that have already been passed. If so, the agent is eliminated (it is clear that this information in the system as a whole is not lost, the other agents continue to operate).
5) Go to step 1.

The algorithm terminates when the path from *A* to *B* is found or when all agents are eliminated.

If you do not pay attention to how many agents can operate simultaneously, then, in the presence of the path from *A* to *B*, you must not necessarily check a loop (item 4). Instead, you can use a more stringent condition of the agent elimination, the condition of visiting this destination by any of the agents. But then you need to memorize *global information* about the network of roads and cities: the attribute is associated with each of the towns and that marks it as passed at the first visit (this is made in step 4 before leaving the current location)[2].

---

[1] Pedagogical aspect of solving this problem is discussed in Chapter 10 “Early learning in parallel programming” of this issue.

[2] If the path from *A* to *B* is guaranteed, it is theoretically permissible another solution, which work capacity is doubtful because of an excessive number of generated processes: we may never check the liquidation condition and reproduce the agents indefinitely because, at least, one of them will reach the objective, and this event could serve as signal for all other agents elimination.

The above algorithm needs remembering information about the past in the local database of agents. This means redundancy of storage: the local data of each agent to be eliminated are stored in vain. However the correct path cannot be obtained for the global storage. This deficiency is absent in the solution generated by the reverse algorithm i.e., by finding the path from *B* to *A*. In this case everything works just the same as in the previous one, but with the exception of the following: local information about agents and their paths is not remembered, but, as a mark of visiting cities, it is stated what city the agent came from to this city (this mark can be called as recommendation), it is *general information*. As a result, when any of the agents reach *A*, the sequence starting with A and built by recommendations, gives the desired path (this inverse algorithm is presented by Dahl and Hoare [11]).

Both forward and reverse algorithms are efficient when all processes are provided by the work. For this purpose, you can use the known wave method which strictly regulates the sequential enumeration of the variants corresponding to the agents.

It is a direct rejection of the processes, since their parallel actions are replaced by sequential execution of their actions not requiring synchronization. Nonetheless, it is possible to consider this approach as a special method:

6. **Means to overcome the interactions complexity can be sometimes served by forming processes in sequence.**

All search algorithms are engaged in such alignment (with a varying degree of success – both in terms of efficiency and clarity). A useful discussion of this topic is presented in [12].

In relation to the subject of this work, the alignment is the degenerate method. There is more interesting approach of languages Simula, Simula 67, etc., which proclaims the simulation of parallelism by sequential computations and, therefore, leaves the possibility of thinking in terms of active agents and behavioral algorithms open.

It is based on a *system with discrete events* as an environment of process activities in which the sequence of their execution is governed by a special structure called *control list*. Each process is in one of four states defined in connection with the queue of processes in the control list, dynamically assigned to execution. The states are:

- *active* when the process is executed;
- *suspended* when the process execution is interrupted but the point of resuming activity (address in the program) is memorized and the process is in the control list;
- *passive* when the process is interrupted, the point of resuming activity is memorized, but it is not present in the control list,
- *completed* when the process is interrupted, and the point of the resuming activity is not stored.

The control list simulates time. Its first process is the only active one. If it is interrupted, the following suspended process becomes active. The process can be *inserted* into the control list (*before any process*, or *after a certain process*) or *removed* from it. It can be *assigned to a certain time*. This means that it is inserted before the process which running time is minimal surpassing the assigned time. It may be random (pseudorandom) inserting the process in a particular place in the list.

So, the processes workflow is clearly built. It is postulated that manipulation of the control list and the state of active processes is a result of certain *events occurring in the discrete system*. While an event has not occurred, the process state and position in the control list are not changed. In this case parallelism is replaced by an agreement allowing simulation of the simultaneous actions of an arbitrary number of processes.

Characteristically, in the system with discrete events, you do not need to withstand time delays explicitly. They only order and reorder the control list.

For the considered problem, agents copy means:

1 the creation of local structures of these processes-agents;
2 placing all processes-agents in the control list according to the *activation time*;
3 the movement of each active agent in the process control list according to its time *delay*.

Of course, we are talking about the model time only! According to the postulate of events, the execution of any process can not change the order of other processes until a special event occurs. It does not require the time attribute, the order relation is sufficient for processes.

Even an infinite loop, as a result of the refusal of inspection of the sequence of agent's actions in paragraph 2 or in paragraph 4, will not prevent the implementation of the algorithm if the capacity of control list is sufficient.

Several important points must be emphasized:

- Instead of real parallelism in the system with discrete events, we have the effect of parallelism which is devoid of unpleasant situations, requiring special care of synchronization (for instance, collapse of "pasta philosophers") because of *ordering execution of processes in runtime* but not in the model time.
- If we try to implement a system with discrete events using real parallelism, all the troubles that needed synchronization appear again because the order is violated.
- In each model point a set of simultaneously existing agents is partially ordered. It becomes fully ordered by an appropriate placement in the control list.
- The control list is a *general data structure for processes-agents*. It could be considered as a global structure but the control list has no explicit access (for example, by the name).

The system with discrete events shows that:

7. Coping with processes multiplicity is possible by complete ordering processes in time of execution with simulated parallelism at the model level.

This approach does not claim universal applicability to real parallel systems, but it gives a reason to think that, in such systems, the process chains are possible, and parallel execution of the chains could be replaced by quasiparallel execution reducing the problem of process multiplicity.

Continuing the discussion of the problem of the shortest distance between cities, it is appropriate to mention an approach based on distributed computing (see [13]).

The approach formally describes the wave method which, as we have already noted, can be regarded as a special organizing method of agents actions.

In this approach, the solution is functionally similar to the agent-based method of Dahl and Hoare, but it does not require the presence of active agents, their copying and other agent-based entities. Instead of this, the activity of computer network processors is used. The decision is motivated by the actual need for finding the routes of data transmitions between nodes. This is not only natural, but also directly connected with the parallel computations. Constructing correct distributed algorithms would be impossible without an accurate description of network interactions models. And it is paying off: on the basis of such models, we can solve the problems of robustness and verification, and calculate complexity estimates. Thus:

8. **Exact description of the model of parallel computing, which is performed on the basis of multiplicity of processes, enables us to increase the reliability and robustness of interactions and data transmitting between processes.**

In fact, when developing programs, it is very useful to assign tasks using a mathematical description of the problem. An accurate and conclusive description of the problem, being solved in accordance with the used calculation model, not only allows one to avoid many errors of non-formal representation, but often to see new approaches to its solution. An illustration of this can be, for example, the parsing techniques, discussed in the previous section, that exhibit good cases of communications between processes. It is largely due to the fact that they are based on a mathematically precise description of the problem by D. Knuth. After the publication of his works [5, 7], where he described the LL- and LR-analysis, the parsing has become quite a practical technology. Another illustration of the usefulness of the problems mathematical description is presented in the next section.

3.3. Character Conversion of Structured Data

The following problems are related to the area that has traditionally been viewed as a sequential process: conversion of character information. It may seem surprising that such problems have attracted attention in the discussion of the processes interaction. However, first, it is not really necessary and, with the knowledge of the structure of character data, it is often undesirable to see the character transformation as a single sequential process. The example of compilation illustrates this. Secondly, we discuss the transformations that can be conveniently expressed in terms of the string structure. These are the cases that are adequately described as interacting processes. From here we obtain restrictions on the languages which are worth to deal. These languages are Lisp [14] and Refal [15].

Snobol [16], for example, is clearly not suitable, since the order of pattern matching steps execution, prescribed by the language, virtually eliminates the ways to overcome the difficulties of parallelization except for building the processes in sequence.

In the context of this work, it would be to explore the unification of Prolog [17, 18], which is well structured and suitable for the description of symbolic transformations. But, unfortunately, it cannot be cleaned from the concept of elementary steps sequential execution.

Thus, in Snobol and Prolog, the sequence of actions predefined by the language rejects the idea of description by processes.

The calculation model of Lisp (and other functional languages, too) is closest to the idea proposed here. As will be shown, the *a priori* standards of data structure both in Lisp and Refal help to overcome processes multiplicity. Choosing between Lisp and Refal can be made arbitrarily. However, Refal has the essential advantage: the elementary act of the data processing is always determined for the entire string, while Lisp gives the opportunity to ask the sequential processing of data presented in a list.

Refal combines the handling of strings with the structure processing and, so, it is possible to trace what advantage this concept gives compared to the traditional sequential conversion.

Furthermore, the Refal calculations model is in a good agreement with deep mathematical results and, therefore, it is easier to read.

The Refal idea is to adapt the theoretical Markov algorithm [19, 20] to the practical needs. The system of rules of this language is the development of the process of Markov's substitutions defined by productions: $\alpha_i \rightarrow \beta_i$ and $\alpha_i \rightarrow \bullet \beta_i$, where α_i, $\beta_i \in T^*$, $1 \le i \le N$ (N is a number of productions, T is an alphabet of input string symbols). Computation of production systems by the Markov Algorithm is a cyclical repetition in a strict order of *search* of α_i in input string (always from the beginning) and replacing the founded α_i by β_i. The calculations are completed when nothing can be found, or when production • is realized.

In Refal, the Markov Algorithm is enriched to manipulate strings with the bracket structure due to the fact that this structure is the base of handling transformation. In the dynamics of calculations, the structural units, needed for processing, are framed by the so-called *concrete definition brackets* **k** and **.**[3] with *determinatives* immediately following the **k**. This construction provides a subroutine-function call for processing a selected structural unit. This is pattern of calling the function with the name specified by determinative and the arguments given by residue of the structural unit. The patterns of the function call provide the binding of processing to the structural data units for local transformation.

The actions of Refal functions are defined by *operators* that are similar semantically and syntactically to the productions of Markov Algorithm. The alphabet of productions is expanded by *variables* of different types. When comparing the left-hand side of productions to the processed string, the variables are obtained as values of the strings balanced by parentheses. The mapping, combined with assignment, is called *projection*. The projection is considered successful if all characters of the left side are mapped with characters in the string, and all variables are assigned to the correct value.

The most simple example of the always successful projection is operator

ke1**.** → **k**/dif/e1**.**

because variable e1 without restrictions can be assigned to any string framed by *brackets* **k** and **.**. Its implementation makes it possible to perform operators with determinative /dif/, i.e., function call dif. If this function implements a symbolic differentiation (for definiteness, on x), it is possible to attempt to project the operator of taking the derivative of the product:

[3] In the latest versions of Refal language [21], developers have moved away from the image concretization brackets by special characters replacing them by < and >, respectively. This is convenient from the point of view of fast writing but, in our opinion, is not so clear.

k/dif/v1*v2. → (**k**/dif/v1.*(v2)+**k**/dif/v2.*(v1)).

Execution of the projection reduces to finding the character * on the upper level of brackets and assignment of variables v1 and v2 to the left and right multiplication operands. If there are several characters *, then its first occurrence will be selected and, so, v2 will be assigned to the rest of expression. Furthermore, if the expression actually consists of addenda, then v2 will be assigned to the remainder of the string. To avoid this error, it is necessary to perform the differentiation of addition before the differentiation of multiplication. This is accomplished by the ordering differentiation operators.

If projecting is successful, then two concrete definition fragments, **k**/dif/v1. and **k**/dif/v1.. appear in the resulting string. In these fragments, the variables are replaced by their values. Otherwise, an attempt is made to perform projection for the textually next operator with determinative /dif/.

Such statements must be provided for all differentiation rules in the order reflecting the syntactic structure of the expression (in particular, the derivative of the sum should come before the presented operator). For the same reason, in the left side of the operator the above variables v1 and v2 should be framed by parentheses. In addition, there should be "obvious" operators (for example, replacement of constants differentiation by zero) and the operator of concretization percolation inside the brackets:

k/dif/(e1). → (**k**/dif/e1.)

As a result of the subroutine /dif/ execution on the input string

a*x+bx*(c+x)+d

a string with redundancy will be likely built:

((0*(x)+1*(a))+((b*((c+x))+(0+1)*(bx))+0))

The root of redundancy is that the subroutine /dif/ is irrelevant for arithmetic transformations (multiplication by 0, addition of constants, etc.) which, if it is necessary, should be scheduled for another special determinative subroutine, e.g., /ar/ that will clear the differentiation result of the debris. The joint launch of subroutines /dif/ and /ar/ is achieved by operator

ke1. → **k**/ar/**k**/dif/e1..

The Refal transformations can be effectively carried out only for a suitable choice of representation of the processed strings. In the Refal-machine this problem is solved as follows. At every moment of computation, the recyclable string is located in the so-called *field of view*, where it is defined as a double-linked list with the elements representing characters, determiners, and brackets. Each substring in brackets becomes sublist. The beginning and the end of the sublist have pointers from the elements representing these brackets. This representation prohibits the input strings with unbalanced brackets.

They are not available in the field of view and cannot appear there during the calculations! The representation is in accordance with the mechanism of projection that does not require viewing nested substrings.

As an example, Figure 1 illustrates the representation of string **k** AB(CD)(E)F**.** in the field of view of the Refal-machine. The example shows that for implementation of variables it is enough to store, for each of them, only two pointers, to the beginning and to the end of a string value of a given variable. This format is free more than in Lisp and allows efficient processing.

Each projection variant can be treated as a launch of a stand-alone process which ends ingloriously if it leads to failure. The language requires the nested concretizations to be executed at first. For a process-based description, it means the suspension of a process for the substring with concretization brackets until the nested process exits.

A separate projection process can be considered as a sequential search of reference symbols (they are defined in the statement explicitly) and parentheses. The search begins with a study of the first character after **k**. If there is ambiguity to continue, the process splits and one of the processes coming to character **.** is considered as *completed with the hope for a continuation.*

Any pair of brackets, occurring in the processed string, generates a *local projection process*, subordinating to the parent process which can continue the projection, i.e., comparison of characters that are not nested in parentheses, but it must wait for the results of all local processes generated by them.

As a result, all production variables consistently receive the values, and there is a base for building the result, or the projection fails, and the process is ingloriously terminated. If the projection is successful, then the construction process of the result string is completed with the hope for a continuation.

A canonical sequence of actions is illustrated schematically in Figure 2, where the bold lines indicate the characters of the field of view that are not parentheses. Bracket pairs A, B, ..., K limit the nested structure shown as a triangle with a serial concretization number.

The program execution begins with the construction of projection F and, then, projection G. If F and G are defined by the concretization brackets, then, in the process description, they are obviously independent processes; their alignment for sequential execution is not principal and they can be run in parallel.

The situation is changed if F and G are conventional brackets. In this case, the projection is performed for substructure B.

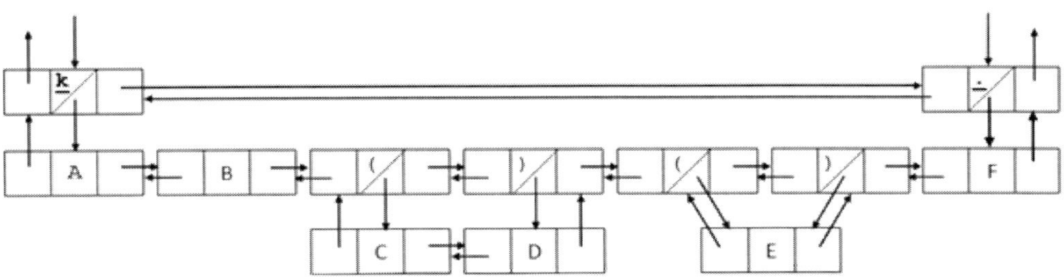

Figure 1. Example of string representation.

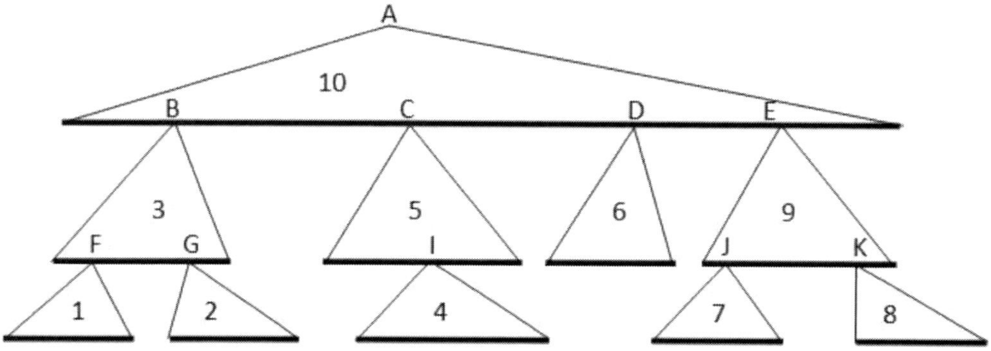

Figure 2. Scheme of running Refal program.

The selected product of B requires the nested substructures generating variables interdependent values. Then projection processes F and G must act in accordance with the computations definition. Essentially, they need to realize interaction for shared data synchronization. The outstanding quality of the Refal is that regulation of such interaction can be computed statically, i.e., it may be based on the productions analysis.

For the independent and dependent F and G, in the general case, the concretization of B cannot be made up until the completion of processes F and G. However, there are special cases that do not require waiting for the completion of these processes: if F and G do not reduce the level of nested parentheses, they do not prevent the parallel computation of the enveloping process. Again, the situation is detected statically and an unpleasant dynamic adjusting can be avoided. But when the suspension of the enveloping process is necessary, nothing complicated happens for the Refal concretization mechanism: it is always clear from the static analysis, what kind of string conversions can be expected.

The question about completion of the Refal process concretization is solved easily. If the successful projection is failed, then all processes, generated by the completing process, should be destroyed. The state of the field of view in this case is not changed, since the substitution is not possible, and all variables that received their values in the projection are localized in the process.

The information, needed for decision-making on all kinds of process interaction, is well localized. It includes:

- rules-products that can be analyzed before computing (*static data*);
- the current values of the variables that are local for the corresponding process of specification (*local dynamic data*);
- the process hierarchy that appears during the computation (*common dynamic data*);
- the current value of the field of view, distributed among processes in strict accordance with the hierarchy of the process creation (*structured global data*).

A set of processes, generated in any time, is partially ordered by the runtime. Each totally ordered chain corresponds to processes alignment into the sequence. Data synchronization of processes is always controlled by the enveloping process.

In fact, this process plays a role of the message broker [22], but, unlike the broker, it has information about the whole chain of the message transmissions.

Therefore, it is more likely to increase the robustness of computing. As a consequence, we can formulate the following good case of the process-based description of the data conversion: when the processed data structure can be represented so that the message broker has the general information about all possible sequels, the broker is able to control the data transmission correctness.

9. **Solving the problem of the communication reliability is possible providing the communication control of complete information about the history of interactions, as well as all possible computing extensions.**

There is another Refal property, allowing to hope that its computation model can be extended to more general cases of interacting processes not associated with the symbolic processing and, in particular, useful for describing the distributed computing[4]. We are talking about how to connect external computing to the executable Refal program. This method is the easiest to explain by the following illustration.

The Refal computation method is certainly unsuitable for the normal arithmetic.

For example, with the computation rules for addition (**k**/addition/) and subtraction (**k**/subtraction/), the rules for multiplication are obvious, but very inefficient:

k/multiplication/v1*1. → **v1.**

k/multiplication/v1*v2. → **k**/multiplication/**k**/ addition /v1+v1.***k**/subtraction/v2-1. .

Of course, this approach to executing arithmetic operations is not good. More reasonable is to take the advantage over a program that does this effectively, i.e., through external functions. The external function call in the Refal program is a concretization with the appropriate determinative that identifies the requirement to obtain a certain result, for example, by conventional computing (in the example it is the multiplication function which could be realized in another language). The concretization of the external function assumes the necessary transformation of the original string arguments into a format amenable to this function as parameters and a subsequent call of this function. The result of this call is transformed by the Refal system into a sequence of characters.

The way to include external functions allows one to move arbitrarily far away from the symbolic computation. The only thing required for this inclusion is an autonomy of functioning and uniform handling of the parameter formats. The sequence of the external functions in a single concretization can be interpreted as a sequence of calls to the atomic processes that do not interact with each other. This concretization can activate interacting processes, but they are already the subject to regulation by Refal computations.

The Refal language syntax is very unconventional. It is quite suitable for symbolic computations, but not suitable for the external one, for example, arithmetic computations. The evaluation of this fact is ambiguous. On the one hand, writing concretization brackets may seem tedious. So, it is desirable to have a possibility of writing the expressions (and other purely operational actions) in the usual manner. On the other hand, it can lead to ambiguity in

[4] The idea of using the Refal-based model, enhanced by methods of operating priorities for the description of distributed computing, belongs to N. N. Nepeivoda. At the time of writing this work it, as much as the author knows, has not been published.

understanding the strings, where the expression characters should not denote computations. Consequently, we need to introduce additional notations on the syntactic level. This question is important, but it has nothing to do with the computation model since it deals with the abstract syntax only.

Essentially, Refal offers a certain interface standard for process interactions. This standard allows the transfer of common information between the processes, if it is necessary. Refal has a solid mathematical foundation and is more flexible than languages for specifying protocols of information transfer, in particular, promoting the reliability of the process interaction. Thus, the analysis of the Refal language means calling the external computations leads to the conclusion that

10. The flexibility of interface standards for the transmission of information between processes and access to common information contributes to robustness of interacting processes systems.

Conclusion

In all the above examples, a common approach to the decomposition of the solved problem can be easily seen. This process-based decomposition transforms (projects) the problem in a form suitable for a particular computer. In some cases, this transformation facilitates the encoding of processes; in other cases, it is used as a special organization of ordering computations. We can say that the essence of this decomposition is to separate the convenient description from further serialization of computations.

Whenever the presented approach is used, there is a need, in common, although not global information, for alignment of processes execution.

When we consider the classical schemes of process interactions in parallel computations, we see that Dykstra semaphores, Hoare monitors, and other synchronization means should be considered as common but not global data. The appropriate hypothesis is that we need to use common data for the achievement of correct processes interactions. It is true, if there is no distortion in the common data access. Unfortunately, in real situations, this condition is not always guaranteed. As a result, an uncontrolled disruption of the system behavior is possible. For example, if a catch sign of the monitor is not exhibited in a critical situation of a capture, the failure may occur or may not occur, but no information is obtained about it.

It is important to know the possible causes of disruptions and to plan actions for failures cases to increase the distributed computing robustness. As a means to minimize the failure losses, we recommend tracking all activities of the processes achievable in every moment of distributed computing. In this regard, we should pay attention to the Refal computation model and its parallel extension. Essentially, here a plan is built for all computation extensions possible after the projection and concretization. If we abstract from the concreteness of symbolic processing and replace it by abstract activation and suspension of processes, then we will see that all cases of the computation continuations may well be tracked. The tracking is a direct consequence of the explicit common data structuring.

A direct transformation of the process-based description of the Refal computing model in a form suitable for a particular computer is not always to be successful. The straightforward strategy can generate more processes than the computing environment can provide. It means that other mechanisms must be involved and, again, we may try to use the cases from the arsenal of alignment of the processes used for sequential computations.

Here the method of constructing control lists for the discrete event system is quite efficient. Of course, the direct interaction modeling by this system is not suitable because it provides the mapping of active processes on a single processor only. Therefore, we need to build the control lists for all real network computers. As a result, it is possible to implement correctly the queues of processes with dynamically assigned priorities. We can expect that in conjunction with the planning of all extensions of computing this will increase the distributed computing robustness.

As our illustrations show, it is very useful to know how processes are terminated for the planning of all continuations of calculations including the error diagnosis. The inglorious process termination typically initiates the inglorious terminations of the processes generated by it. This indicates that these processes do not affect subsequent computations. For this reason, a set of the processes, that must be analyzed in the error diagnosis, is narrowed. The completion of the process with the hope of continuation provides information about the processes that can be influenced by this action. It can be useful for accuracy of diagnostics in the future. In both cases the analysis is refined by engaging information about the semantics of interacting processes.

Of particular note is the multiplicity coding. As we know, this technique becomes quite common for sequential processes, but it is not used in the case of parallelism. This issue needs further investigation.

Outside the scope of this work, a significant number of good cases of distributed computing, which experience is appropriate to be used, remained. In particular, we did not study the approaches to the description of distributed computing based on a dataflow model. As is pointed out in [23], it is very natural to consider the so-called data flowcharts as a representation of the network of computers interconnected by the data flows transmitted between them. Good instances of such network are caused by the network functionality: the history of past computations does not affect the behavior of each computer. Essentially, other networks are not considered. We can assume that the traditional data flow computing solves the network problems by fairly strong restrictions. Such restrictions can be considered as another example of overcoming difficulties, perhaps the most effective. But it is correct only if the scope of the system applications is not narrowed more than allowed.

The materials presented here should not create the impression that all the existing network solutions are bad. On the contrary, in many situations, they demonstrate acceptable robustness and plenty of good cases. For instance, this is true with respect to the protocols that have been criticized above. This criticism is not aimed at denying the past experience. Its purpose is different: we try to show that acceptable solutions can be found not only by correcting errors, but also by analyzing the existing solutions in areas that, at first sight, seem very far removed from the studied problems.

It is quite clear that the search of private good solutions does not guarantee the absence of errors if we try to apply the search in another area. This search is not good for the straight introduction, but it is useful for forming a base for the development of applications: generalizing concepts, theories, and principles, promoting conscious coping.

References

[1] *Robustness. // Pedagogical terminological dictionary.* - URL: http://pedagogical_dictionary.academic.ru (used 04.18.2014).

[2] Orfali, R., Harkey, D., (1998). *Client/Server Programming with Java and CORBA.*

[3] Fielding, R., Irvine, U. C., et al., (1999). *Hypertext Transfer Protocol - HTTP/1.1.*, Network Working Group, W3C/MIT.

[4] Hoare, C. A. R., (1974). Monitors: An Operating System Structuring Concept, *Comm. ACM*, 17 (10), 549-557.

[5] Knuth, D. E., (1971). Top Down Syntax Analysis, *Acta Informatica*, 1 (2), 79-110.

[6] *Document Object Model (DOM) Level 1 Specification, version 1.0*, W3C Recommendation 1 October, 1998.

[7] Knuth, D. E., (1965). On the Translation of Languages from Left to Right, *Information and Control*, 8, 6, 607-639.

[8] Levine, J., Mason, T., Brown, D., (1992). *lex and yacc*, O'RELLY®.

[9] Skopin, I. N., (2011). Early learning in parallel programming, *Bulletin of the Moscow City Pedagogical University, Series Information and education informatization*, Moscow, MCPU, 2 (22), 46-55.

[10] Dahl, O.-J., Myhrhaug, B., Nygaard, K., (1968). *SIMULA 67 Common Base Language* - Norwegian Computing Center.

[11] Dahl, O. J., Dykstra, E. W., Hoare, C. A. R., (1972). *Structured Programming*, Academic Press.

[12] Nepyivoda, N. N., Skopin, I. N., (2003). *The Foundations of Programming*, Moscow-Izhevsk: Institute of Computer Science (In Russian).

[13] Tel, G., (1995). *Introduction to Distributed Algorithms*, Cambridge University Press.

[14] McCarthy, J., (1962). *LISP 1.5 Programmer's Manual*, MIT Press, Cambridge, Mass.

[15] Turchin, V. F., (1974). *Basic REFAL. Description of the language and basic programming techniques*, Moscow, CNIPIASS (In Russian).

[16] Griswold, R. E., Poage, J. F., Polonsky, I. P., (1971). *The SNOBOL4 Programming Language*, Prentice-Hall, Inc.

[17] ISO/IEC 13211-1:1995, Information technology - *Programming languages - Prolog - Part 1: General core.*

[18] ISO/IEC 13211-2:2000, Information technology - *Programming languages - Prolog - Part 2: Modules.*

[19] *Markov algorithm.* - URL: http://en.wikipedia.org/wiki/Markov_algorithm.

[20] Markov, A. A., (1954). The Theory of Algorithms, *The mathematical. Inst. Steklov proceedings*, 42, Moscow, Leningrad, AS USSR.

[21] Turchin, V. F., (1989). *Refal-5: Programming Guide and Reference Manual*, New England Publishing. Co., Holyoke.

[22] Squibb, J. *Configuring WebSphere Message Broker V. 6.1 on z/Linux* - IBM developer > WorksWebSphere > Technical library http://www.ibm.com/developerworks/websphere/library/techarticles/0804_squibb/0804_squibb.html?S_TACT=105AGX99andS_CMP=CP.

[23] *Lucid, the Dataflow Programming Language*. - London: Academic Press, 1985.

In: Parallel Programming
Editor: Mikhail S. Tarkov
ISBN: 978-1-63321-957-1

Chapter 10

EARLY LEARNING IN PARALLEL PROGRAMMING

Igor N. Skopin *
Institute of Computational Mathematics and Mathematical Geophysics SB RAS,
Novosibirsk State University, Novosibirsk, Russia

Abstract

The current approach to teaching programming is analyzed. We underline its problems related to training in parallelism. An alternative approach based on rejection of thinking patterns in teaching is presented. The main idea of the approach is separation of two types of activity in the program construction: development of the program sketch, which does not take into account the resource constraints, and mapping the sketch to a real computer. We show the advantages of this approach for the development of thinking and, in particular, when teaching parallelism.

Keywords: Cognitive development, activity-based approach to learning, teaching patterns, problem tasks, parallel programming, computational model, resource constraints

1. Introduction

Traditional teaching programming is based on the premise that the student should instill algorithmic thinking skills through the study of a simple programming language. Gradually, as the familiarization of language is developed, the range of the language features useful for algorithms program representation is extended. Inherently it is the way of stereotypes and pattern formation. It combines different templates by available methods for algorithmically meaningful texts. This approach is comfortable enough in teaching to motivate the students to master a new material.

However, the presentation of algorithms in programming languages will always limit the programmer, make him describe a set of possible actions the language, and not express what

* E-mail address: iskopin@gmail.com.
The chapter presents the work that is supported by grant RF RSF № 14 – 11 00485 "High-performance methods and technologies of electrophysical processes and devices modeling"

he can imagine at understanding the problem. As a result, a programmer restricts, step by step, his natural ways of data manipulation and actions to the level of linguistic resources. Formed thinking patterns are caused by the language, which is often perceived as a way of thinking that is characteristic for programming.

Restrictiveness of the programmer mindset manifests itself clearly when problems are solved involving concurrency. This statement confirmes an approach to the development of a parallel program when, first, its serial version is built, and then it is parallelized. To support this approach, the market offers specialized systems (OpenMP [1], MPI [2], etc) whose means are superstructures over sequential languages.

Comparing sequential and parallel programming in terms of teaching, it is appropriate to mention that many of our programming languages inherit the properties of the von Neumann calculation model, which postulates commands sequential execution by the only active item called processor. As it was noted by J. Backus [3] in 1975, this fact is a major obstacle to the mass transition to programming based on more developed and expressive computation models, for example, with the active memory and flexible structure of control organization.

The conclusion from the above is paradoxical: the focus of learning programming to the development of thinking actually leads to its decline and, perhaps, the only useful thing is a student ability to adapt to objectively existing restrictions. The highest level of thinking, which is usually able to achieve a programmer, is combinatorial thinking [4]. Such thinking is not conducive to the development of new methods. They appear not because of, but in spite of the objective combinatorial activity of a programmer. In other words, the methods are developed at the expense of natural talent of some outstanding individuals abilities, unspoiled by a routine of programming work.

This is indirectly confirmed by the problems that arise from those who begin to study parallelism and interaction of autonomous processes after a study of sequential programming. If it is necessary to take into account the consequences of the fact that the program fragments will run concurrently, then the student mentally attempts to order processes in time. As a result, he or she does not notice the well-known errors that do not appear in the sequential execution.[1]

In the following sections we motivate the need for new approaches to teaching parallel computing and, in particular, the study of parallel programming at the same time or even earlier than the sequential one. This statement is developed as an idea of the program design division into two components: drawing a sketch without restrictions on the use of resources and, then, mapping the sketch to a real computation model taking the limitations into account. The idea, illustrated by several examples, leads to a special methodology of programming called sketch programming, which has good prospects for the teaching that develops thinking.

2. Motivation of Early Parallel Computing Study

The most effective method of teaching is to create a new need which is natural for a student. If there is no need, then there is no interest and, as a consequence, the training activity falls. Applied to the study of parallelism, the skill of serial programming creates a

[1] The situation is similar to that when a programmer does not consider that because rounding an arithmetic calculator does not lead to the results corresponding to well-studied algebraic structures. Here, fundamental knowledge is in conflict with the fact that sometimes happens in numerical calculations.

barrier that is overcome only when a student faces the problem of insufficient performance of a single processor to solve the problem. The student, uninitiated in sequential programming methods, is spared from this barrier, and there is a reason to believe that it would be easier for him to learn the concurrency before the sequential programming.

Let us consider an illustrative example which the author repeatedly used in teaching to demonstrate a parallel solution of the classical problem of finding the best route (path) between two cities *A* and *B* connected by a system of roads.[2] We shall state a hypothesis that an individual, who does not have serial programming skills, probably, proposes an algorithm (even with quite typical errors) which can be characterized as a multi-agent decision [5]. Similar quasi-parallel solution was proposed by U.-I. Dahl and C. Hoare to demonstrate the capabilities of systems with discrete events of Simula and Simula 67 languages in the collection of articles entitled "Structured Programming" [6]. We call it a competition of agents dispersed over different roads during the time of goal achievement [4].

The hypothetical decision of the uninitiated man is in the concept of a forbidden city, i.e., the city in which the agent is not allowed to fall. The city is considered forbidden if it was previously visited by any agent. Initially, all cities are declared as allowed to visit, the only one existed agent is located in *A* and its traversed path is empty.

The solution, as the behavior of each agent in a certain city, is described as follows. Two parameters are given for each agent:

1) the agent location (city);
2) the length of the road along which he moved to this location from the previous city.

The agent's behavior includes the following actions:

1) the current location of the agent is appended to its traversed path. The path length is increased by the second parameter value.
2) **If** the agent is in *B*, **then** the goal is achieved and the traversed path is a solution, **else**
   a) the agent checks whether the city is forbidden. If so, the agent is eliminated (it is clear that the information about the system as a whole is not lost, the other agents continue to operate).
   b) The city is declared forbidden if it has the agent.
   c) The agent copies (sons) are generated. The sons number is equal to the number of roads coming from the current location of the agent. As the local data of new agents, the path, traversed by the parent agent from *A* to the current location, is specified (no matter, the agent becomes one of the copies or destroyed). If there are no roads from the location except for the one on which the agent came to the city, the agent is eliminated: it is deadlocked.
   d) Each new agent is directed to a dedicated road, passing which it comes to the state (1).
3) The agent is liquidated.

[2] The best path can be defined in different ways. Correct is to assume that this is an integral characteristic of any path from *A* to *B*, down from the local characteristics of the roads. In particular, the characteristics, such as the path length, can be chosen. Assuming that the speed of movement is the same for all roads, this criterion is equivalent to the time for which one can cover the way. The scheme below does not depend on the choice of the criterion. To be certain, we speak about minimizing the path length.

The process begins as generation and activation of a single agent in A, i.e., as running a scheme with parameters A and 0. Calculations are completed when all agents are liquidated.

Note that the goal achievement by the agent does not mean the completion of the computation process in general. In this case, other agents may try to pass on their ways down, but it is extra work, since their fate is to be liquidated in any forbidden city. It should be noted that a trainee's motif appears here to solve, in general case of parallelism, the problem of the calculation completion which does not occur in a sequential programming. This is a clear example of the barrier which was discussed above.

The scheme shows what errors can be made by an uninformed individual, and how to turn the idea into a solution by errors correction. Note an error of the scheme which is essential for teaching parallelism methodology. At first sight, this error can be invisible. It is associated with the agents concurrent actions. We are talking about potential conflicts that arise when two or more agents must act in the same city at the same time. Even not a very skilled expert in parallel computing knows what can occur and how to eliminate the conflict, and we shall not discuss this issue (see, for example [7]). What synchronization tools would be shown by a teacher to trainees in this case is the subject of a particular methodology. Here it is worth discussing another question of how to implement the proposed solution on a real computer.

The above-mentioned scheme is not a program for any computer because it does not involve restrictions on the number of available processors that implement the scheme behavior. So, we need a special movement to transform the idea into the program.

Dahl and Hoare propose an elegant solution in which the actions of dynamically generated and liquidated processes are regulated by the so-called control list, a global data structure specially organized for ordering calculations. This solution shows the possibility of agents retention in the structure of real computation. It provides a deterministic procedure performed on a single processor (see [6]). The solution is constructed as a dynamic mapping of dispersed agents to a linearly ordered structure of the control list directly associated with the control of computing.[3]

Two well-known classical solutions are based on the traversal in width and in depth of the tree of all possible passes in a graph. These solutions require calculations, too, but, due to the structure of data rather than actions. Thus, we have three variants of mapping multi-agent decision to the sequential computer: control list, breadth-first search and depth-first search. Comparing them in terms of efficiency, it is easy to conclude that the breadth-first search is preferable. However, this overlooks the fact that the classical solutions can be obtained from the agent approach identifying all possible movements in advance before computations. Using conventional teaching, this fact is always overlooked, and a teacher immediately talks about the structure of the roads, marks of vertices and other concepts that are not related to the above-presented natural approach of an uninitiated programmer.

Note that the problem of parallelizing classical solution is very difficult for beginners. It inevitably leads to management and synchronization of the flows. Inherently, the flow is a veiled hypostasis of the agent which has no place in the classical solution. This is precisely the difficulty of parallelization for the novice. A natural question arises: why do we introduce new complicated concepts instead of talking about natural agents?

[3] Details of the Dahl and Hoare's solution are given in Chapter 9, "The approach to building robust systems of interacting processes" of this book. It is used as an excuse to discuss the possibility of its using control lists for distributed computing organization.

Streaming and agent-based parallelization cannot circumvent the problem of mapping solutions to a finite set of available processors. Note that the proposal of Dahl and Hoare to use the control list is mapping of an agent-based solution, assuming unlimited set of processors, onto a single processor, i.e., the action inverse to parallelization. It is possible to set the parallelization problem both for classical and for agent-based solutions. Figuring out which of them is more difficult is beyond the scope of this paper. More important for us is the above-mentioned reducibility of agent-based and classical solutions to each other.

3. Program Sketch and Mapping It on a Real Computer

The above-mentioned example can be criticized indicating that streaming is not quite parallel programming due to assuming that the CPU resource is unbounded. This statement is denied for the following reason. A hypothetical solution of the uninitiated person is constructed under ignoring resource constraints. The variants of transforming this solution to the program demonstrate the capabilities of mapping it on the real computer. This work can and should be considered as an independent activity, other than "unlimited" programming. Combining these activities is always more difficult for a person than their sequential run. It is particularly undesirable in the learning because of dramatically reducing effectiveness (see [8, 9]). That is why we proclaim early learning parallelism considering programming as the following two-step scheme:

- *First*, the unrestricted algorithm development is made: a sketch of the future program is constructed. The closeness of the result to the actual program may be different; we shall call it sketch (of solution, program or algorithm).
- *Next*, a map of the sketch on a real computer is constructed, taking in account the restrictions. If you keep in mind a quality criterion, the second stage can be regarded as an optimization, and it must be spoken in teaching programming.

An important aspect of this approach is the removal of restrictions on the amount of allocated memory at the first stage. Here, common teaching practice explicitly or implicitly follows the provision on the division of activities (presumably that it is easier to tell, and because successive languages do not prevent these activities separation).

As the problem is often used to examine how beginners possess the combination method, we show the Gris example which is required to interchange two successive parts of the array [10]. Additional conditions, requiring the minimization of read and write operations, are considered merely as a measure of quality, and not as CPU time limitation. It is enough for the learning task. Memory unlimitedness leads to a trivial solution: rewriting data to a new location. That is what beginners do. Its criticism is nothing more than a proposal to build a map of the trivial sketch of a solution onto the computer with memory deficit.

Here is another learning task which, at the very beginning, is formulated with a demand for parallel program construction. It is given in [11] to illustrate the usefulness of operating data which have different and existing simultaneously structures. In this case, we are talking about matrices and the comparison of their row or column structures with their diagonal structures.

Suppose you want to convert a 3-diagonal matrix to another matrix in which the main diagonal value is replaced by the arithmetic average of the diagonal matrix element and its upper, left upper and diagonal neighbors:

$$a_{ii} = \frac{a_{ii} + a_{i-1,i} + a_{i-1,i-1} + a_{i,i-1}}{4} \tag{1}$$

From the very beginning, the problem formulation focuses on structuring the matrix as a string and column because it appeals to the indices. As a consequence, the programmer, not thinking about the formulation, is immediately ready to implement a sequential iterative algorithm (apparently, he or she realized quite quickly that it is necessary to organize a cycle from a larger value to a smaller value of *i*). This decision leads to the fact that parallel algorithm implementation on multiprocessor architectures requires a special analysis discovering that iterations are actually independent from each other.

At the same time, this problem is formulated in a very natural manner if we use another data structure that immediately follows the definition of a 3-diagonal matrix. In such a matrix with dimension $n \times n$ three vectors are informative:

- The main diagonal is a vector whose length is equal to n.
- The above located main diagonal is a vector whose length is equal to $n-1$.
- The located under the main diagonal is a vector whose length is equal to $n-1$.

For brevity, they are denoted as a, a^+ and a^-, respectively.

If we define the concatenation of vectors x and y as $x \bullet y$, discarding the last (first) component of vector x as x' $('x)$,[4] and component-wise arithmetic operations (they are indicated below with underlining), the required transformation is described as

$$a = a_1 \bullet \frac{a^+ \pm a^- \pm a' \pm 'a}{4}, \tag{2}$$

where a_1 is the first component of vector a.

The second formulation of the problem leads to the naturally parallelized solution. Perhaps, the developers of computational schemes, not related to the fixed programming language structuring, could formulate the algorithms more suitable for parallel computing.

Note that the separation of programming to the sketch design and mapping the sketch on the computer led, for this simple task, to the operating structure, nonexistent in terms of programming languages, but substantively very natural.

Thus, we have constructed a sketch solution which is almost trivially mapped on the computer. It is noteworthy that the mapping on the traditional single-processor computer (i.e., the program representation as a loop through the matrix elements) is more difficult. Note that if vectorization requires splitting the structural units, then the mapping ceases to be quite

[4] These operations are used to align the vectors with different number of components. It is required for componentwise operations. Perhaps, it would be better to determine the alignment operations directly, but this task is beyond the scope of this work.

trivial, but is still simple enough. This situation shows that the mapping can be constructed gradually by a consistent introduction of certain restrictions related to the real computer.

The problem formulation using (1) seems more understandable than (2) because we use the index notation a_{ij} and consider composite structural units manipulation as a special way of writing. The learning tasks of linear algebra are the reason. They all are related to computations (whether manual or mechanical) leading to the elements indexing. If we turn to the discipline's origin, then we see that, for example, the problem of solving the equations system is naturally formulated in the vector form:

Find a vector X satisfying AX = B, wherein A is a matrix, and B is a vector.

The vector-matrix form is suitable for the proofs of many linear space operators properties. It is well suited to explain a number of methods for solving systems and, in other cases, when the indexes are irrelevant. Applied to our problem, it would be better to formulate it as a construction of a suitable operator in the linear space. Then expression (1) will have no advantages over (2). As a consequence, the solution becomes directly parallel. To map it on a real computer, we need to impose a restriction on the number of vector elements allowed for the real parallel operation and to split the diagonal units to the corresponding parts.

The illustration of feasibility to decompose the programming into a conceptual sketch design of an algorithm without restriction and mapping the sketch on a real computer can be made in the field of playing chess. It is easy to write a program, without restrictions, which builds all the possible sequences of movements starting at the initial position as a total tree whose vertices are all possible chess positions. If this tree is built, we can offer the computer player's behavior as a choice of one of the winning branches (in principle, any of them) outgoing from a vertex of the current position. Note that the problem of constructing the total tree is naturally parallel: you can define as many independent threads as allowable movements are in this position for each item.

Since the total tree is so huge that all of the world computing resources are not enough to work with such a "simple" program, it must be regarded as a sketch decision needed a mapping on a real computer and taking restrictions into account. Clearly, this mapping can reduce the quality of the choice of a movement, because we have to choose it from the stripped-down tree. Instead of the preconstructed tree in choosing the next movement from the current position, we can request building the initial fragments of the tree branches trimmed to a depth of a fixed number of analyzed movements.

In this case, the choice of movements, i.e., the choice of one of the resulting fragments, is based on a preference criterion. It is essentially a stripped-down mapping:

- The "infinite" total tree cannot be saved, so, we need to build local fragments actually used in the selection (this subtask is naturally parallel);
- The choice of the guaranteed winning (no man's) branch is impossible, so we need a criterion with the verification localized by a dedicated set of fragments (this subtask is also naturally parallel: the parallel processes for computing the criterion values and sequential process, non-critical with respect to resources, for comparing the criterion values, are distinguished here.

Implementation of the presented idea is very expressive when we use the tools of functional programming based on the concept of lazy evaluations allowing the functions of infinite structures. The function laziness is manifested in the fact that this function is never executed "to the end". It provides the results by the portions defined by the need for another function that calls this function. The article by J. Hughes [12] provides details of operating such functions, particularly as applied to game programs, where the function of the total tree construction is "glued together" with the function of selecting a movement. Functional structuring simplifies the sketch program mapping in the case of processing infinite structures, separating the mapping from choosing a movement. Mapping the choosing movement program on the limited computer resources is constructed independently from processing the total tree, but it takes into account the fact that choosing the right tree pieces is provided.

4. Construction of the Method Based on Sketches

The success in solving the problem using separate sketching and then mapping the sketch motivates the student to repeat the experience in similar, just solved, problems. It is the beginning of the method's construction. To arouse the interest, the students should be invited to sketch solutions for the problem which is conceptually close to that having just been solved. In this case there are two versions of the offer:

1) a task which can be obtained modifying and mapping the finished sketch,
2) a task for which the sketch is fundamentally not suitable.

The first option gives grounds for confidence that the new method is obtained, and it is only needed to transform the scheme of a solution to an independent format, noting what modifications may be required. For the second variant, we need to discuss the reasons for failures and try to find the ways to overcome them. It is not very important whether another method is formulated or not. It is more important that the trainees can see the limitations of the approach's applicability and get an idea of incorrectness of the statements about the total method's universality.

These general theses are applicable to illustrate the development of the problem of searching the shortest path between the cities. The sketch presented in section 3 is good for generalizations that are associated with assigning roads weights or finding the shortest path as the number of passed cities. Such problems should be discussed to reinforce the skills of using the agent-based approach.

The similar problem for applying the ready sketch is to finding all acyclic paths from A to B. The original sketch can be applied if it is possible to consistently forbid the already passed paths. However, it is a particular problem which may cause difficulties for students. It is more simple to prompt them to find a reverse path from B to A using the original sketch and change the concept of the forbidden city and the agent's behavior during their visit. Additionally, we need to decide how to save information about the found paths. This is a solution associated with subsequent sketch mapping. The question is critical for a new problem, and it is very reasonable to discuss it during the sketch construction and to consider possible options, one of which shall be approved of when restrictions on the minimization of local agent memory and/or a shared one for all agents are introduced.

It is useful to compare the old and new problems and their solutions, and show the general principles of dynamic programming. Note that this method can be useful to study it after solving the problem and not before.

A fundamentally new similar problem is finding the shortest acyclic paths for all pairs of cities *A* and *B*. A ready agent-based sketch may be used to solve the task in a trivial but not tenable case when the previous solution is run for all pairs of *A* and *B*. To improve it, one should attempt to glue common fragments of different agent ways, but each agent does not know anything about the behavior of other agents. Overcoming obstacles is possible due to more general information that may be applied to agents to select the desired behavior. There are different possible problem solutions but this is beyond our discussion. We note only that the well known technique of constructing the so-called wave algorithms [13] can be eventually built. It is important to emphasize that this technique is given to trainees not as a finished scheme, but it is derived from the needs for specific tasks.

The development of the sketch decisions in conjunction with their analysis is very productive not only in the curriculum. The goal is to summarize the decisions in the parallel program development schemes. The sufficiently general schemes can be offered as specialized techniques. The Ian Foster's approach [14] is an example of this technique. It obviously resonates with the agent-based sketch and can be obtained from it by generalization. This approach presented the process of designing a parallel program as four distinct stages: *partitioning*, *communication*, *agglomeration*, and *mapping*. In the first two stages, the developer focuses on concurrency and scalability and is aimed at the discovery of algorithms with these qualities. In the third and fourth stages, attention shifts to locality and other performance-related issues. The stages of the methodology called PCAM (acronym for the first letters of stages names) can be summarized as follows:

1. *Partitioning.* The computations to be performed and the data processed by the computations are decomposed into small tasks. Practical issues, such as the number of processors in the target computer, are ignored, and attention is focused on recognizing opportunities for parallel execution.
2. *Communications.* The communications required to coordinate task execution are determined and appropriate communication structures, and algorithms are defined.
3. *Agglomeration.* The tasks and communication structures defined in the first two stages of a design are evaluated with respect to performance requirements and implementation costs. If necessary, the tasks are combined into larger tasks to improve performance or to reduce the costs of development.
4. *Mapping.* Each task is assigned to a processor in a manner to satisfy the competing objectives to maximize the processor utilization and minimize communication costs. Mapping can be specified statically or determined at runtime by load-balancing algorithms.

The last stage of the methodology clearly indicates that the mapping is based on the results of the first three stages, i.e., it is performed as a development of the program sketch. The methods of stages 2 – 4 are not associated with the use of formal languages (but they do not eliminate the use of them). So, these stages should be considered as a sketch programming that adds the appropriate restrictions step by step.

Introducing his approach, Foster rightly warns that the PCAM technique is not universal and it is not the only one. He demonstrates its use in solving a number of problems as a design pattern. Thus the Foster's teaching concurrency is solved within the traditional teaching methods opposite to what is proposed in this chapter.

Conclusion

The discussion above shows that early learning parallel programming should be associated with a more general provision on the division of programming into two activities: a logical construction of a program sketch and mapping it on a real computer. Of course, the design must be fitting for building computable sketches, i.e., they should be represented so that mapping is simplified. But the mere fact that the division of two activities during programming promotes liberated training and allows one the effective teaching methods. Applied to the study of concurrency in programming, it means that the teacher has to abandon the traditional display of the template solutions. He or she should focus on offering the greatest number of sketches for discussion. Comparing the sketches from different points of view, the learners come to a decision for which the mapping should be constructed. In other words, we encourage the learners to set the problematic tasks involving an analysis of options for choosing the optimal solution [15] that has good prospects for the skills evolution in the methods creation and development.

Selection of activities for constructing the program sketch, for a good reason, may be regarded as a special kind of programming which is naturally called the sketch preliminary programming. It differs from conventional programming in only one thing: the programming language is not fixed. Everything else remains usual: the sketches of data structures and the operators retain their meaningful understanding, and "manual" mapping of the sketch program on a real computer is completely analogous to a usual compilation. Thanks to the freedom of choice of the language means, the sketch programming can be regarded as the most high-level program design. If we turn to the traditional sense of programming which uses a fixed language, then such development can be considered as a sketch programming for which the compiler implements automatic mapping of the sketch on the real computer. Thus, the sketch programming, highlighted this chapter, can be defined as the process for which the compilation remains manual work. This does not mean that the sketch programming should not be automated. On the contrary, it needs an adequate support which, in particular, pointed to possible errors so as the compilation does.

In developing the early learning parallel programming methods, the main problem to be solved is how to find problems that provide solutions with a natural parallelism. To realize this, traditional learning should be analyzed, especially the tasks that allow one a parallel solution. It is needed to reconstruct these tasks to select the sketch components allowing the parallel solutions and mapping them on real computers. The examples above may be regarded as the first step in that direction.

References

[1] The OpenMP® API specification for parallel programming. URL: http://openmp.org/wp/.
[2] Message Passing Interface Forum. URL: http://www.mpi-forum.org/
[3] Backus, J., (1978). Can Programming Be Liberated from the von Neumann Style? A Functional Style and Its Algebra of Programs, *Communications of the ACM*, 21, 8, 613 – 641.
[4] Nepyivoda, N.N., Skopin, I.N., (2003). *The Foundations of Programming*, Moscow-Izhevsk: Institute of Computer Science (In Russian).
[5] Wooldridge, M. J., (2009). *An Introduction to MultiAgent Systems*, University Of Liverpool.
[6] Dahl, O.J., Dykstra, E.W., Hoare, C.A.R., (1972). *Structured Programming*, Academic Press.
[7] Hoare, C. A. R., (1985). *Communicating Sequential Processes*, Prentice-Hall.
[8] Skopin, I.N., (2010). Role Playing in the Methods of Teaching Management of Project Activities, *Science and Education*, 1 (57), 74 – 77 (In Russian).
[9] Halperin, P.Y., (2000). *Four Lectures on Psychology*, Moscow, Yurait (In Russian).
[10] Gries, D., (1981). *The Science of Programming*, Springer Verlag, New York.
[11] Skopin, I.N., (2006). Multiple Data Structuring, *Programming and Computer Software*, 32, 1, 44–55. (In Russian).
[12] Hughes, J., (1989). Why Functional Programming Matters, *The Computer Journal*, 32(2), 98 – 107.
[13] Tel, G., (1995). *Introduction to Distributed Algorithms*, Cambridge University Press.
[14] Foster, I., Designing and Building Parallel Programs. URL: http://wotug.org/parallel /books/addison-wesley/dbpp/
[15] Skopin, I.N., (2011). Challenge Tasks for the Study of General Methods of Computer Science and Programming, *Bulletin of the Russian Friendship University. Series: Education Informatization*, 4, 21 - 33. (In Russian).

INDEX

A

B

C

D

E

F

G

H

I

K

L

M

N

O

P

X

Y